Aesthetics
in Twentieth-Century Poland

Aesthetics in Twentieth-Century Poland

SELECTED ESSAYS

Edited by

Jean G. Harrell and Alina Wierzbiańska

Lewisburg
BUCKNELL UNIVERSITY PRESS

Associated University Presses, Inc.
Cranbury, New Jersey 08512

Library of Congress Cataloging in Publication Data

Harrell, Jean Gabbert, 1921–   comp.
    Aesthetics in twentieth-century Poland.

    Includes bibliographical references.
    CONTENTS: Witkiewicz, S. I. On pure form.—Chwistek,
L. Plural reality in art.—Ossowski, S. What are aesthetic experiences?
[etc.]
        1. Aesthetics, Polish. 2. Aesthetics, Modern—20th century.
I. Wierzbiańska, Alina, joint comp. II. Title.
BH221.P63H37   111.8′5   78-38984
ISBN 0-8387-1100-6

CONTENTS

ACKNOWLEDGMENTS

The editors wish to thank the following publishers for permission to use the following copyrighted material:

British Journal of Aesthetics, for permission to reprint the English translation of the essay of W. Tatarkiewicz.

Mouton & Co., The Hague, Paris, for permission to reprint from the Series Minor, no. 90, of *Janua Linguarum* the English translation of the essay of J. Pelc.

Państwowe Wydawnictwo Naukowe, PWN—Polish Scientific Publishers, for permission to reprint the essay of J. Białostocki and the essays of R. Ingarden and S. Ossowski in English translation.

Instytut Filozofii i Socjologii PAN (the Editorial Board of *Estetyka*) jointly with *Państwowe Wydawnictwo Naukowe,* publishers, for permission to reprint in English translation the essays of K. Piwocki and M. Wallis.

7

INTRODUCTION

I

The primary aim of this volume is to present important Polish essays in aesthetics that are largely unknown to the English reading public. Bibliographies of contemporary issues in aesthetics in English generally list only English sources. It is well known, however, that Polish philosophers have made substantial contributions to the field. W. Tatarkiewicz's *History of Aesthetics,* in three volumes, is undoubtedly the most comprehensive work on the subject in any language. Increasing interest among English readers is being shown in the work of Roman Ingarden. Several English translation projects of his writings are now under way. I. M. Bocheński writes: "Roman Ingarden's main work *The Controversy over the Existence of the World* . . . is one of the most significant publications of the present time. . . . We protest against the unfortunately widespread custom of issuing serious philosophical works in languages which are known only to more or less minor groups, for example, Finnish, Polish and Dutch. The decision should be made to issue all such works in *one* language, and in the present state of things English would doubtless be most suitable."[1] Bocheński's conclusion may be unnecessarily extreme. The present group of essays, however, should be a step in one right direction.

With the exception of the essays of Tatarkiewicz and Białostocki, none of those presented in this volume has appeared elsewhere in English. The English version of Tatarkiewicz's essay has been revised by the author; that of Białostocki has been available only in Poland. Translations of the other essays have been made at the request of the editors expressly for this volume. The suggestion for

9

this particular selection was originally made to the editors by W. Tatarkiewicz. Most of the essays were selected by him around the very broad central topic of art and reality. Some choices were left to the authors themselves. The essay of Stanisław Ossowski was selected for this volume by his widow, Dr. Maria Ossowska, and is the only portion of Ossowski's *Foundations of Aesthetics* that has been translated into English. The final collection is not exactly according to the original plan. It was hoped that the essays would be more nearly equal in length than later proved feasible. Variation in length, however, should in no way reflect editorial judgment of the contributions.

II

It is useful to make some short comparisons here between the ideas expressed in these essays and those of prominent British and American writings concerned with the same or similar issues.

There is a marked similarity between S. I. Witkiewicz's theory of *pure form,* published in 1921, and Clive Bell's theory of *significant form.* The theories were developed almost simultaneously, are almost identical, and yet it does not appear that Bell influenced Witkiewicz in any way.

Both of these theories are primarily directed toward visual art, but both authors recognize that they seek a principle common to all art. (Witkiewicz *does* name the novel as an exception.) In *Art,* Bell initially calls this principle "significant form," but later he slips into frequent references to the same terms as Witkiewicz's "pure form." Bell refers to a peculiar "aesthetic emotion" characteristic of significant form, and Witkiewicz to "aesthetic satisfaction" emanating from pure form. Bell stresses the intensity of this more than Witkiewicz, at times referring to "ecstasy." Indeed, Witkiewicz never terms "satisfaction" an "emotion." However, both authors recognize that this satisfaction or emotion is a personal or subjective experience. "It is obvious," Witkiewicz writes, "that objective evaluation and criticism of a work of art is an absolute impossibility, since the essential relation to it is based on subjectivism. The critic should only know who he is, and whether he is looking at a given thing from the point of view of form or content. . . ."

Both authors consider qualities of nature that people call beautiful to be different from those which they call beautiful in art. "Beauty in reality and beauty in art are two completely separate domains," writes Witkiewicz. Bell writes, "I am satisfied that, as a rule, most people feel a very different kind of emotion for birds and flowers . . . from that which they feel for pictures."[2]

Both Bell and Witkiewicz claim that the product of pure form is unique to the individual artist. "We can define a work of art," Witkiewicz writes, "as a construct of arbitrary elements . . . created by an individual as the expression of the unity of his personality, that acts on us in an immediate way by reason of its very structuring." Bell says, ". . . the peculiarity of the artist would seem to be that he possesses the power of surely and frequently seizing reality (generally behind pure form), and the power of expressing his sense of it, in pure form always."[3]

Bell suggests as a "metaphysical hypothesis" that, since the expression of one artist nevertheless affects the perceiver as an "end in itself," the perceiver of significant form becomes aware of "essential reality." Similarly, Witkiewicz acknowledges a certain "metaphysical feeling" resulting from the "expression of the unity of personality." "The deeper justification of this theory (of pure form)," he adds, "must have a basis in the fundamental laws of existence in general, in other words, in the laws of General Ontology."

Two writers have recently indicated an influence of G. E. Moore on Bell. George Dickie writes: "Now recall two things: (1) Bell's praise of Moore's moral philosophy, and (2) Moore's statement of his basic method, which is: 'In order to define Ethics, we must discover what is both common and peculiar to all undoubted ethical judgments. . . .' These two considerations strongly suggest that Bell is attempting to set forth an intuitionist aesthetic theory parallel to Moore's intuitionist ethical theory." Again, Ruby Meager writes: "As a denizen of Cambridge in 1913 he (Bell) would have been writing under the immediate shadow of Moore's *Principia Ethica*, treated then as an epoch-making work; and indeed the whole theory of *Art* might be regarded as an attempt to fill out by careful examination of experience part of Moore's own answer to the 'first question of ethics' propounded in *Principia Ethica*, namely: 'What kinds of things ought to exist (Moore's way of saying 'are valuable') for their own sake? Moore himself answers *inter alia* 'consciousness of beauty,' and Bell's claim that 'works of art are immediate means to good' so that to judge a work to be a work of art is to judge it to be of the first ethical importance in itself, and that in this sense art is superior to the morals of conduct, can be regarded pretty clearly, I think, as deriving from Moore's question and answer."[4]

These comments stress two aspects of Bell's theory as dependent on Moore: the suggestion of a correlation between ethical and aesthetic "good," and the suggestion that "good" is an intrinsic quality, either something "for its own sake," or something immediate. It will be noted that Witkiewicz is not concerned in his essay to correlate ethical with aesthetic "good." His development of "pure" form, however, may stress the nonpractical, or the immediate and intrinsic, even more than does Bell's. In the first chapter of *Art*, Bell's primary concern is with the nonrepresentational. He shifts, then, in chapter 3, to an almost exclusive concern with the "end in itself." Both Bell and Witkiewicz, however, confuse the "non-real" with the intrinsic or immediate. (That which is real may yet be valued intrinsically. That which is of instrumental value may yet be "formal.")

Herbert Read has noted a similarity between Bell's theory and observations made by Vernon Lee. He refers especially to more than one passage in Lee's *The Beautiful: an Introduction to Psychological Aesthetics*, published in 1913, that suggest a definition of aesthetic responsiveness in terms of shape. In the light of these, and of influence indicated by

Lee herself of Lipps, Karl Groos, Wundt, Münsterberg, and Külpe, Read concludes that Bell did not originate the theory of significant form.[5] It should be noted, however, that "the" theories of significant or of pure form are in fact collections of several different concepts. What is most striking is the number of these that are the same or very similar in the statements of Bell and Witkiewicz. "The" theories include the following: art must be described in terms of either form or content. It is possible to find a necessary condition of art, and also of aesthetic significance. The latter is independent of representation of the "real" world. It is an intrinsic or immediate, rather than an instrumental or future-oriented value. Artists express their aesthetic feelings to perceivers of their works. Natural objects do not possess significant form. Art and/or aesthetic significance is related to something "metaphysical." The result of the juxtaposition of these concepts is a philosophical blur that goes by the name of a single theory.

Bell's *Art* was published in 1914. From 1914 to 1917, Witkiewicz was a soldier in the Russian Army. There was a trend similar to Bell's in Russia, but its first "constructivist" defender was Malewitsch, who began painting in 1913, but who wrote his essays later than Witkiewicz did. In the opinion of Tatarkiewicz, it would have been impossible for Witkiewicz, as a front-line soldier, to have come into contact with painters in St. Petersburg and Moscow. Since the death of Witkiewicz's wife, Tatarkiewicz has been in possession of all the manuscripts Witkiewicz left. None of them deals with Bell or the Russian constructivists. "Witkiewicz," Tatarkiewicz notes, "was a man for whom it was a mental necessity to polemize with every book he read. . . . It is of course difficult to prove a negative proposition. I am, however, certain that Bell's and Witkiewicz's theories are independent."[6]

In contrast with Bell, Witkiewicz has been described as having "no proper systematic education," and as "having been at the university for a short time only; he never held any academic or official post."[7] Both authors, however, have been criticized for logical weakness, Bell especially for arguing in a circle. (Significant form in art is that which evokes aesthetic emotion, and aesthetic emotion is the appreciation of significant form in art.) Kotarbiński criticizes Witkiewicz thus: ". . . at the end of his life (he) was quite well read in philosophy, but he was never able to overcome the lack of basic, elementary logical training. . . . I do not know any work of his which could be considered as fully mature and free from strangenesses, weaknesses and blots."[8]

Criticisms of the theories of Bell and Witkiewicz have generally amounted, however, to criticisms of parts of "the" theory, rather than wholesale rejections. Ruby Meager notes that Bell's theory is still being reissued in paperback, in spite of having "been shot at with pretty well all the bolts in the philosophical locker; charges of subjectivity, vicious circularity and even—last and worst of philosophical insults—of irrefutability." She suggests that the theory "says something that someone wants to hear" and that although Bell's theory lacks "systematic adequacy" she agrees with him in this: There may well be a peculiar aesthetic emotion, generally the same in response to different arts, and it may well be located in "formal" coherence and a thing "evoked directly." She thinks, however, that Bell was wrong to exclude representational significance as a conditioning factor.

Several American writers have argued against the possibility of finding a necessary condition both for art and for a peculiarly aesthetic type of response to it. These writers clearly reflect the influence of Ludwig Wittgenstein's *Philosophical Investigations,* especially Wittgenstein's reference to "family resemblances" (a term itself borrowed from William James).[9] W. E. Kennick, for example, rejects Bell's theory of significant form for having mistakenly assumed that there is a single "common denominator" of art. Kennick acknowledges, however, that Bell did find a "new and profitable way of looking at pictures," although he does not attempt to explain wherein lay the "profit."[10] In a similar fashion, Marshall Cohen argues against the possibility of finding a necessary condition of that which is pecu-

liarly aesthetic. He analyzes in detail possible interpretations of Edward Bullough's concept of "psychical distance"
and finds them wanting. He concludes that "aesthetic criteria are numerous and make a reference not only to the
sensory and formal features of objects and to expressive
and technical qualities of media but also to the intentions
of artists, the dialectical demands of particular arts, the
expectations of aesthetic elites, and the impersonal progress
of the institutions of art."[11]

The analysis of Stanisław Ossowski, in his chapter "What
Are Aesthetic Experiences," is strikingly similar to these.
Ossowski's essay does not mention Bullough, but is extensively concerned with the vagueness of Kant's concept of
disinterested contemplation. It should be noted that Ossowski's *Foundations of Aesthetics* was published in 1933, over
a decade prior to *Philosophical Investigations*. Ossowski was
not influenced by Wittgenstein or British analysis, but was
influenced by Polish teachers adherent to Twardowski, especially by the logician Łukasiewicz. They were primarily
concerned with philosophical method, especially with the
objective of clarity and precision. On the other hand, extensions of certain aspects of Wittgenstein into aesthetics, such
as those mentioned above, are among the most recent American developments, dating from this and the last decade.

Ossowski finds that no necessary or sufficient condition
of the peculiarly "aesthetic" can be found in immediate
sensation, in representation, in "reality," or in some special
aesthetic experience. He suggests, however, that the "aesthetic" may always be characterised by "enjoying the moment." This refers to the temporal aspect of "disinterest,"
and has not been isolated in quite this way by Anglo-American writers. It is perhaps closest to J. O. Urmson's reference
to the aesthetic as that which is "present to the senses," or
to David Prall's "aesthetic surface," but is certainly not
identical with these.[12]

In his essay "Plural Reality in Art," Leon Chwistek criticizes Witkiewicz's theory of pure form in a way that is not
reflected in critical comments in English of Bell's theory.
One of the faults of the theory of pure form, Chwistek

argues, is that Witkiewicz entertained only a single concept of reality. Chwistek thinks that no notion of reality can contain contradictory elements, and that no single concept of reality is possible. Chwistek's theory of plural reality is similar to some very much later thinking of Anglo-American writers. In his most recent book, *Languages of Art* (1968), Nelson Goodman reminds his readers that "in 'The Way the World Is,' *Review of Metaphysics,* vol. 14 (1960) pp. 48-56, I have argued that the world is as many ways as it can be truly described, seen, pictured, etc., and that there is no such thing as *the* way the world is. Ryle takes a somewhat similar position (*Dilemmas,* Cambridge, England, Cambridge University Press, 1954, pp. 75-77) in comparing the relation between a table as a perceived solid object and the table as a swarm of atoms with the relation between a college library according to the catalogue and according to the accountant."[13] Again, in *Ways of Being,* Herbert Schneider argues that no single definition of "what it means to be" is compatible with the ways in which being is actually conceived—ways that "cannot be correlated analytically." Schneider, however, distinguishes his "natural," "cultural," and "formal" ways of being from theories of "reality." "Because the theory of the real is so confused, it seems prudent to try to get along without it. Let the world be made of nature, culture, and structure, in varied combinations, and let this be all that analysis can do to make the ways of the world more intelligible."[14]

Chwistek does not consider it to be the job of philosophy to find out what is true or false. Philosophy is concerned with method of making meanings clear and precise, and Chwistek is concerned here to clarify the meaning of "reality." His essay, published in 1921, is complex. It combines analysis of different meanings of "reality" with a philosophy of visual art, especially with ideas of reality that he believes always condition the practice of painters and sculptors. The essay contains observations about visual perception almost identical with those made by Wittgenstein a quarter of a century later. The similarity of Chwistek's "monk-eagle" example to Wittgenstein's famous "duck-rabbit" example is striking. So also is that between Wittgen-stein's white and black "double cross"[15] and Chwistek's observation: "if . . . a white design is made on a black background, it might rightly be said that a black drawing has been made on a white background. Careful observation shows that neither of these two alternative possibilities could hold, for oscillations in both directions enable us to see either the first phenomenon or the other, alternatively."

Wittgenstein did not extend his observations on visual perception to philosophy of art. One possible correlation has been made recently by Isabel Hungerland, in her refer-ences to "perceptual viewpoints" determining "aesthetic ascriptions." "Painters," she notes, "have always resorted to a variety of 'tricks' to break down habitual ways of looking at things and every new style in painting represents, one might say, a new perceptual viewpoint."[16] This is rather similar to Chwistek's claim that every new style in painting reflects a different concept of reality. Mrs. Hungerland, however, identifies perceptual viewpoints as conditions of "aesthetic ascriptions" and as sufficiently unstable to pro-hibit the making of "non-aesthetic ascriptions." Chwistek does not draw this dichotomy between the "aesthetic" and the "non-aesthetic."

An explicit suggestion for an extension of Wittgenstein's observations on visual perception to philosophy of art has been made by Virgil Aldrich in his book *Philosophy of Art*. Aldrich defends the existence of an "aesthetic mode of perception," which he calls "prehension." His claim that there is a different mode of perception from a scientific one has been criticized. Joseph Margolis, for example, asks: "Is seeing a camel in a cloud, in some significantly exclusive sense, aesthetic perception; and must the camel, in some significant sense, be 'there' to be seen?"[17] Chwistek does not posit a special "mode" of aesthetic perception. Indeed, he almost ignores the question of what is "aesthetic." He is rather concerned to demonstrate a necessary condition of visual art, good or bad. However, he is not entirely clear about whether he is naming a condition of all visual art, or primarily of good art. For example, he notes that the chief factor distinguishing painting and sculpture from ornament lies in a difference between "even and uneven oscillations" in visual perception, and that "no great works of art were ever composed of objects distinctly modelled and clearly separated from each other."

Chwistek's correlation of visual art with "realities," however, might be considered a partial, though crude answer to issues raised by several British authors recently on what the critic "brings us to see," what "there is" to be seen, and how the critic does this. Frank Sibley finds that "with so much interest in and agreement about *what* the critic does, one might expect descriptions of *how* he does it to have been given. But little has been said about this, and what has been said is unsatisfactory."[18]

In his introductory statement, it will be noted that Chwistek mentions two realities, but that in his main essay he mentions four. This is not explained. The distinction of four realities, however, seems to lend a more complete analysis of different styles of painting.

Chwistek finds form and content in art to be distinguishable but not separable. He also recognizes initially that these concepts are ambiguous, but claims that, contrary to popular opinion, exclusively "formal" aspects are far simpler and more constant than those of "content." He finds, by a certain polemic, that the only justifiable reference of the term *content* is to "elements of the real." Chwistek makes it clear that the "real" in art is not a copy. He means to indicate that some idea of the real determines what the painter does and what the perceiver sees. If shapes, proportions of their various sizes, and degree of complexity are aspects of visual "form," one may well ask how these are identified. "Oscillations" characteristic of visual perception are even and uneven. What determines the route of oscillation?

Chwistek identifies four fundamental types of painting: primitivism, realism, impressionism, and futurism. The bulk of his essay is concerned with the first three, and with the ideas of reality that determine them, respectively, namely: the reality of things, the reality of physics, and the reality of sense impressions. The fourth reality, that of images, is most difficult to describe, but conditions a variety of recent aspects of futuristic painting. Reflections of different realities may be mixed in one painting, as where a realistic head appears on an impressionistic background. Chwistek argues generally, however, that development of new types of painting is determined by new ideas of reality. He is not clear whether he thinks there can be *only* four concepts of reality, or whether yet other concepts may develop that will condition the practice of future artists. In any event, the most recent concept, that of images, can best be understood in the language of poets and mystics, or through personal experience of a reality that is completely indeterminate. It is reflected in painting in a relaxation of demarcating lines that separate objects from each other, in what might be called an attempt to "overcome content."

It is in this general way that Chwistek argues that all visual art is related to some reality and that Witkiewicz's and others' defense of pure form was mistaken. Skolimowski notes: "A modern painter and a theorist of modern art, Chwistek wished to integrate into his philosophy all aspects of life and art, and therefore was inevitably at odds with analytical philosophers who concentrated only on those problems which have cognitive content and can be tackled rationally and formulated unequivocally. The fullness of life and the richness of art cannot be grasped, in Chwistek's view, by rational means alone; therefore, a sort of irrationality is inevitable. On the other hand . . . Chwistek was a zealous defender of rationality in the philosophy of mathematics. This inconsistency among others made him unpopular and unacceptable to the analytical movement (in Poland)."[19]

The essays of Władysław Tatarkiewicz, "Abstract Art and Philosophy," and of Ksawery Piwocki, "Husserl and Picasso," reflect Chwistek's correlation of ontological commitments and the practice of painters and sculptors. They are, however, more limited in their claims and more exclusively historical. These authors do not argue that a painter *must* operate with some idea of the "real." They suggest, rather, that the thinking of a time, and not necessarily that of "professional" philosophers, has in fact determined what artists have done. Piwocki suggests a relationship specifically between phenomenology and cubism. "Husserl's attempts," he says, "tend to visualize the image of the essence of the object. According to the quoted texts, this does not concern the image corresponding to sensuous perception, but the integral, or as Husserl says, 'pure' image, free of every fortuitous element of sense experience." Tatarkiewicz's final comments are striking. Having suggested that two principal types of visual art may be discerned, which he calls "aspect-ism" and "prospectism," he argues that "Plato not only formulated both aspectist and prospectist theories, but in 'Philebus' . . . he also cleared a way for abstract art." He adds that those who think that their theoretical justifi-cation of abstract art is new "for the most part do not realize how old their lineage is."

These authors do not claim that looking at paintings will disclose the "meaning" of whatever theory supposedly de-termined what the painter did. Nor do they argue for some sort of "knowledge by acquaintance," such that "knowledge" which may be claimed in a theory that has conditioned a painting can be found in the painting itself. The essays develop theories of picture-derivation, rather than of picture-meaning or picture-knowledge. It might be argued, however, that the thesis of philosophical determination of the prac-tice of visual artists could be extended in divergent direc-tions. For example, a correlation might be found between Picasso's paintings and Bertrand Russell's theory of the "ultimate constituents of matter." After confessing that he first attended the "cinematograph" to check out a theory of Bergson, Russell concludes that the cinematograph is a better metaphysician than common sense, physics, or philoso-phy, and that a "real" man is, as on the picture screen, a "series of momentary men." Real objects are classes of momentary particulars from various points in a six-dimen-sional space.[20] Might not Picasso's painting be said also to reflect Russellian realism, as well as Husserlian phenome-nology or Chwistek's "reality of images"? Such possibilities, of course, raise the question of the method whereby these correlations are established. (They may also raise a kind of reverse question: if such correlations of ontologies with visual arts are correct, to what extent may ontologies themselves be based on visual perception? P. F. Strawson, for example, suggests in his chapter on "Sounds" in *Individuals* that we might not have avoided solipsism or have obtained an idea of independently existing objects, if our sole sense data had been auditory).

Tatarkiewicz's essay presupposes not only a knowledge of history of philosophy, but also of history of art and aesthetics. Tatarkiewicz has been concerned extensively with method in these fields, upon which such conclusions as those in his essay presented here clearly depend. At the beginning of Volume 1 of his *History of Aesthetics,* he notes: "The historian of aesthetics has not only to study the evolution of various kinds of aesthetics, but he has to apply himself various methods and points of view. In studying older ideas about aesthetics it is not enough to take into account only those which have been expressed under the name of aesthetics, or have belonged to the definite aesthetic discipline or have applied the terms 'beauty' and 'art.' It is not sufficient to rely solely on explicit written or printed propositions. The historian will also have to draw on the taste he observes of a given period and refer to the works of art it has produced. He will rely not only on theory, but also on practice, on works of sculpture and music, poetry and oratory. . . ."[21] This statement does not include reference to another methodological expectation of Tatarkiewicz, namely, familiarity with the languages in which aesthetic theories are stated. One of his most important short essays, which shows the fruits of this complex method perhaps more clearly than the essay included in this volume, is titled "Romantic Aesthetics of 1600." By a detailed consideration of utterances of characters of Shakespeare, Tatarkiewicz finds that they "express a number of thoughts germane to aesthetics" that Shakespeare himself did not assert, and that were "not formulated until Romanticism." He also notes that the Polish poet, Sarbiewski, "seems to have been the first to apply the idea and the name 'creation' to artistic (poetic) works. ("The poet is a creator who 'finds' [*confingit*], 'constructs' [*quammodo condit*] and 'creates his work from what is new' [*de novo creat*]."")[22]

In the wake of recent language analysis, aesthetic writings in English concerned at all with relations of art to "reality" have referred primarily to literature. In music, the nineteenth century opinions of Eduard Hanslick (*On the Beautiful in Music*) and Edmund Gurney (*The Power of Sound*) are still prominent in contemporary bibliographies. In contrast, bibliographies in philosophy of literature differ more radically from nineteenth-century sources. They center on problems of "truth" and the definition of fiction. The most popular opinion expressed in English writings is that propositional truth is irrelevant to music and visual arts and, though relevant to literature, is not or may not be significant.[23] The suggestion has also been made that literary fiction can be distinguished, in part at least, by logical uses of language.[24] The essays of Roman Ingarden, "On So-Called 'Truth' in Literature," and of Jerzy Pelc, "Nominal Expressions and Literary Fiction," are welcome additions to English sources, largely for their suggestiveness in answering some of those special questions about literary art which are still outstanding. Some answers to these questions differ among different authors.[25] Implications of others on which authors may agree have not been fully worked out.

Ingarden's contention that literary sentences are quasi-assertions, whose references can be determined only by the context in which they are found, which are products of "poetic fantasy" and not translatable into "strict" judgments, is close to the conclusions of several British and American authors. Similarity may be found in Monroe C. Beardsley's "Nonpredication theory,"[26] in Gilbert Ryle's contention that propositions of *Pickwick Papers* are "only a pseudo-designation,"[27] and in Arnold Isenberg's observation: ". . . it may well be that in poetry it is the idea—the bracketed, fictive 'assertion'—that matters."[28] Isabel Hungerland argues that differences between literary and other discourse are found in "language situations," that there are nonpropositional ways in which perceptiveness can be articulated, and that no literal paraphrase can duplicate the effect of metaphor.[29] (Her observation that "one cannot isolate the effects of rhythm and sound" in poetry is also close to Ingarden's reference to the "word-sound stratum" developed in his early work, *Das literarische Kunstwerk*.) Margaret MacDonald, in probably the best-known essay in English on literary fiction, argues that fictional sentences cannot be verified by any factual discovery, and that they are neither self-contradictory nor nonsensical. Her contention that fiction yields a story through imagination and a "mutual conspiracy" between author and reader, is close to Ingarden's reference to the literary work as a product of a "double-intentional act."[30] Joseph Margolis repeats Miss MacDonald's points on fiction, and finds them "conclusive."[31] Yet Margolis argues that fiction is not to be explained by "psychological" uses of language.

Although Ingarden is generally recognized as one of the world's leading phenomenological aestheticians, it is probable that his work is attracting increasing attention in Britain and the United States also because of his marked subtlety in analysis of aesthetic terminology. Note has been made of his analysis of nine meanings of the form-content distinction since its publication in English translation in 1960.[32] In the chapter immediately preceding the one translated here from *Studies in Esthetics*, the author finds eight meanings of "truth" in art. "Truth" may refer to: 1) that which is logically or universally cognitive, 2) objects represented in art, 3) a correspondence of means of presentation to the subject presented, 4) cohesion of a series of qualitative "moments" in art, 5) a relation of art to the point of view of its author, 6) the forcefulness of effect upon a perceiver, 7) "the true" work of art (as when we speak of "the true diamond" in relation to polished glass), 8) the "idea" that a work of art contains.

In his present essay on "truth" in literature, Ingarden finds that quasi-judgments function like axioms, "*vis-à-vis* the objects which they determine*," and that predicated statements in a lyrical work "must be regarded as quoted statements." He finds that literary language plays a role in discovery, and provides "an element of understanding" that would not otherwise be possible to conceptualize at all. The points he makes in this essay are consistent with his analysis of Aristotle's *Poetics,* especially with his interpretation of what Aristotle meant by *mimesis* and *mimeisthai.*

Ingarden divides literary sentences into three types: "sentences clearly quoted in the text and uttered by one of the characters presented in the work; sentences appearing in lyrical works . . . like Shakespeare's 'Love is not love Which alters when it alteration finds . . .' "; and sentences that Ingarden finds are "borderline" cases, some of which are strict judgments, and some of which are quasi-judgments. Ingarden argues, however, that even in borderline cases, the works cannot be read simultaneously as literary art and as scientific or philosophical treatises. Such a dialogue as Plato's "Symposium" can be read either as a philosophical treatise or as literary art, but not both ways simultaneously. When the "Symposium" is read as literature, it is of considerable importance which character utters which statement. As quasi-assertions, which are neither true nor false, they depend upon a speaker and a contextual point of view. But it is of no importance which character utters which statement when the dialogue is read as a philosophical treatise. Studied as philosophy, "nothing apart from the truth or falsity of its statements is at stake and no aesthetic charm can save it if its most important statements are false or even if they are merely unsupported or improbable." The double nature of such works, Ingarden thinks, contributes to their "weakness."

The interpretation of Plato's dialogues made by F. J. E. Woodbridge in *The Son of Apollo* would apparently be, by Ingarden's distinction, purely "literary." "The dialogues evidently define their own audience . . . ," Woodbridge writes. "In them we are not taken to a university, but to the steps of a court-house, to the court itself, to a plane tree by a limpid stream. . . . With generals there is talk about courage, with sophists on wisdom, with rhetoricians on rhetoric. . . . A curious, ugly man goes about with his questions and talk springs into being as naturally as blows from a quarrel."[33] On the other hand, Arnold Isenberg's description reflects an exclusively "philosophical" reading: "One who sits back and admires the give-and-take in the *Protagoras*," he writes, "is aestheticizing the dialogue. He does not share the main concern of the author and the characters, who are interested in the truth and who stop at the point of view only because the truth of the matter, embracing so many aspects is too hard to get at. But in Shakespeare the points of view are somehow final."[34] Although Isenberg does honor a distinction between reading the dialogue as philosophy and "aestheticizing the dialogue," his concept of the role of author and characters differs from Ingarden's. His interpretation affords no clear reason for the appearance of characters in the dialogues at all, since their "point of view" stops at the truth.

Amid general agreement that literary sentences are different from true statements, several questions are still outstanding. A likeness of the fictional "world" to the "real" world has been acknowledged. This has most commonly been called "verisimilitude." However, we are told by writers in English more clearly what verisimilitude is *not* than what it is. It is not propositional truth. It is not verifiable. It is not nonsensical. Its statements are not self-contradictory. Ryle suggests that Mr. Pickwick is a "complex predicate," but Miss MacDonald rejects this ("no one would ever say this"), and Margolis finds it difficult to see how such a complex predicate can be "imagined" to refer to someone, though not to any actual person. Again, affirming what verisimilitude is not, Margolis notes "the story as a mere story does not assert . . . a resemblance (to events in the world) and does not refer to whatever it does resemble."[35]

Again we find references to "pure fiction" or "whole fiction," although criteria of distinguishing this from some-time-fiction are far from clear. Miss MacDonald notes: "The content of very little fiction is wholly fictitious. . . . A story which introduces Napoleon or Cromwell but which departs wildly from historical accuracy will not have the verisimilitude which appears to be its object and will be implausible and tedious."[36] Margolis notes: "As far as I can see, it is perfectly possible to hold that historical novels are not pure fiction . . . or that a formulation of the alleged implications of a story obliges us to construe the story as more than a fiction . . . and, *at* the same time, to hold that we are *aesthetically* interested in verisimilitude and in truth or implication in novels."[37]

Jerzy Pelc's essay is not a polemic concerned with the authors just mentioned. His consideration of the role of "nominal expressions" in fictional sentences, however, offers an extremely clear and positive contribution toward answering questions that arise from their analyses. Pelc begins by acknowledging that there are several meanings of "fictitious subsistence." He concentrates here on analysis of semantic function of nominal expressions (nouns, adjectives, pronouns, and noun and adjectival phrases) in "fictitious subsistence." "The traditional explanation of the problem of literary fiction consists in linking it with the problem of the truth-value of the sentences occurring in a literary work. This is a good method of analysis, but I think that it can be usefully expanded by the study of the function performed by non-sentential expressions in creating fiction; we mean here nominal expressions in the grammatical sense of the term. . . ." Pelc's success appears to depend on his taking fictional sentences apart and examining their parts independently of the truth value of the sentences in which they appear.

Pelc classifies nominal expressions into "empty, singular and general—according to the number of the designata of a given nominal expression in a given language and a given use; into those with a singular, a general, and an empty intention—according to the way the meaning of a given expression determines its denotation; into individual and general—according to whether they can function only as subjects or as predicates as well." Pelc also distinguishes a token of an expression, the use of an expression, and an expression; and also between the dictionary value of an expression, "as isolated from the context and the situation accompanying its use, and the contextual value, modified by the context and the situation." He then distinguishes "fictive" use and "real" use according to whether a nominal expression is part of a "real" language or "fictive" language, having a real model consisting of a real object, or a fictional model consisting of a fictional object. He argues that "real" and "fictional" languages are different languages even if their lexicon is the same, *i.e.,* "if their expressions are pairwise equiform, if their expressions are pairwise equisignificant, if the grammatical structure of both languages is the same, and if the models of those languages are isomorphic."

Consider the example that Pelc gives, the fictional sentence "John was a secret emissary." The subject name *John* occurs in a fictive use, "as an empty expression with a singular intention; its counterpart is the imaginary hero of the story. But the predicate 'secret emissary' occurs in a real use, as a general name, and the whole sentence may be interpreted so that it states the inclusion of the class of the subject in the non-empty and non-singular class of the predicate. It would be contrary to the intention of the author to interpret the sentence as stating that fictitious John was a fictitious secret emissary; no, fictitious John was a 'true' secret emissary." In such a case, Pelc thinks we "oscillate" between an empty use of a nominal expression with singular intention, often functioning as subject, and a general and real use of another nominal expression, often functioning as predicate. Pelc suggests that literary fiction is a "mixed language." One and the same sentence may be "bipolar," containing both a fictitious and a real referent. He thinks that the "world of literary fiction" is not solely an imaginary world, "but in fact that world includes concrete objects in addition to imaginary ones. . . . It combines that which subsists in fantasy only with what exists objectively."

In the light of analyses of "truth" in fiction, preservation of the law of excluded middle has appeared irrelevant. Isenberg observes: "No one has ever thought of asking whether a law of excluded middle applies to art: can there be statements in poetry which are neither 'poetically true' nor 'poetically false'?"[38] Isenberg implies that "no one"

has lacked the sense to realize that truth references are not
to true propositions in poetry. Pelc's attitude differs from
this. He considers it a disadvantage of Ingarden's analysis
of literary sentences as quasi-true that the law of excluded
middle must be renounced. He thinks, however, that the
law can be saved if one accepts Russell's theory of descriptions. But this also has disadvantages. Not only must one
accept Russell's theory, and also adopt what to many is a
too cumbersome translation, but all nominal expressions in
a fictive use would have to be interpreted as descriptions in
Russell's sense.

Results of recent analyses of "truth" in art have been so
consistently negative that we are left with little explanation
for the persistence of truth references, or for the disagreement between those who were once dubbed the "yea sayers"
and the "nay sayers."[39] Pelc's essay offers some positive
explanation in the field of literature. One may see more
clearly, also, in what sense a sentence that as a whole is
neither true nor false, may yet have "verisimilitude" that
can be explained semantically. Again, if Pelc's theory of
literary fiction as a mixed language is correct, it becomes
difficult to see what so-called pure fiction amounts to.

Toward the end of his short history of aesthetics, Monroe
Beardsley writes: "Future historians of ideas, I believe, will
record with some astonishment—but also, I hope, with sym-
pathetic understanding—the remarkable preoccupation of
the twentieth century, through many of its best minds, with
the meaning of meaning. In so many varied concerns and
achievements—symbolic logic, linguistics, the interpretation
of dreams and neurotic behavior, the explication of poetry,
cultural mythology, religious symbolism, communication,
philosophical analysis—our attention has concentrated on
the problems of *semiosis,* the process in which one thing
functions as a sign for something else."[40] Mieczysław Wallis's essay, "The World of Arts and The World of Signs,"
is a more modest development of a theory of relation between art and signs than many have been. The author is as
aware of differences among arts and of their differences
from signs as he is of similarities. He does not attempt to

identify art *as* sign or symbol, and does not think it tenable even to divide all arts into those which are "semantic" and "asemantic." "Asemantic and the semantic works of art may be connected together in the most varied ways." His essay is more suggestive than conclusive, in effect ending on a question mark that invites further inquiry.

In aesthetics, Wallis has been mainly concerned with the value of aesthetic experience and appreciation. He has attempted to trace what he has called "non-valid" aesthetic appreciations to "inadequate" aesthetic experiences, and to analyze the logical structure of ratiocinations by means of which we motivate aesthetic appreciations. He has also tried to make more precise the fundamental concepts of semiotics, conceived as the science of signs, and to apply them to the theory of art and to the history of visual arts. From a detailed examination of different arts of different times and cultures, Wallis in the present essay finds that two independently complex "worlds"—that of arts and that of signs —are nevertheless intricately interrelated with one another. He indicates the extensive dependence of many arts on signs for their recording and their reproduction. Maintaining two "worlds," however, Wallis assumes that works of art can be identified and "communed" with independently of signs that may serve to record or reproduce them. For example, although he acknowledges that "musical notation is a system of conventional signs," he says that musical works "are, for the most part, not signs." This is in agreement with Ingarden's opinion: "The musical score . . . is only a schematic set of prescriptive signals as to how a given work should be played." It is also in agreement with Ossowski's conviction that "musical forms have no semantic functions."[41]

The question of the identity of a work of art in relation to signs is clearly a complex one. A good review of some extended considerations of this problem that have recently been made by several British and American authors is given in Margolis's chapter "The Identity of a Work of Art" in *The Language of Art and Art Criticism*. At the risk of exaggerating the importance of the particular art of music in the consideration of Wallis or others, it is interesting to note a marked divergence of two authors, both American, from the usual opinion that music as an art has no semantic function, or is not "itself" a sign or symbol. These are developments different from those mentioned by Margolis. Indeed, one of them—Susanne Langer's definition of music as a "presentational symbol"—Margolis considers "paradoxical" and one to be avoided.[42] Where music has generally been thought least likely candidate as an example of a semantic art (generally following Hanslick), Mrs. Langer has considered this art and poetry first in her development of Cassirer's theory of "dynamic forms." Again, Leonard Meyer has devoted an entire book to a theory of "emotion and meaning" in music.

Although Meyer's and Mrs. Langer's theories differ from each other, it appears that the development of both of them has depended in part on familiarity with the music theory of Heinrich Schenker. Schenker's writings were banned by the Nazis and were brought to the United States by a colleague, Hans Weisse, where largely through Weisse's explication they have gained considerable following. Mrs. Langer became familiar with the writings of Schenker when she was doing reading preparatory to writing *Philosophy in a New Key,* published in 1942. Meyer acknowledges that the influence of the concepts and methods of Schenker (and others) on his work is "obvious."[43]

Schenker's theory itself is not one of musical signification or of meaning. But his principles of score analysis have lent themselves especially well to definitions of musical form as "motion" or "dynamics," or as having "referential" functions. His theory would not be cordial to a definition of musical notation simply as a system of signs, or as a set of instructions for executing a work. Mrs. Langer's theory was largely worked out independently of Schenker, and her references to his writings, appearing in both *Philosophy in a New Key* and *Feeling and Form,* are brief. Nevertheless, she looks at the score analyst as having access to the truth about musical composition, much as one who would consult the composer himself, notes that Schenker's doctrines have been "corroborated" by "scientific evidence" of *gestalt* studies, and refers to them as though they verify her own theory.[44]

Schenker interpreted harmonic composition as a process of working out (*Auskomponierung*) the tones of either the Ionian (major) or Aeolian (minor) triads. The tonal relations that obtain in these triads function as means for determining harmonic identity of other tones in any given composition and these relations obtain essentially successively, rather than simultaneously. Harmonic structure develops through a process of hearing through time, such that the whereabouts of an established tonic must be maintained even when it is not momentarily sounding and such that a projection of possible future sounds is made. (Schenker thought of harmonic melody as self-contained counterpoint.)[45] The "backward" and "forward" process necessary to identify harmonic structural relations between tones executed successively, produces an impression of "motion" that can, depending on the case, reach considerable intensity. In the light of such an analysis of harmonic hearing, it is easy to see how a defense of music as "presentational symbol" like that of Mrs. Langer might be made by describing that which is "symbolized" as dynamic "forms" of feeling, and the "symbol" itself in terms of experienced motion, "presenting" what is symbolized. It is also easy to see how one may begin to think in terms of "probability" and even of "necessity" and as though tones are "referring" to one another, as Meyer did (although Meyer did not restrict his references to tonal music).

Schenker found a "natural" relation between the perfect fifth (dominant) and major third (mediant) and any ground tone, because the former tones are contained in the overtone series of a ground tone. Although Schenker did not draw an analogy with color, this is similar to the claim that there is a "natural" relation of green to blue and yellow because blue and yellow are "in" green. Indeed, they can often be "seen" enough in certain greens for us to speak of these greens as "yellowish" or "bluish." If a painter, then, wishes to "keep track" of green (let us say he is doing a "Study in Green"), he will do better to exploit

yellow and blue to this end, than purple and red. The greatest composers, Schenker thought, were those who exploited
the natural relation of fifth and major third (he gave explanations justifying also the minor third) to a tonic. The
close relation of these tones enabled introduction of a greater
complexity, and the extension of a composition through
longer periods of time than other systems of tone relation
without the subsidiary tones in these complexes losing their
harmonic identity, without the hearer's becoming "lost."

Since Schenker found the origin of harmonic musical
structure to be "natural," the particular composition would
not be interpreted as determining its own basic direction, nor
would the fundamental relations upon which it depended be
intersubjective, or merely culturally determined. We may
say that a musical composition does not reflect "reality,"
when that reality is thought of as the world of physical
objects. But in Schenker's opinion, a harmonic composition
is an exploitation of a reality of tone relations that anyone
should hear "implicit" in a single tone, just as anyone, regardless of conditioning, should see an affinity between
yellow, blue, and green.[46] Schenker's ontological specula-
tions, primarily his Platonic reference to the "Chord of
Nature," are generally disregarded by those who find his
insights into harmonic composition and the nature of harmonic hearing otherwise revealing and constructive.

A paper by Polish author Zofia Lissa, "On the Evolution
of Musical Perception," which is readily available in English
and is not included in this volume, clearly differs from
Schenker's references to "natural" tone relations. Mrs.
Lissa stresses dependence of different musical styles on
changes in psychology of musical perception, and would
base "correct conclusions" about musical structure and value
on what the particular historical period happens to have
brought.[47]

It would not be the case for Schenker, then, that musical
notation is merely a system of signs whose function can be
identified independently of a sounding composition and which
it merely serves to record or reproduce, any more than
logical symbols on a page can be interpreted as identifiable

aspects of a sign system that is independent of logical theory. The central question here is, of course, what "is" the score? To what exactly do we refer when we speak about musical "notation"? Wallis acknowledges in a footnote that "musical notation has yet to be investigated in a comprehensive way from the semiotic point of view. I for my part know of only one paper dealing with it from this point of view, namely the paper 'The Description of the System of Musical Notations,' by M. Langleben. . . ."

Stefan Morawski's essay "On Mimetism and Realism," is again concerned with the role of signs in relation to art, specifically iconic signs related to visual art and linguistic signs related to literature. This essay is presented as a Marxist extension of theory of realism in art, but also reflects several ideas of other Polish aestheticians. Chwistek's theory of plural reality is interpreted in the light of semiotic "models," which Morawski thinks are always sociohistorical. He does not take these models to be cultural "stereotypes" or "mere conventions," such that any plastic work, for example, may be interpreted as realistic or nonrealistic, mimetic or nonmimetic according to some momentary cultural slant. Many signs are quite accessible to a number of cultures. Indeed, the "essentials" of reality that realistic art probes are apprehended, Morawski thinks, on the basis of certain "natural" historical laws. Mimetism, he thinks, is based on "recurring modes of reality." Even beauty that is ascribed to nature he interprets as a projection of "cultural perspectives."

Morawski criticizes the method of some American authors, especially Beardsley, Weitz, and Margolis, in their analyses of literature. He finds that their examination of differences between fictional sentences and predicating propositions fails to recognize that the central mimetic function of literature is "global" and dependent on whole systems of signs. Morawski does not think that denotative function of literary language can be reduced to denotation in the logical sense. "Cognitive content" and "verisimilitude" in literature, he thinks, depend on "integral semantics."

s that all Marxists do not interpret realism

in art the same way, but that they all agree that realism is a "transformation" of reality. The usual dichotomy between a reproduction of reality in art and a "creation" of something new is not a tenable one. Art is semiotic, based on models from the world of nonart, but as a transformation of these models, it is also creative. Morawski distinguishes between mimetism and realism, although he finds that these functions of art overlap. Much realism is mimetic, but some of it is not. The mimetic, by Morawski's interpretation, is a reflection of "specific" aspects of a real model—its forms and "external" characteristics. The greater the degree of "transformation" of real models, the more condensed and selective the result, and more it "probes" essentials, the more it tends toward realism. Realism is concerned with the "essential," and may probe products of fantasy, devils, gods, and so on in a way in which mimetism does not. "The realist is a creator who is not content with a simple description of reality, but who, in addition, evaluates that reality by adopting definite points of view."

Morawski's essay is the only Marxist essay in this volume. However, Jan Białostocki's essay "Ars Auro Prior" is oriented historically in a way similar to Marxist historical orientation. Białostocki's exploration of a consistent downgrading of gold as a suitable artistic medium is an unusual detailing of the common assumption that artistic activity is superior to the value of its materials. One is hard put to name any British or American scholar who has put such wealth of scholarly detail into the minute examination of value judgments made in the past of one artistic material: gold. Primarily an art historian, Białostocki has been a favored collaborator of Erwin Panofsky, and has translated several of Panofsky's essays into Polish.

Jean G. Harrell

NOTES

1. *Contemporary European Philosophy,* trans. Nicholl and Aschenbrenner (Berkeley: University of California Press, 1957), p. 130.

2. *Art* (London: Chatto and Windus, 1914), p. 13.

3. *Ibid.,* p. 57.

4. *BJA* 5, no. 2 (April 1965) : 141, 126.

5. *Ibid.,* pp. 108, 109.

6. From a letter to the editor, March 25, 1969.

7. Henryk Skolimowski, *Polish Analytical Philosophy,* International Library of Philosophy and Scientific Method (London: Routledge, Kegan Paul, 1967), p. 210.

8. *Ibid.,* p. 211.

9. This connection has been pointed out by Prof. Allan Shields.

10. "Does Traditional Aesthetics Rest on a Mistake?", *Mind* 67 (1958). Reprinted in F. Coleman, *Contemporary Studies in Aesthetics* (McGraw Hill, 1968), and in H. G. Duffield, *Problems in Criticism of the Arts* (San Francisco: Chandler, 1968).

11. "Aesthetic Essence," from *Philosophy in America,* ed. Max Black (Ithaca, N. Y.: Cornell University Press, 1965), pp. 115-33. Reprinted in F. Tillman and S. Cahn, *Philosophy of Art and Aesthetics* (New York: Harper & Row, 1969), pp. 641-56. See also Paul Ziff, "The Task of Defining the Work of Art," *Philosophical Review,* no. 1 (Jan. 1953), reprinted in Tillman and Cahn; in Coleman; and in Duffield; also M. Weitz, "The Role of Theory in Aesthetics," *JAAC* 25 (1956) : 27-35.

12. "What Makes a Situation Aesthetic?", *PAS* Supplementary Vol. 31 (1957) : 75-92. Reprinted in J. Margolis, *Philosophy Looks at the Arts* (New York: Charles Scribner's Sons, 1962) ; David Prall, *Aesthetic Analysis* (New York: Crowell, 1936).

13. (New York: Bobbs-Merrill Co., Inc., 1968), p. 6.

14. (New York: Columbia University Press, 1962), pp. 113, 114.

15. *Philosophical Investigations,* trans. Anscombe (New York: MacMillan, 1953), pp. 194, 207.

16. "The Logic of Aesthetic Concepts," *The Proceedings and Addresses of the American Philosophical Association* (October 1963), pp. 43-66. Reprinted in Tillman and Cahn. See also Mrs. Hungerland's later development with some changes, "Once Again the Aesthetic and Non-Aesthetic," *JAAC* 26, no. 3 (Spring 1968) : 285-95.

17. *The Language of Art and Art Criticism* (Detroit: Wayne State University Press, 1965), p. 27.

18. "Aesthetic Concepts," *Philosophical Review* 48 (October 1959) : 421-50. Reprinted in Tillman and Cahn, and in Margolis, *Philosophy Looks at the Arts.*

19. P. 205.

20. In *Mysticism and Logic* (New York: Barnes & Noble, 1917). Reprinted by Doubleday Anchor (New York, 1957), pp. 120-39.

21. *PWN* (The Hague, Paris: Polish Scientific Publishers and Mouton,

1970), p. 4. See also Tatarkiewicz, "History of Philosophy and the Art of Writing It," *Diogenes* (Winter 1957).

22. *BJA* 7, no. 2 (April 1967): 140.

23. See, for example, Monroe C. Beardsley, *Aesthetics: Problems in the Philosophy of Criticism,* pp. 367–99; Bernard C. Heyl, *New Bearings in Esthetics,* Part 1, chap. 3; John Hospers, *Meaning and Truth in the Arts* (Chapel Hill: University of North Carolina, 1946); Arnold Isenberg, "The Problem of Belief," *JAAC* 13 (1955): 395–407; Kingsley B. Price, "Is There Artistic Truth?", *J. Phil.* 46 (1949); Albert Wm. Levi, "Literary Truth," *JAAC* 24, no. 3 (Spring 1966).

24. Joseph Margolis, *The Language of Art and Art Criticism,* chap. 11. Also his reply to F. E. Sparshott, *JAAC* 27, no. 3 (Spring 1969): 256–60.

25. On the question of truth in literature, for instance, see F. E. Sparshott, "Truth in Fiction," *JAAC* 26, no. 1 (Fall 1967): 3–7; R. K. Elliott, "Poetry and Truth," *Analysis* 27, no. 3 (January 1967): 77–85. Reprinted in Tillman and Cahn, pp. 631–40. Also M. Weitz, "Truth in Literature," *Revue Internationale de Philosophie* (1955), pp. 116–29.

26. Pp. 413, 414.

27. "Imaginary Objects," *PAS* Symposium, Supplementary Vol. 12 (1933).

28. P. 405. In Coleman, p. 258.

29. *Poetic Discourse* (Berkeley: University of California Press, 1958), pp. 44, 61, 120, 127.

30. "The Language of Fiction," *PAS* Supplementary Vol. 27 (1954): 165–84. Reprinted in Coleman; Margolis, *Philosophy Looks at the Arts;* and Tillman and Cahn.

31. *The Language of Art and Art Criticism,* p. 153.

32. "The General Question of the Essence of Form and Content," trans. Max Rieser, *J. Phil.* 57, no. 7 (March 31, 1960): 222–33.

33. (New York: Houghton, Mifflin Co., 1929), pp. 52–53.

34. P. 402. In Coleman, p. 255.

35. *The Language of Art and Art Criticism,* p. 156.

36. In Coleman, p. 273.

37. *JAAC* 27, no. 3 (Spring 1969): 260.

38. "The Problem of Belief," *JAAC* 13 (1955): 407.

39. Alexander Sesonske, "Truth in Art," *J. Phil.* 53, no. 11 (May 24, 1956): 345–46.

40. *Aesthetics from Classical Greece to the Present* (New York: Macmillan, 1966), pp. 342, 343.

41. Quoted by Max Rieser, "Contemporary Aesthetics in Poland," *JAAC* 20, no. 3 (Spring 1962): 423–24.

42. *Ibid.,* p. 43.

43. *Emotion and Meaning in Music* (Chicago: University of Chicago Press, 1956), p. 54.

44. See *Philosophy in a New Key* (Cambridge: Harvard University Press, 1942), p. 231n.

45. For good extended descriptions see: Allen Forte, "Schenker's Conception of Musical Structure," *J. Music Theory* (Yale School of Music Theory, New Haven, Conn.) 3, no. 1 (April 1959) : 1–30; Michael Mann, "Schenker's Contribution to Music Theory," *Music Review* 10 :3–26; Oswald Jonas, trans. Elisabeth Mann Borghese, *Introduction* to the English translation of Schenker's *Harmony* (Chicago: University of Chicago Press, 1954).

To date only *Harmonielehre* and *Der Freie Satz* have been translated into English from Schenker's 3-vol. work *Neue musikalische Theorien und Phantasien* (1906–35), the latter as *Free Composition* by T. Howard Krueger, Iowa University Ph.D Dissertation, 1960.

46. This is at variance with Ingarden's "one stratum" analysis of music. See his *Untersuchungen zur Ontologie der Kunst* (Tubingen: Max Niemeyer, 1962), pp. 3–115.

47. *JAAC* 24, no. 2 (Winter 1965) : 273–86.

Aesthetics
in Twentieth-Century Poland

1

ON PURE FORM*

by

Stanisław Ignacy Witkiewicz

("Witkacy")

Translated from Polish by
CATHERINE S. LEACH

S. I. Witkiewicz was born in 1886 in Warsaw, and committed suicide September 18, 1939, as the Germans were entering Warsaw. Although his father was an eminent writer and one of the leaders of the Polish intelligentsia, Witkiewicz was not a technically trained scholar. He was primarily a playwright and painter. Not only did he propose new ideas in both these fields, but in the last years of his life he invented a complicated amateur system of philosophy. He was author of more than 200 publications, chiefly plays, and including several voluminous novels. His "New Forms in Painting" was published in 1919, "Outlines of Aesthetics" in 1922, and what he termed his "opus magnum," titled Concepts and Propositions Implied by the Concept of Existence *in 1935.*

All of Witkiewicz's writings were republished in one volume in 1959. A group of twenty-one authors have also published a volume on Witkiewicz that contains an exhausive bibliography.

I do not intend to say anything new, only to give a general

---

*This essay, written in 1921, was first published in *Zet,* under the title "O czystej formie."

outline of the so-called theory of Pure Form. People have accused me of being long-winded and obscure on this subject; so now I wish to condense myself as far as possible and simultaneously treat the matter with a maximum of informality lest there be implied that some special knowledge is needed to understand the idea presented here.

I maintain, in spite of the opinion that the so-called new art is already outdated and its theory even more so—and in Poland perhaps the theory of art is of no concern at all to anyone except to a few specialists—that the elements of the idea, even the simplest ones, are worth recalling in view of persistently repeated misunderstandings on the part of various critics (such as Irzykowski, Boy, Piwiński, and the like, who would persuade the reader that everything has long since been settled and overcome through another approach); for the idea illuminates not only the new, but also earlier, artistic phenomena.

First of all, I should make it clear from the start that it is practically impossible here to discuss properly all the questions I intend to raise. I can simply sketch a general outline of the topic. This will not be a systematic exposition but rather a digression, which can only provide a stimulus to thought in the direction of my arguments, and material for debate.

Those who would like to have the question of the new art explained in a few words do not realize the difficulty of the problem. To tackle the subject of new art is unthinkable without having explained what art in general is; and that is tantamount to constructing a system of aesthetics. I have to add that those theories with which I am familiar do not satisfy me, and I must begin from the beginning, sometimes covering areas that have never been investigated and oftentimes areas that are thoroughly contaminated by the naturalistic ideology I am combatting. Therefore, I must ask him who would understand me to take an attitude of good will and forbearance instead of the programmatic resistance with which I have so often met; since, as Bertrand Russell has rightly declared, the desire to reject *par force* the opinions of a given author is not the best way to understand his ideas.

I would like to set forth what I mean as simply as possible without the admixture of any philosophical arguments, and even with as little as possible of my own terminology, which seems to discourage many from my theory of art. Whether I will achieve this in practice is completely another question. I will have a few words to confide about this at the end of the lecture.*

People have accused me of being complicated and unclear in the exposition of my theory. That objection may be partly correct. But besides a given author's formulation, which can be almost perfect or less close to perfection, a certain hierarchy does exist among topics themselves. I must point out that the problem of art belongs to the most difficult of all, which, however, does not prevent the great majority of people from speaking of it lightly and without serious reflection. Above all, critics behave this way, and they are responsible for the aesthetic breeding of the general public. But they are far from fulfilling their task. On the contrary, they accustom everyone to a complete lack of respect for artistic problems. Every man, without having thought through the basic difficulties at all, considers himself prophetic in this sphere.

As long as realism existed everything was still all right. Each man could talk about works of art, comparing the reality represented with that which he saw and heard. "I see nature, I see what it is like in the painting—why shouldn't I talk about it?" Well, everybody can talk about it, both the critic and the so-called layman, who differs from the former mainly in that he does not write reviews.

This is the way it was in painting, and in the other arts too, with the exception, perhaps, of music alone. The latter is the more fortunate because not so much can be said about the real-life emotions which are its nonessential though necessary content as there can about real life and objects in connection with painting, poetry, and the theater.

---

* Witkiewicz does not do this in writing.-trans.

But a renaissance of Pure Form has occurred—I will explain this term as far as I am able a' little while later— and this is a renaissance in forms unlike any previous ones. Suddenly everything has grown muddled in what appears to be inextricable chaos.

Everyone has begun to speak of real art with that same negligence that people acquired when speaking of represented life in relation to real life. Those who act in this way are similar, for me, to the people who talk about physics, criticizing Einstein and his theory, while all the time it was only yesterday that they barely knew physics existed and that before Einstein there were a Newton and a Galileo.

I will state the basic problem as follows: how do we distinguish a work of art from other objects and phenomena? I introduce this last distinction because certain works of art exist in time, for example, musical works, poems, and theatrical plays; others exist in space, like sculpture and painting. The first I call phenomena; the second, objects. In real life, we have both types of essences.

Posed in this way, the problem seems childishly simple. In solving it, however, we encounter apparently insurmountable difficulties. I must note that in aesthetics we have to proceed similarly as in other sciences.

The greater the number of phenomena we can comprehend in a uniform manner with the help of a given hypothesis, the more nearly perfect that hypothesis will be. We are obliged, however, to start from certain basic concepts that are indefinable and from certain primary assumptions that cannot be proven. Natural scientists and physicists proceed in this way, and even logicians and mathematicians. So much the more can the aesthetician. Everyone knows that the attempt to define all the concepts of a given system results in a vicious circle and everyone knows that you cannot build any system of ideas without at least one fundamental assertion, which much be accepted without proof.

In philosophy and aesthetics, the creation of something completely new is almost impossible. For centuries, one and the same problem has been formulated in ever-different ways. Perhaps the school of psychologists in philosophy has created a relatively new view, although, according to some, its roots go back to Descartes's system, and maybe further.

The problem of Existence and the problem of Beauty, along with the problem of Good, is as old as thinking humanity. The problem is to build a system in the most nearly perfect way, *i.e.,* the simplest and most economical way, by means of the least possible number of new conceptual formulas, creating concepts only when they are absolutely needed and when they actually correspond to some sort of reality.

The problem is also to build a fecund system, which means that it should be capable of bearing far-reaching consequences and of describing new phenomena as they arise in a given sphere. I have the impression that my system possesses these characteristics, provided we agree about its fundamental assumptions. For me, the difficulty of formulation is due to the lack of familiarity with my theories on the part of most people, and their ignorance of my books. It is for this reason, not being able to devote myself to one part of the problem here, that I must start at the beginning and present in summary the whole of a rather complicated theory.

In philosophy and aesthetics, we are usually dealing with systems that can be divided into two basic groups; and this has to do with the duality of Existence and the duality of Art. Since Existence is both temporal and spatial, we shall have, depending on which side of that duality the emphasis is placed, systems that are more materialist or more psychological and vitalist. Please note that I am speaking very generally here, and that there can exist a whole gamut of intermediary elements, among which the psychological monism of Mach, Avenarius, and Cornelius occupy a rather exceptional place. In aesthetics, we shall have the duality of form and content, and we shall have systems favoring one of these elements over the other, that is, we shall have realist and formist systems. Since it is impossible to negate either of these components, it would be a question of creating such a system as would recognize the relationship between them and assign to them their proper place in the whole of artistic phenomena. In my view, philosophy should proceed in the same manner. I want to indicate that my system will be formist. I shall arrive at it through a consideration of the question previously posed: what is the distinguishing characteristic of a work of art that makes it different from other objects and phenomena; why do we designate such different essences as sculptures, poems, paintings, musical works, and stage plays by the common name of art? For the time being, we shall accept as a primary fact that these essences must possess a common characteristic.

The method I am going to make use of will seem somewhat artificial. I will have to give examples of series of objects and phenomena which, at first glance, will look rather crazy.

Let us take a man who is howling in pain. Here, we shall have a certain succession of changing sounds, filling certain segments of time. First of all, therefore, we have qualitative elements that are irreducible and indefinable, namely, sounds. Next, we have pitches, tonal colors, and their intensities. If we could register accurately the duration of each invariable tone, we would get a division of the whole segment of time into shorter and longer partial segments, filled with various sounds of differing intensities. This scheme would express precisely the form of the suffering man's howl. All phenomena in time will have their own more or less definite form, which will be observable directly, sometimes more easily, sometimes with more difficulty. In this case, we can define form as a certain sequential pattern in time. We will distinguish sequences that are more ordered or less. We can, according to the degree to which they are ordered, set up a whole series of phenomena that are completely continuous, at least theoretically. In this series, two neighboring elements will be more alike than two distant ones, insofar as we abstract from other characteristics and examine only their form. Starting from the howl of our suffering man, we can go on, in an almost continuous line, to a symphony. As intermediate elements, we can accept,

for example, various types of singing, from indistinct humming all the way to a definite melody, until finally we end
up with a perfectly constructed musical work. All these
kinds of phenomena will have qualitative elements, *i.e.,*
sounds arranged in a certain form—from absolute arrhythmia to a definite rhythm, and in addition, the form can
complicate itself in such a way that the last elements of
the series can, at first sight—or rather hearing—give the
impression of being completely formless.

Besides this, the combination of sounds can express something for us; they can be symbols of other phenomena. The
above-mentioned howl will be an expression of pain. A song
can express a whole gamut of different feelings that do not
lend themselves to interpretation and presentation in any
other way. That which given combinations of sounds express, we shall call their real-life content, in contrast to
form, which we shall define as the only certain sequential
pattern in time.

In this sense, we can say that form serves as a receptacle
for a certain content. Since all these phenomena possess
qualitative elements, *i.e.,* sounds, and they all possess form
and express a certain content—which, in the case of music,
is apprehended directly—we do not have any data, apparently, for classifying some and not others as works of art.

Let us take another example: a certain moment in a real
battle we are watching. The order or form of this phenomenon will be a disorder of figures or of certain complexes of
colored shapes within our field of vision, which we accept
at once as limited—let us imagine we are looking at the
battle through a window. Next, let us take a tableau showing
the battle, then a part of the battle panorama, and finally,
a realistic painting and a formist painting of the battle. In
the first case, the battle will present itself to us in all its
haphazardness, in spite of its probably having been thought
over in its entirety by a commander of genius, and executed
according to his idea.

The person who put together the tableau stopped the
movement of the figures and regrouped them in order to
make the picture of the battle clearer for the viewer. Its

form has become more distinct. The person who painted the picture, and who was forced to deal with surface alone, introduced still greater order into that battle: the commander stands in the foreground amid a group of warriors, which sets off his figure even more; banners are silhouetted against sky, and so on. Kossak,* for example, composed his pictures in this way. Here, the form is still more distinct, although it only serves to bring out the content better, which is the battle itself, as battle. The formist—to whom only the form matters, as is obvious from the term itself—was, from the standpoint of real life, absolutely arbitrary in composing his battle. However, some people will see immediately (others only after reading the titles) that his picture is of a battle, more or less distorted, both in its general composition and in its parts, the individual figures.

Again, we have a series of phenomena, or of objects really, with both form and real-life content, and with qualitative elements, *i.e.,* colors as their material. Again, we apparently have no special characteristic that would enable us to classify this series into objects that are works of art and those that are not.

Similarly, we can pass in a continuous fashion from an agitator's speech at a rally to a recited poem, adding more and more new characteristics, none of which, however, will tell us unequivocally at which point in the series poetry begins. The agitator can become more and more eloquent; his speech can acquire better and better form; he can slowly fall into a frenzy, begin speaking in rhythmic prose and then improvise in both rhyme and rhythm. But when the transition occurred, no one will be capable of saying. In absolutely the same way, we can go from any sort of real-life adventure—some street incident, or bedroom drama—to a stage play. For those who say that make-believe is the essence of theater and who assert that the stage begins at the point where everyone begins to pretend something, we can assume that in every succeeding element of the series, real people, but for the moment not actors, will slowly start pretending, then improvising more and more, then

---

* Wojciech Kossak (1856-1942), Polish painter of battlescenes.-trans.

planning their actions, and in connection with this, they will perfect the form of the whole phenomenon until they arrive at a splendidly constructed drama and afterward a formist drama, in which, as the name indicates, the form is the main thing. Yet, if a continuous passage is possible, again, we apparently cannot define where art begins and life ends. The situation becomes hopeless.

Without having made any assumption as our point of departure, we shall be unable, theoretically, to separate art from other phenomena. The most we shall be able to say is that all phenomena have form and content, and we shall define art like any other phenomenon, as a certain content in a certain form and, when writing about art, we shall analyze the real-life content enclosed in it—which art and theater critics do mostly, less so critics of poetry, and least of all music critics, since, as I have observed, the feelings expressed in music are difficult to express in general. And from time to time, as critics do in the above proportions, we shall say something about form as about a receptacle for a certain content. Without a fundamental assumption, all additional assumptions—for example, that art is the expression of the human soul, that it is the desire to please, the imposition of one's own feelings and thoughts on others, even the saying that it is Beauty—turn out to be unsatisfactory. A great many other essences are the expression of human soul, but are not art. Thoughts and feelings we also impose in completely unartistic ways and likewise endeavor to please by means having nothing to do with art. Even an undifferentiated concept of Beauty does not apply, nor does the additional definition that art must be the creation of man. We think some view or other is beautiful, a woman for a man is beautiful and vice versa, a horse can be beautiful, a cow, a machine, and other objects, without being works of art; and technology is creation, as is science and civic activity.

If we adequately differentiate the concept of Beauty, it may appear suitable at first, but then it must be replaced by concepts that are more precise. The concept of Beauty implies the concept of pleasing. Liking or not liking is something immediately given, capable of being described but not justified. We have one certainty: that our relationship to art is immediate, which means that liking or disliking does not result from intellectual understanding, even though we may speak figuratively of liking a philosophical tract, or a machine whose construction we have understood through explanation.

Since the single, undifferentiated concept of Beauty appears to be unsuitable, we must accept a primary assumption that the essence of art is form. The concept of Beauty can be broken down, then, into concepts of Practical Beauty, connected with the usefulness of an object or phenomenon, and Formal Beauty, which consists in order alone, in form, or in the structuralization of an object or phenomenon. This will be beauty in the precise artistic sense. It should be noted that there can be objects which possess both kinds of Beauty; correspondingly, we shall have practical likes and formal likes. Because, however, all the previously described elements of all the series had form, we can like all of them artistically, or not. And this is how it is, of course, but we can like them more artistically or less, depending on the proportion of the two components: the formal and the practical. To the extent that the formal and the real-life or practical elements remain secondary, we will be talking about artistic pleasure.

Form is that which imparts a certain unity to complex objects and phenomena.

And what I call aesthetic satisfaction, in contrast to other, purely practical pleasures, is precisely the apprehension of that unity, an apprehension that is immediate, not run through any intellectual calculations. I can put it in another way as the integration of a multiplicity of elements into one whole. Having thus defined Artistic Beauty, we can now designate, in the series mentioned above, the places from which we can start reckoning works of art. They will be wherever form begins to predominate over content in our experiencing of the objects and phenomena in those places and wherever the unifying of the many into the one comes about, without any subordinate considerations, solely within a purely formal construct of these objects and phenomena, which directly affects us. Such a form, which acts through itself alone and evokes aesthetic satisfaction, I call Pure Form. It is not, however, a form deprived of content, because no living creature can create such a thing; but it is one in which real-life components are secondary. In the abstract, we can view every object and every phenomenon from the standpoint of its form. Here though, we are concerned not with the abstract but with direct experience; and only form that is felt, that acts directly upon us, do I call Pure Form.

What then will be the role of the real-life elements, which adulterate even the most abstract Pure Form? In music, feelings are the real-life ingredients. Music can be the means of their expression, or they can serve merely as the pretext for a certain dynamic tension and qualitative coloring of the parts that make up a musical work. In the case of the latter, we have to do with Pure Form in music. In painting, a similarity of the parts of the composition to certain objects will impart directional tensions. This concept will enable us to eliminate from aesthetics the notion of the object and its distortion, a notion that involves the idea of the imitation of that object, and further, the idea of reality in general, which so clouds a simple view of art. From the moment we have an artistic composition, consisting of individual shapes within a closed space, it makes a difference to the whole where, for example, a given partial shape begins and where it ends, and in which direction we think it tends. The similarity to objects, precisely, indicates those directions in an unequivocal way and imparts to them a directional tension. Of course, just as feelings in music are fused into a unity with a given subject, so too in the composition that arises in the imagination of the painter, the shapes are conceived together with their directional tensions. The creative process is a homogeneous one; only, to describe it, we must break it down into its limited, constituent moments.

Passing on to poetry and theater, I must observe that the situation in these spheres is far more complicated. Here we are dealing not with simple, qualitative elements as in painting and music, *i.e.,* colors arranged into partial shapes and sounds into rhythms, but with mixed elements. To the sound value of a word is added meaning and the image it evokes. Not every word calls forth a picture to the same extent. Sometimes a private semantic complex, namely, the sum of that which is connected with a given sign and which is the reason why that sign is not an empty sound but precisely a concept with a certain meaning, can be made up of other qualities: touch, taste, muscular sensations, and inner feelings.

The novelty of my theory consists precisely in that I have recognized the semantic element of a word as an artistic element. Only in this way, I feel, can the theory of Pure Form apply to mixed arts, and I have the impression that it takes precise account of reality. The elements of content are simultaneously artistic elements. It all depends on their being blended into a unity with the elements of sound and image, thus giving new, mixed elements, the structuring of which is Pure Form in poetry. Sound, image, and meaning must form a unity in order for the construct to make an aesthetic impression. I call that new quality a poetic quality. The good poet will be the one who can, like a chemist joining elements in a new chemical combination that is different from any one of them taken separately, make an absolute unity by using the three above elements in a formal poetic conception that arises within him. This constitutes the strange effect of good poetry. Listening to such poems, we cannot really tell what world we are in: that of pictures, of sounds, or of meanings of words. We apprehend directly their amalgamation in the general construct of the poem, but when the poem is over, we awaken as if from a dream, as if we had been in some unknown dimension. For this reason, it is perhaps most difficult to be a good poet without having that mysterious capacity for creating amalgamations of apparently heterogeneous elements. At the most, one can learn how to write correct exercises in rhymed form on an assigned intellectual or emotional subject. To reconstruct in memory an impression from poetry one has listened to is almost impossible, just as is the reconstruction of certain bizarre dreams.

It is a more difficult thing still with theater, which has a fourth and additional ingredient: action, which, like the word, also has the element of meaning. The action, however, is a part of a changeable, real image, to which are joined the images suggested by the words. In addition, combinations of sounds can be infinitely varied, beyond the sounds of the words themselves. To combine these diverse elements into the amalgamations that make up the complex whole of the construct is the task of the formist playwright, the director, actors, and set designers. Actually, the author only provides these artists with a pretext for creation. They create the essential play on the stage. That new quality, arising from the amalgamation of the aforesaid elements, I call the theatrical quality. New poetry may already have realized its Pure Form, but formist theater is still in the germ, and who can tell yet what horizons may open up for it. This can also lead to a new way of staging the classics (for example, Słowacki in Poland), which are mainly played and produced realistically to the detriment of the formal values of these works. In Poland, Wyspiański* and Miciński** should be recognized as the precursors of formism in the theater. With the former, the pictorial element predominates, while with the latter we have an ideal equilibrium of all the elements.

Here is still another definition of a work of art: although its execution and working out can be a collective deed in certain instances, the idea, the formal postulate by which it is forged into a unity, must arise in one individual. I maintain that even in those arts where the action occurs in time— music, poetry, and theater—the first conception must have a spatial character, since we cannot picture, or think of a simultaneous image of the whole temporal complex, unless we are dealing with improvisation, or with the juxtaposing

---

* Stanisław Wyspiański (1869-1907), painter, poet, and playwright.

** Tadeusz Miciński (1873-1919), poet and novelist, author of weird, amorphous prose poems, sometimes called dramas, sometimes novels.–trans.

of pieces side by side. But a work so conceived cannot be a construct to the same degree as a thing built up from a formal postulate given at the base as the potential whole.

Since all that exists, and therefore, we ourselves, both psychologically and physically, along with objects and large complexes of phenomena in nature—since all things have this fundamental characteristic, that they form to a greater or lesser degree a certain whole and a unity and are made up of parts joined together in that whole—in other words, they are a unity in multiplicity, or vice versa—I consider this law the basic law of existence. For this reason, I assert that art always expresses one and the same thing: that law. And it is expressed in an immediate way, not subject to any subordinate considerations, either biological, practical, or intellectual. This feeling of unity in multiplicity is given to us directly in the form of the unity of our personality, our "I," and for this reason, I call art an expression of the unity of personality. Since this feeling is basic, I have called it a metaphysical feeling in contrast to other feelings, and due to this, many misunderstandings have arisen between myself and my opponents. It may be that this term was an unlucky choice. But if it is one term that is being disputed, the sense in which it is used by the given author must always be remembered, and in general one ought to remember the definitions of the ideas he introduces; otherwise discussion is senseless. I shall not go into the philosophical justification for these assertions here. What I want to point out is that although we may create a theory of Pure Form without bringing in philosophy, a deeper justification of this theory must have a basis in the fundamental laws of existence in general, in other words, in the laws of General Ontology.

Generally, then, we can define a work of art as a construct of arbitrary elements, both simple and mixed, created by an individual as the expression of the unity of his personality, that acts on us in an immediate way by reason of its very structuring.

It is also characteristic of a work of art that elements that are unpleasant in themselves—a bad juxtaposition of colors, musical dissonances, combinations of words and ac-

tions that are bizarre, unpleasant and disturbing in themselves—can, in the sum total of a given work be the necessary elements of its unity or artistic beauty. This making of
the whole out of elements that are unpleasant in themselves
and their predominance in a given work, I call artistic perversity. Heretofore it has been possible to conceive of a
work of art without the use of perverse means, but today,
in view of the feverish pace of life, social mechanization,
the exhaustion of all means of action, and a blasé attitude
toward art, it has become necessary to employ perverse
means. Creative artists cannot survive in the older, quieter,
simpler forms; nor can today's viewers and listeners experience anything, meaning those of course, who want to
experience something, not those who search in art for am-
plified reality or even just plain reality.

The worn-out forms of old yielded realism as a symptom
of temporary decline. Realism is presently going through a
crisis due to complete exhaustion, and it shows up in the
theater as a feverish search for new subjects. Typical manifestations of this process—and they are manifestations of
decadence in the full force of its expression—are Bernard
Shaw, Pirandello, and to a certain degree, Evreinov. Although the end of certain processes can resemble the begin-
nings of a completely different order of phenomena, I do
not see in these authors—in spite of all the recognition
awarded the first two—the beginning of a new creativity,
only the final, powerful twitch of a long process of dying.
The curiosities in both Shaw and Pirandello, whether strictly
naturalistically or symbolically justified, have a strong after-
taste of decadence, of futility, of hopeless impasse.

To those who are interested in further explanations—
from my point of view—of the process that has led to the
present state of affairs, I must recommend the fourth part
of my book entitled *New Forms in Art*, also *Aesthetic
Sketches,* and my book *The Theater*. In our time, the highest
art, in which the condition of modern man is expressed
indirectly, without hypocrisy, must of necessity be complicated, or as the case may be, artificially simplified, artistically
perverse, disturbing; and the old calm, with very few ex-

ceptions, can only be in the form of reproducing earlier, now dead, styles, but not in the creation of new formal values. And art is always concerned with the latter, with that fresh, never-before-existing form in which an artist must essentially and sincerely experience creation and which can awaken us anew, after having been satiated by the old forms, to aesthetic satisfaction. Besides, the reproduction of the past, the re-creation of reality, occupies people who are incapable of artistic creation but who have a strange, inexplicable desire and even necessity to paint and write. "I see the world, I know something about life; why shouldn't I paint the world and describe life?", they think, and cover thousands of canvasses and reams of paper. But as artistic good breeding becomes more widespread, they will be less and less needed, and will slowly disappear, perhaps simultaneously with real creativity and that same artistic breeding which, after passing a certain high point, will also become unnecessary as society grows more and more mechanized and, in connection with that, as personality disappears. Such is, I hold, the irreversible law of social development. Society creates certain splendid, deep, and beautiful things in order to destroy them mercilessly for one purpose: to make all mankind happy in more material dimensions.

So too religion will die sometime, as will philosophy and art, which flow from one and the same source: the Secret of Existence, the experience and understanding of which will become inconvenient for a socially perfect, mechanized man. I want to add here, in connection with what I said about realism, that I exempt the novel, which does not belong to Pure Form, from the formal requirements in my system.

Returning to the series of phenomena and objects I described above, we have to affirm that it is impossible to define precisely and objectively the line between realism and formism, due to their being nearly continuous and to the scarcely perceptible transitions from one element to the other. For each individual that line must lie at a different point in the series, even though we shall certainly be able to define elements that are quite far apart as realistic or formist. For one, Gauguin's paintings will still be too realistic to be felt as Pure Form, and for him the line will begin, for example, at the works of Derain, or Picasso. Another will feel them as Pure Form already and in the case of this individual, the line will shift according to the changing state of artistic ennui and other inner states. It will be the same in music and poetry and with the representation of life in the theater.

Further, elements at the same point, as far as Purity of Form is concerned, will always be subject to our likes and dislikes. In zoology, we also have many species of objects arranged in a series according to certain characteristics, and a person can prefer beaches, for example, to mammals and insects. But a zoological description of a given species will be objective. Regardless of our sympathy or antipathy to certain animals, we shall necessarily have to accept this description. I can be afraid of and I can be disgusted by a rhinoceros, but from the time the zoologist describes his anatomy and functions and the mutual connections between his organs, I will have to accept that description. No description and explanation of a mutual connection between the given parts of a composition can force me to recognize works of art that I do not like immediately, as beautiful. I can, at the most, recognize intellectually that they possess a certain construction but do not give me, immediately, aesthetic satisfaction—in a given moment, of course. For we must, in general, admit that adjustment to new forms in art is an undeniable fact. It is obvious from this that objective evaluation and criticism of a work of art is an absolute impossibility, since the essential relation to it is based on subjectivism. The critic should only know who he is, and whether he is looking at a given thing from the point of view of form or of content, and then he should take account of his subjective artistic impressions with the help of a system of unequivocal concepts. But critics do not even fulfill this modest requirement. Mostly they talk about only the real-life side of a work of art; as for their system of ideas, they are probably the most elusive creatures on our planet.

Naturalism left in its wake the delusion that there was

an objective criterion, namely, reality, to which the artistic re-creation of reality can be compared. How illusory that criterion is, is proven by the systematic overturning of both critics and public by new individuals in art. Neither the public, nor the critic usually, thinks about the essence of art and they demand that it represent life, of which they should really have enough in the course of their everydays, and even holidays. For this kind of experience, one need not go to the theater at all. One can find it—perhaps not so condensed as it is in the theater—at home, in the street, or at the coffee-house. This is the result of having been long oppressed by the products of naturalism, with which the nineteenth century renounced real art, and the naturalistic ideology connected with those products, which is just as difficult today to overcome. People make improbable demands on artists, as if they were machines and not live beings. They require of them consistency and conformity with a given theory, which a quietly working scholar might have, but not someone who is a prey to the heartrending contradictions of form and content, which are contained in the very essence of art. A given critic will always find a reason for "picking on" a given artist and it is always an unessential reason.

Let them criticize the artist for his formal mistakes, and everything would be bearable then. But that constant complaint about inconsistent feelings, improbable situations, lack of credibility, unnatural colors, sentences that are senseless either in logic or in real life—such things can beget a complete reluctance to teach anybody anything. When will this finally end?

The process of conceiving a work of art and the development of the artist himself must be understood: first he achieves his own form of expression, which gives a shape to his feelings and thoughts and represents his own images. This is the first stage, at which even the most talented sometimes stop, then fall into naturalism, unable to wade through to the sphere of Pure Form.

Next, having conquered the material of real life, the artist simply employs it as a pretext for creating an abstract, formal construct with directional and dynamic tensions and qualitative coloring. Of course, this development must be accomplished in a natural, not a programmatic, way. Since the given individual does not create his own style *par force,* this process goes on slowly and can fluctuate considerably. The battle with real-life content in art is a complicated and difficult story, and sometimes one cannot demand of a given artist complete continuity of development and conformity to his theoretical or even nonintellectualized assumptions, which might be deduced from his previous works. However, one should demand from viewers and listeners a certain disposition for receiving formal and not real-life values in works of art. Despite the pressure from naturalistic ideology in our day, one can achieve this by teaching them what the essence of art consists in, which they have forgotten or did not know at all, as a result of an upbringing and of living in an atmosphere of naturalism. Of course, no one can hold it against a person for not liking a given work. What matters is that his liking it or disliking it be for the right reason. It is hardest, of course, to dispose oneself to receive formal values in the theater, but it is not impossible, even with the most hardened naturalists, as I have already managed to confirm several times.

People who are up in arms today about the distortion of reality in art show that they have no artistic understanding either of yesterday's or of today's art. They understand undistorted reality as it was represented in old pictures and in old plays; emotionally, they understand relatively uncomplicated old music; they understand the intellectual content of old poetry. Thus, if they are shown that same reality transformed in a certain manner for artistic purposes, *i.e.,* for the whole of the construct and its individual tensions, they cannot understand how anything so pretty as the visible world, or how feelings and the meaning of life can be so mercilessly transfigured, twisted, and caricatured. Beauty in reality and beauty in art are two completely separate domains. When people will learn to see and hear, they will cease to be preoccupied with reality and will enter a world of experience, hitherto closed to them, that of Pure

Form, and perhaps someday they will be thankful that this world was opened to them. It is an interesting fact that, due to the atmosphere of the epoch, even people who have not been saturated with impressions in a given sphere of art accept works by new artists relatively easily; and once they acquire an understanding of them, they begin to understand all previous art differently, which before they had not understood in its essence; and the realism that used to delight them will begin to bore and tire them. The atmosphere of the life that surrounds us acts in such a way that people who have never drawn, or children, for example, express themselves in forms that are completely modern, and oftentimes completely original. It is possible that the styles of today's artists are easier to imitate than earlier ones; it is even possible that in view of the general riotous proliferation of forms it is easier to become an artist today than before, due to the democratization of art generally. But at a certain level of artistry, these problems become irrelevant and Picasso is no less a startling phenomenon than Titian or Botticelli.

Returning to the question of being open to impressions of form, observe that one can look at a whole painting, or, as the case may be, at a certain part of it, *e.g.*, one can look at a certain shape just as a shape, or also, abstracting from reality, one can see it only as a certain mass joined to others within the total construct and possessing a definite directional tension, expressed precisely through its similarity to a certain shape.

If, however, that shape will have been realistically executed by imitating the plasticity of the real object in a given light, then no one, be it with the greatest good will, will see anything in that part of the picture except the thing represented and that impression will only destroy the whole of the picture, which, but for this, could have even made a certain construct. But for defining the point where the execution starts making it impossible to experience Pure Form, we have no criterion. It is the curse of the whole domain of art that there exist no objective criteria in it, and if someone should obtain from one of Chełmoński's* paintings or from one of Grubiński's** plays, impressions that are purely formal, or if someone should assert that a painting of Picasso's or a play of Shakespeare's is too realistic for him, nothing can be done about it. In the case of plays, there is the added question of staging. However, just as no one will ever create Pure Form in painting out of a badly composed picture by darkening the outlines of shapes and destroying their modeling, so too no theater performance will ever make Pure Form on the stage out of a realistic play, since the very point of departure for these things, as well as the process of their conception, is completely other than for works of Pure Art. Likewise, if one were to model the shapes in a formist picture or produce a formist work realistically, he could destroy their essence and make it impossible for the viewer to have a purely aesthetic experience.

A work has a certain self-identity and it is an uncrossable line that no interpretation can overstep. If a given play or, for example, a musical work loses its value, on the whole, through a realistic or sentimental interpretation, without retaining some worth in precisely these dimensions, it shows that the formal element predominates in it. The wrong interpretation can make a worthless, realistic hoax out of a perfect, formal thing, or can change a good realistic drama into formal nonsense. Paintings and sculpture are fortunate, since they are dependent only on the disposition of the viewer; but with poems, musical works, and plays, one can do things to them that are simply monstrous, that destroy their whole value, and added to that is the problem of how viewers and listeners will feel about them. If, therefore, a person wants at all costs to see in art the outer world as such, either distorted or undistorted, and wants to see in the theater reality that is either faithfully reflected or grotesquely caricatured, he will never experience aesthetic satisfaction.

There is still another type of person who is not satisfied

---

* Józef Chełmoński (1850–1914), Polish landscape and genre painter.
** Waclaw Grubiński, Polish playwright and novelist.

with anything, nor, as I maintain, can anything satisfy him. Like those who are unable to surmount reality in art, they cannot experience artistic impressions. These people do not understand Pure Form any more than the realists do, and in art they search precisely for reality that is distorted. They are realists *à rebours*. Such were our futurists in theory, but luckily not so often in practice. Thus, looking at Picasso's paintings, these people say that they see too much of normal nature in them and not enough of the strange. While listening to formist poems, they lament not hearing a bellow from sort of unimaginable metaphysical beast; and while watching a play, which for others has quite enough abnormal life, they are bored because the actors are not abstract triangles, or do not devour ironclads, or twist themselves into steel discs like corkscrews. To satisfy these people is as hard as satisfying realists. Both these species are not looking for artistic impressions, but only for normal or abnormal real-life experiences. As long as they are not satisfied with circuses, snake-swallowers, and other tricksters, they must remain unsated. Maybe sometime in a dream they will satiate themselves, provided destiny permits them to dream up something sufficiently monstrous.

While we are at it, we can clear up still another misunderstanding. We have seen that a work of art must be conceived with reference to the whole of the creating psyche, that all the artist's thoughts, feelings, and images go into the make-up of the work, as an element nonessential in itself, but necessary. In poetry and the theater, the connection between real-life content and Pure Form is much closer than in the other arts because in these two spheres the emotional elements are not rendered into a form that is indeterminate, as in music, and the semantic content emphasizes real-life elements far more strongly than do the shapes in a painting, for example. Then, too, reality is distorted for purposes of composition, due to the insatiability for form, and in poetry and the theater, this distortion strikes the eye far more strongly as something out of the ordinary, for both logic and life, even as a senseless combination of words and situations, than does a strangeness of feelings in

music, for example, or even a distortion in painting. Of
course, in theater, where artistic perversity is so closely
linked with perversity in life, the overcoming of a true-to-
life position is the hardest. If, in the place where we have
been accustomed to seeing the most normal life, we see
something that even slightly deviates from it and is not
justified by any blatant, easily deciphered symbolism, the
majority of people begin to burn with a holy flame of indignation, even though nothing more wicked is happening than
what takes place in a hundred realistic plays. But if we take
into consideration how really monstrous are the infamies
that occur in practically every French farce, which everyone
digests with an agreeable smile and no one gets annoyed at
in the least, we must admit that even a slight distortion of
real life, as in my plays for example, is innocent child's play
compared with what occurs in realistic dimensions in the
normal theater, and that the viewers' indignation derives
from a bad disposition and prejudice. The average viewer
can take a lot, as long as the monstrousness of the life that
is represented does not diverge too much from the monstrousness of daily life, and as long as the guilty are pun-
ished and there is no so-called glorification of crime or
immorality. But in how many normal plays, under a very
thin lid, as it were, of ultimate justice, whereby sin is pun-
ished and virtue rewarded, simple nastiness is presented, for
the observation of which moralists, who are outraged by
distortion, go to the theater. I am convinced that the moral
level of my plays is not at all lower than the average level
of theater today. But a certain category of people comes
to them with a prejudice. It is because of this prejudice
that completely innocent sentences are entirely misconstrued
and the meaning of my heroes' noble pronouncements is
twisted around. If the word "God" falls from the lips of
one of them, this is, in advance, considered a blasphemy,
which makes understanding my simplest thoughts, which
are not sacrilegious but the opposite, impossible. The force
of prejudice and an *a priori* attitude about what is indecent
or abominable have induced certain people to hear, in completely innocent words, similar words that are coarse and

vulgar. It is the same with so-called programmatic nonsense. Since the feelings and thoughts of the given poet and playwright must enter into the process of conceiving even the most abstract Pure Form, as long as he does not think up his works in cold blood but creates them under the dictate of a primary, initially undefined, formal conception, each work will contain at least a particle of his world view and, to a certain degree, will be unconsciously symbolic, just as every dream is, according to Freud's theory—even the most senseless. This symbolism presents no obstacle at all to Pure Form, as long as it is not programmatic and does not impose itself as such on the viewer, forcing him to puzzle out rebuses, thus preventing immediate artistic experience. Realism in the text and in the staging imposes itself immediately, as soon as it comes into being on the boards, and it excludes the simultaneous understanding of the artistic construct because two different things cannot be the content of our existence at one and the same point of time.

The symbolic content can be thought over after the end of the spectacle, when the receiving of impressions does not prevent this.

I have been endeavoring to talk about each of my plays "in my own words," as they say, and to explain their connection with the whole of my real life, my social and my artistic convictions.

Once at Szyfman's in Warsaw they put on my one-act play entitled "A New Liberation."

A propos that, I explained the real-life content of that play to someone for the first time, seven years after its writing. On the day after, I heard an almost identical interpretation from a person whom I had never seen before in my life. But even if interpretations differ, depending on the psychic content of a given individual, that will not discredit the Pure Form of a given work. Everybody explains a given thing, which is not completely unequivocal in its meaning, according to his own view of the world and according to those elements that predominate in him.

Because I assert that a creating artist should not confine himself to either logical or true-to-life meaning in the constructing of his works, I am suspected at once of programmatic nonsense as such, which releases the viewer from verifying whether the artist's assertion is even correct.

These misunderstandings stem mainly from the lack of an artistic disposition on the part of viewers and also, perhaps, from the fact that plays are, for the moment, still burdened with real-life and symbolic content and are far from that abstraction of form which I would like to achieve. This, of course, depends on the style of staging too, which is not always unified enough so that real-life elements can be entirely absorbed into an artistic experience from the whole construct. I assume that the relative success of my play entitled *Jan Maciej Karol Wścieklica,** has been due to various, minor misunderstandings. I say nothing about its being, of all my things, the most heavily laden with real life, in other words, from my point of view, perhaps, the least successfully executed. However, I did not write it in a compromising mood, calculating on success, of which I am suspected by several of my enemies. Although I do allow compromise in art, by drawing almost naturalistic portraits,** this, however, is not without benefit for one's draftmanship and can keep one in "shape," in the sporting sense of the word. That compromise I regard as immeasurably less than a compromise in the theater, which I would have to characterize as a dishonest social act.

---

* The title is simply a man's name: "John Matthew Charles Wścieklica" –trans.
** Witkiewicz painted portraits for a living.–trans.

2

PLURAL REALITY IN ART

by

Leon Chwistek

Translated from Polish by
HANNAH ROSNEROWA

Wielość rzeczywistości (Krakow, 1921). Reprinted in Leon Chwistek, *Pisma logiczne i filozoficzne* (Logical and Philosophical Writings), vol. 1 (Warsaw, 1961).

Leon Chwistek was born in 1884 and died in 1944. Unlike Witkiewicz, he was a recognized scholar highly valued for his studies in formal and mathematical logic. He was only incidentally a diplomat and artist. He received his Ph.D. in 1906 and became a professor in 1930. His first essay, "Über das Verschwinden der kleinen Punkte," appeared in the German Zeitschrift für Innerphysiologie, *1906. His first essay in logic was on Bertrand Russell's principle of contradiction and was published in Polish in 1912. His major book on epistemology,* The Boundaries of the Sciences, *appeared in 1935.*

Introduction

1. The aim of this study consists in establishing the meaning of the word *reality*. The original concept of reality is quite adequate for purposes of everyday life, but proves insufficient in certain complex cases. There is no reason to

66

doubt that surrounding objects are real; no reason to question the real nature of events we learn of from history, and of our sufferings or joys as well. This assumption is the starting point of any sound theory of the real. But, on the other hand, there are many examples that show that it is impossible to decide whether we are facing reality or merely fictions; this state of things is due to a certain lack of clarity in the original concept of the real.

1) To begin with, are the sufferings of other people and animals real or unreal? Their being real seems plausible, and yet a shade of doubt remains just the same, particularly as concerns animals on a low level of organization. Now, let it be assumed, for the sake of the argument, that this question has found a satisfactory solution. But this would only mean that the original concept of reality has been liberated of its vagueness and hence actually replaced by a new notion.

2) The system of physical science is not dependent upon the concept of reality: it consists of certain mental constructions conceived in such a way as to enable us to grasp given kinds of phenomena. But in order to achieve this sort of construction a certain picture of reality is necessary, and hence a reference to what we consider as being real.

The history of physics shows that in this case the original concept of reality proves insufficient, for either its extension has to be supplemented with unperceivable objects, such as ether, atoms, electrons, and the like, or certain connected notions, such as the concept of simultaneousness (cf. Einstein's principle of relativity), have to be modified. Consequently, the original concept of reality seems to be undergoing fundamental changes under the influence of the development of physics.

3) The need of a clearly determined concept of reality is striking in certain concrete situations.

Let us take as an example the problem of a man sacrificing his life for the sake of his country. We are told by common philosophy that any man should be ready to make this sacrifice, when needed, for the death of an individual is of no great importance as compared with the resulting events that might prove very advantageous to his neighbors. But, on the other hand, the instinct of self-preservation leads to a different reasoning: whatever happens after my death, it can be said, will be inaccessible to my knowledge, and, as such, is nothing else but a kind fiction; thus I am supposed to sacrific my life to a fiction. Now, since a sacrifice to a fiction is undoubtedly absurd, then no one should sacrifice his life for the sake of his country.

The above dilemma is well known and many people seem to be concerned with the issue in some of its aspects. It is obvious that its solution depends upon the meaning assigned to the word *reality*.

4) Let us take another example of not so fundamental an importance, but interesting just the same.

Suppose I want to make a portrait of a person I am fond of, and I am trying to find out the best way of doing it. In this case, obviously, my concern is not purely artistic; true, my effort is intended to provoke the delight resulting from a perfect combination of colored shapes; but, on the other hand, the product of my activity as an artist must necessarily involve a specific relation to its object. Consequently, I have to make a choice: either I simply face certain visual impressions, which I group into objects, and then the best way would be to proceed in the manner of impressionist painters and to present a configuration of color patches I find the most interesting, or else I have to believe in the existence of a real object, independent of my visual impressions, and then I have to search for a much more complicated method of presenting it on the canvas. The solution will depend entirely upon the notion of reality at my disposal.

2. The analysis of the original concept of reality enables us, in theory at least, to draw a list of objects considered as being undoubtedly real, and, accordingly, a list of objects considered as being surely unreal. If such lists could actually be made, they would be of some help as a sort of guidance; for our purpose, however, we shall simply assume that they *have been* drawn. Now, the construction of the notion of reality would consist in putting all objects of the same type on one or the other of our lists, respectively. The estab-

lishing of a distinct rule of distribution of objects on both lists would be equal to the construction of a definition of this notion. The fixing of the notion of reality in the form of what is commonly designated as a basic concept, would consist in the reference to well-defined criteria difficult to be formulated, though infallible.

The above examples point to the fact that in constructing the notion of reality two ways may be taken: either by using the criterion of "common sense" or by referring to direct knowledge.

In the former case, we must take into account the possibility of existence of real objects we can not *see,* and in the latter we have to deal exclusively with perceivable objects. We shall assign the former notion the name *common concept,* for its acceptance means our being in no conflict with the common picture of the world; we shall, accordingly, denote the latter notion as the *psychologistic concept,* for its application means our following the philosophical views held by psychologists. Both these concepts are implied by certain ideologies, and through these ideas we shall try to grasp the notions themselves.

Common philosophy says the world consists of things, persons, and events. The divisions between these notions are somewhat vague. In the nineteenth century popular ideology was commonly considered as leading to paradoxes (cf. Kant's antinomies), but this prejudice has been destroyed by advances in formal logic: contradictions, generally linked with the notion of things, proved to be of a purely logical character, and thus could be radically removed. Consequently, the system of common philosophy, liberated from contradictions, seemed no longer to be utopia doomed to death by its very nature.

The psychological method proves highly efficient in theoretical research, but often fails in practice. On the other hand, it can easily have a hold on the life of individuals, and even social groups, as has often been the case with mysticism and autosuggestion. Modern literature emphasizes an increasing role of psychological states in practical life. . . .

3. It follows from the above that *a*) the original concept of reality is unsatisfactory as a means of clarifying certain fundamental phenomena; *b*) this state of things implies the necessity of a new notion of the real that would be capable of fulfilling this task; *c*) the solution seems to be obtainable in two different ways at least.

Thus, I think, the importance of the problem of reality becomes obvious. It remains to deal with certain general objections brought by positivists against any philosophical investigations. Their main argument consists in claiming that it is impossible to discuss and formulate these problems in the form of clear reasoning corresponding to scientific thinking. But this is an erroneous argument, for any clear and well-defined idea has to be preceded by uncertain thinking, and if all ideas involving a certain amount of doubt were to be rejected *a limine,* then all progress should be given up as well. Moreover, it is to be borne in mind that there is no discipline—including the systems of symbolic logic or textbooks of geometry—quite free from uncertainty and, therefore, the only way of avoiding it would inevitably consist in refraining from all mental activity. What we have to be satisfied with is the degree of distinctness available in a given case. For one of the main tasks of philosophy lies in a careful classification of theoretical systems with respect to the degree of clearness they succeed in attaining.

Philosophy, unlike mathematics, has no ready-made apparatus of symbols at its disposal, and, as a rule, does not apply the method of formal demonstration that is appropriate to sciences. Therefore, I think, the saying that the aim of philosophy consists in discerning between truth and falsehood may be objected to as unjustifiable. That task is the concern of scientists, while a philosopher should aim at finding out the difference between meaningful and meaningless expressions, or, strictly speaking, at a systematic search for more and more clear concepts. It follows that definitions, rather than theorems, are the actual subject matter of philosophy. The history of human thought shows that all sciences in their origins belonged to philosophy and did not begin their independent existence until their notions were utterly defined. Recently, progress in formal logic was an extremely interesting example of this phenomenon. Thus, philosophy itself will never develop into science; whether new disciplines arise out of it and what they be like, will be seen in the future. Nor would it be possible to predict the rise of a new science making a proper use of the *notion of reality*. If any such science were to be born out of the attempts undertaken so far, it should be named the *theory of knowledge*. In our present state of preparatory research we are still on purely philosophical grounds and, therefore, in the realm of concepts *to be* defined. Under such circumstances, we have to oppose ideas belonging to the field of instincts, prejudice, and beliefs.

Since we shall apply the method that has been tested and verified, no unpredictable obstacles will hinder our task; the main difficulty lies elsewhere; it consists in adjusting intuition to results of conceptual constructions. This would be meaningless in the sciences, and particularly in mathematics, where intuition proves very humble and easily follows step by step the results of formal reasonings in spite of their often being apparently paradoxical. In philosophy, the scaffolding of formal demonstration is unavailable and hence the refutation of prejudices frequently presents extreme difficulties. Strictly speaking, the full justification of a given construction might be possible exclusively through complete elaboration of the whole system of philosophy. As it is, any construction is inevitably arbitrary, at least beyond the very restrained limits, and proves insufficient in attempts at the removal of well-fixed beliefs. Yet, we have at our disposal general considerations capable of standing for the above-mentioned method.

4. As has already been stated, there are two notions of reality. Now, their respective scopes are overlapping. The psychological notion does not include objects unperceived in a given moment, or objects that could not be perceived in certain conditions, properly prepared and defined; on the other hand, the common notion is utterly consistent with unperceivable objects. If we believe in the reality of impressions, then the traffic in the streets of Paris is real only

on the condition of our being present in these streets or believing in the (theoretical) possibility of our being present there imminently. But to persons using the common notion of reality in everyday life the above condition is of no importance, since they conceive events as occurring independently of their presence as witnesses. It is therefore impossible to reconcile these two notions without sinking into hopeless metaphysical divagations. Moreover, we shall see that there is no possibility of making a choice between the two notions until we agree to accept this choice as arbitrary and as implying no need of justification. We have no other way out except the admission of such an equality of rights of both these concepts, and no other possibility beyond an attempt at understanding this state of things. It must be assumed that there is not a single well-defined system of real objects, but at least two such systems, to be referred to as the *reality of impressions* and the *reality of things,* respectively.

In our considerations both these systems will be dealt with, and thus one *or* the other will be utilised. The event consisting in our taking a step into one of the realities is an event of a higher level and does not belong to the scope of any of these concepts, which follows from the application of the theory of logical types; without this theory all philosophical considerations become merely paradoxical. . . .[1]

Plural Reality in Art

1. In painting and sculpture the theory of plural reality has a double aspect:

1) It entails the rejection of imitating nature as a principle contradicting all true art.

2) It gives a foundation to justifying all essential types of painting and sculpture.

We shall endeavor to prove the above statements. But such a proof requires a previous clarification of certain terms: in the modern theory of art most misunderstandings have their origin in the lack of clear notions constituting the basis of the theory itself, and, in the first place, the concepts of form and content. Therefore, our first task will consist in establishing the denotations of these concepts.

The expression "content of a work of art" can be used in three different ways: it designates, respectively:

a) The totality of the mental states evoked as a response to a work of art during its perception.

b) Its plot.

c) Elements of the real, susceptible of being found in a work of art.

With regard to *a*) the analysis of aesthetic sensations has advanced very far in the last decades. Most eminent authors have suggested their explanations. But it is not my intention to refer below to the various views they represent. Such a discussion would be impossible simply because aesthetic sensations known from one's own experience have a specific character irreducible to other mental states, just as in the case of impressions given by the color green or the taste of salt. These states are extremely complex and, therefore, involve certain elements we can find elsewhere as well. An analysis of these emotive states might prove important and forms in itself an interesting part of psychology. But a theory of art must ignore it; sooner or later it will necessarily assume *the existence of some direct criteria distinguishing works of art from other objects.* Deprived of such an assumption it would remain pure verbalism, which, of course, is not our aim. If the word *content* is to be useful in the theory of art, it cannot be connected with the notion of mental states resulting from the perception of a work of art.

With regard to *b*) for decades now, the problem of the "story," or plot, of a work of art has been clarified in art criticism. At present everybody knows that a dance, for instance the American two-step, can evoke aesthetic sensations as something "beautiful," and a national hymn may seem an ugly noise; the raw meat painted by Rembrandt is a masterpiece, and the portraits of handsome statesmen in shop windows are hideous daubs. The object represented by a work of art is no longer an issue in the analysis of its "content" and hence we may dispense with this use of the word.

With regard to *c*) thus, the elements of reality involved in a work of art remain the one and only relevant meaning of the word *content*.

These elements appear in painting and sculpture throughout the art of all centuries and nations: in naturalistic prehistoric frescoes and in modern art as well. The same holds for poetry. Poetry deals with sentences, each having a defined meaning that asserts certain relations occurring within elements of reality or elements of the world of ideas and abstract concepts, and thus brings us into contact with the real or the ideal world, respectively. In contrast with painting, sculpture, and poetry, the case is different with such arts as music, ballet, architecture, and ornament, although these happen at times to deal with elements of reality, too (*e.g.*, voices of nature in music, scenes of life in ballet, tree limbs in architecture, leaves or flowers in ornaments); nevertheless they eliminate these elements quite easily, and thus may be considered as devoid of content. The constant presence of content (in the sense of elements of the real) in painting, sculpture, and poetry has led the theory of these arts astray, and at present it is no longer associated with the fulfillment of its own actual task. This phenomenon cannot be grasped without a proper analysis of the second fundamental notion in the theory of art: the form.

The concept of form is essentially much simpler than that of content, but its elaboration needs a high degree of intimate contact with art, and this is why the term *form* is commonly assigned an inadequate meaning.

We shall therefore try to eliminate these misunderstandings by emphasizing such elements of form as can be easily grasped:

1) Composition, or the mutual relation connecting the elements of a work of art.

In painting and sculpture it consists in the general arrangement of various shapes, proportions of their respective size, degree of complexity, and so on; in poetry, the accentuation, the rhymes and rhythm, the structure and distribution of sentences, and so forth.

2) Color, *i.e.*, the quality and configuration of color spots in painting, distribution of light in sculpture, types of sounds in poetry.

3) Technique, *i.e.*, the general size and shape of the canvas; the quality of the paint and the way of using it in painting; size, material, and the way of treating it in sculpture; the "style" in poetry.

These items do not exhaust the entire meaning of form, nor do they denote its full scope; yet, they will enable us to fix the meaning of the term *form* as used below. We shall also ask the reader to bear in mind that the possibilities involved in form are enormous and, therefore, we shall encourage him to put the following question: Is it right, when dealing with a work of art that satisfies all the postulates of a perfect form, to look for anything that goes beyond the form, anything external to the form itself? It is generally believed that while the criteria of content are distinct and rigid, criteria of form show an apparent lack of clarity; this view is, I think, the reason for the above-mentioned misunderstandings in the realm of concepts. The importance of the theory of plural reality in art lies precisely in the assumption that formal criteria of art are far more constant than criteria of content, the latter being necessarily and entirely dependent upon the kind of reality involved.

2. It follows from prior discussion that the main difference between music, ballet, architecture, and ornament, on the one hand, and painting, sculpture, and poetry, on the other, is due to the following circumstances: in the former group the absence of the elements of reality and a relative simplicity of form lead the theoretical interest toward formal problems; in the latter, on the contrary, the multitude of formal problems and the apparently unquestionable and obvious presence of the elements of reality result in an overemphasizing of these elements, *on the principle of the line of least resistance*. Such is the origin of the most paradoxical criterion ever imagined; painting and sculpture

should imitate nature as faithfully as possible, with, at the most, a certain idealization, while poetry should formulate true statements in conformity with moral principles, social conventions, and the like.

The above criterion is so widespread that, on the face of it, it may be difficult to discover how absurd it is in the light of pure theory. The products of an art practiced on the basis of such ideas show clearly how impossible it is. The radical naturalism of our time is a good example: exhibitions of its products become *salons* of wax figures, and naturalistic poems, whether rhymed or not rhymed, function as textbooks of *savoir-vivre,* or history, or geography. No one should be surprised at the fact that many great artists, having failed to find a way out through an appropriate theoretical analysis of the problem, simply went astray toward symbolic and "literary" art; they could not cope with the duty imposed upon them, the imitation of nature. On the other hand, it is quite understandable that some other artists have simply obeyed their artistic passion and have put forward their art against this theory, without looking for any theoretical justification that seemed to contradict whatever actually interested them in art itself. This instinct of the artists themselves helped the putting forward of a new theory by painters and poets. True, it has often lacked accuracy and has advanced certain obscure and fantastic ideas, but still it was of an immense value as a spontaneous protest of creative minds against an imposed and erroneous doctrine. It would be useless to give a full account of their respective writings published in France, Germany, Italy, Russia, and Poland. I shall point only to an extremely interesting book of Stanisław Ignacy Witkiewicz.[2] It prevails over similar German literature on the subject by a higher degree of artistic intuition, and over other authors by competence and theoretical training. These efforts, however, failed to refute an objection advanced by all the followers of the doctrine that conceives art as imitation of Nature.

Let us assume, they say, that a perfect form proves possible in a work of art, irrespective of its compatibility with nature. But, just the same, what would be the reason for abandoning the search for this compatibility that all great masters of the past have endeavored to find? And, moreover, it certainly gives a work of art an additional value that should not spoil the form, since the form is an independent factor. This argument implies a new objection: those artists who refuse to adhere to old patterns are accused of lacking education and are encouraged to try their hand in naturalistic painting, which is alien to their art. Such procedures result in a general chaos and confusion.

There is, I think, only one possible answer to these objections.

Since we have to copy reality, then what is the reality to be thus followed? Is it the real that stamps itself on photographs or paintings aiming at such an imitation? But what am I supposed to do if I believe that knowledge of the real can be reached indirectly, throughout beams of light, as is stated by rational realism? How am I supposed to behave if I live within a reality of sense impressions and conceive the doctrine of radiation as merely a convenient and plausible hypothesis? Would a photograph then mean for me anything other than a diagram, a factor both external and alien to reality, a kind of dictionary for the purpose of translating reality into conventional terms? And what if I live within the framework of the natural reality? How can I then possibly be concerned with shortenings, lights, and shades of a photograph, since I know that, for instance, the human body has a symmetrical structure and is of a uniform color: white, black, or yellow? If, on the other hand, I find myself—which in our times can easily be the case—in such a situation that the reality of images begins to force itself upon my mind and removes to the background the realities of any other kind, then the photographic postulate becomes merely a paradox, something I cannot possibly take seriously. What, therefore, could be saved out of this apparently unshakable principle? Nothing whatever! The fact is undeniable. It seems that the principle of reality cannot play a positive role in the theory of art; for a genuine artist will simply look for criteria of art on the ground of nothing but the form; but there is still another reason, more easily understandable: the principle of imitation is devoid of any determined meaning, and, being meaningless, is able neither to help nor to harm any artist conscious of the fact.

Thus we can consider our first fundamental statement as proved. It still remains to be proved that the relation of a work of art toward reality cannot *a priori* determine its artistic value, its good or bad quality; in other words, it can be perfect in respect of form and may disregard the kind of reality it deals with, and there is always the danger of its artistic value deteriorating still further when it tries to reflect too many features of this reality. The demonstration will be based on the classification of paintings and sculptures with respect to their relation to one of the given realities.

When adopting this point of view, we must necessarily distinguish the kinds of painting and sculpture corresponding, respectively, to the four types of reality they represent. . . .

3. These fundamental types that are the object of our analysis are the following: *1*) *primitivism, 2*) *realism, 3*) *impressionism,* and *4*) the so-called *new art,* which, for the sake of convenience, we shall term *futurism.*

These main types appear in the art of various epochs, and with varying intensity but, generally speaking, art had its origin in primitivism, then it went successively to realism, to impressionism, and, finally, to the deformations of futurism. Each of these currents subsists, and even preserves, a certain capacity for further evolution. A careful analysis of the conditions of their development shows that each of the currents was intimately connected with one of the four realities, respectively: primitivism with the reality of things, realism with physical reality, impressionism with the reality of impressions, and futurism with the reality of images. We shall now pay some attention to details involved in all four cases, in order to make the above conclusion convincing.

1) Primitivism seems to be in discord with reality, for we are used to moving within physical reality or the reality of impressions. Yet, it is worth while to reconsider this problem from the standpoint of the reality of things.

A primitive artist does not paint things as we see them,

but tries to represent them as they actually are. In order to achieve his aim, he refers to all resources of his knowledge about properties of things. His knowledge depends upon his experience, which is, as we have seen, very limited; this fact is the very source of the extraordinary creative power of primitivism. Owing to certain obscurities and ambiguities involved in concepts of particular things and of relations between them, he is free in combining shapes and colors and therefore is capable of attaining formal perfection. Among the properties of objects, he preserves those which are universally known and, consequently, he does not shock the spectator who remains within the framework of natural reality; on the contrary, he makes it possible for the spectator to contemplate a work of art without objections and distortions.

Owing to this attitude toward reality, a primitive artist need not bother about the paradox of content; he is genuine, because he does not seek artificial constructions aiming at formal effects, but he simply paints the world that attracts him and pleases him. He is not "copying" reality, for the knowledge of things is given to him directly at the moment of creating a work of art, and thus his creative activity is a performance carried out "from memory." Neither does he falsify reality, for in his ignorance of perspective and chiaroscuro he eliminates only that sphere of visual phenomena which he does not conceive as belonging to reality. Finally, he does not lack competence, because he has the skill of representing with utmost precision[3] all the details evoking his interest; he may seem somewhat inefficient if we require from him something that is alien to his reality.

2) The situation is much more difficult in the case of the realist—painter or sculptor. He believes the reality of objects to be perceived indirectly, through visual perception resulting from vibrations of light. For him the use of direct knowledge of things is out of the question; he must inevitably undertake an assiduous study of nature and fill the gaps resulting from constant changes occurring in visual impressions with his knowledge of perspective, optics, anatomy, and so on. His freedom in the choice of colors becomes

therefore rather limited, and his attainment of perfect form on the canvas is determined—as in a colored photograph—by a perfect choice of a model. Now, this task is extremely difficult, which explains why the great majority of realistic pictures (unlike the primitive ones) fail in achieving a good form and give the impression of bad taste when focusing our attention chiefly on content. We are often told that naturalistic art (radical realism) alone is really difficult to attain and that, on the contrary, primitivism is mere child's play. Such a view is the exact reverse of the truth; what seems the most difficult in naturalism, *i.e.*, the faithful reproduction of the model, is often achieved easily by minor talents after a few years of training; from the standpoint of the ideal of art, it has no more value than no studies at all. On the other hand, the essential and immense difficulty consisting in obtaining the perfect form in realistic art is seldom taken into account. This fact, duly emphasized, can easily lead to the conclusion that realism is incompatible with true art. Since the goal of art, it may be argued, is perfect form, and, accordingly, the imitation of nature means its denial, how can we possibly attain this objective within the framework of realism that imposes such far-reaching limitations?

In order to refute this objection we may point to the fact that the notion of realism is not univocal. The realism of the ancient Greeks differed from the realism of the Renaissance; there was a realism of Rembrandt and a realism of Ingres; and there is a realism in photography and its ally, *i.e.*, modern realism called naturalism. A careful study of the history of physical realism in science will show that realism in art corresponds to it constantly, and as physical realism became more deeply rooted in science, realism in art was losing successively its vitality and artistic value. Realism was at the height of great art only at the beginning of its development (*Venus of Milo*, Titian, Tintoretto, Rembrandt), when a certain freedom in its theory enabled it to focus its attention entirely on the search for perfect composition and color; and in these epochs realism was even able to create different styles (*e.g.*, the baroque). It is not until physical realism in the theory of science had definitely killed in realistic art its power of evolution that it became, like photography, merely a kind of illustration, having a purely practical or anecdotal significance.

3) Among different types of painting, impressionism reveals the strongest connection with its corresponding reality. It is a relatively young trend in art and, therefore, the details of its evolution are generally known. This trend was possible only in a society whose connections with the realm of visual impressions was intimate. That is why, together with the climax of impressionism, we witness an unprecedented increase in psychological investigations and a general vogue of psychologism; accordingly, the decline of impressionism was marked by reduced interest in psychology.

The main device of impressionism, consisting in marking patches of color on the canvas at the very moment of their perception somewhere in the environment, was linked with the pointilistic theory of the synthesis of pure colors occurring in the eyes of the spectator. It shows that the reality to which impressionism referred had nothing in common with the world of things of primitive art, and it has nothing to do with the physical reality of the realists, either. Theirs was an entirely new world and this very fact made its impact upon creative activity so powerful: the world of color spots directly given in visual impressions. By consciously introducing form (conceived as a harmony of colors) as the fundamental and unique postulate of art, the impressionists believed they were able to attain this form through a complete surrender to the effect of the color patch. Thus, their relations with the reality of impressions was perhaps as close as the respective relations of realists with physical reality. The impressionists have formerly been accused of a deliberate deformation of reality, but such an objection could have been raised only by a public lacking in proper education and thus conceiving the real one-sidedly. Oscar Wilde was quite right, too, in stating in his aphorisms that it was not until the world itself changed through its art, *i.e.,* until the public became familiar with the reality of impressions, that the impressionists became representatives of the official style in painting and, at the same time, lost their ability of further evolution.

What is interesting to note is that the impressionists have succeeded with their doctrine not only in painting, but—which seems more difficult—in sculpture as well. Impressionist sculpture shows the following features: *1*) it disregards the equal rights of foreground and background; *2*) the treatment of various parts of the whole is fragmentary and out of proportion. Obviously, these properties correspond to the qualities of the reality of impressions.

Before discussing the fourth of the main types of art, which is still in the process of elaborating its features and thus demands a somewhat different approach, I would like to stress some general characteristics common to the three currents already described.

What I want to say is this: any copying is a contradiction of art, and, consequently, any reality highly developed and imposing itself with great strength is not conducive to the development of art. On the other hand, any artistic activity that is compelled deliberately to search for the harmony of colors and shapes conceived exclusively as elements or ornament, may be very short-lived, since all possible combinations would soon be exhausted. This is the argument used by many thinkers who believe in the existence of a single reality to advance a very skeptical view on the development of art in the future. Such is the opinion put forward by Witkiewicz in his book that has already been mentioned, and by Spengler in his huge volume predicting the "decline of Western civilization."[4] Obviously, it is impossible to hold such a view if the theory of plural reality is true. Indeed, a failure threatens any art that develops within a reality that is both static and being gradually grasped by a constantly growing knowledge. The rise of a new reality implies necessarily an outburst of a great art for two reasons: *1*) it becomes an incentive to creative activity, which excludes any "cold" combinations of shapes and colors, and *2*) it offers great freedom in elaborating the form, owing to the relative vagueness involved in the notion of this new reality. This remark will enable us to grasp the significance of the new art *in statu nascendi,* which, I think, will find its place among the three above-described types of art as their equal partner. We shall be dealing with it in the next paragraph.

4) The fundamental revolution in art performed before our eyes was due to the appearance in the foreground of the reality of images. Within this rising reality, which as yet has not taken its final shape, all objects of the reality of impressions dealt with by impressionists are involved. But, first of all, they appear in a totally different form, and, on the other hand, they somewhat disappear among the multitude of objects of a different kind, governed by radically different laws of existence. For example, a woman I had been meeting only from time to time and seeing on these occasions in a similar way, in an intimate contact with the reality of impressions, seems suddenly settled into different shapes, growing more and more strange, and what is the most important feature of this experience is her constant presence.

These phenomena are extremely difficult to grasp. The so-called inner sight dealt with by Bahr[5] is but one of many elements involved in such cases. It is matched by a very vast and direct knowledge of the object, similar to the knowledge used in the reality of things, but utterly deprived of any theoretical information. Moreover, the appearing phenomena are of a much more complex nature and extremely difficult to describe; when not known through one's own experience, they can be featured only through the few available descriptions by poets and mystics.[6] One of such accounts has been given by Saint Theresa.[7]

She spent a few days in the palace of the princess Alba. There she saw a vast hall containing many valuable objects displayed in such a way as to be grasped in a single glance. She was deeply impressed by this picture and overwhelmed by a feeling of its ineffable charm. This general impression remained present in her memory while the details vanished, so that she could no longer say what she actually saw. She described her mystical visions in a similar way. This is undoubtedly an experience consisting precisely in the *overcoming of content* through a relaxation of demarcation lines separating objects from each other; and this is exactly what modern painting is aiming at, more or less consciously. This state of things explains why the theoretical issue—an extremely difficult one—consisting in the shifting of painting toward ornamentation, has recently approached its satisfactory solution. This was due to the familiarity with the reality of images attained by artists nearly at the same time in the most remote parts of Europe, as a result of their being oversaturated with the reality of impressions, and their helplessness after the criticism of this reality made by Bergson. This phenomenon has been a confirmation of his sound remark (though perhaps somewhat overemphasized by that author when applied to philosophy) stating that a man who instead of simply swimming would rather investigate the theoretical question of the very possibility of swimming, would undoubtedly reach the conclusion that he could never succeed in keeping his body above water—which indeed is not so difficult a thing to do.

The complete indeterminacy of the reality of images strongly marks the modern art, which has been unable so far to elaborate its own homogeneous style. Various kinds of painting and sculpture inspired by this reality consist of featuring its essential properties. Thus, the Italian futurists were chiefly concerned with the extreme mobility of the reality of images, and the cubists with its relative simplicity; the expressionists insisted upon its close connection with the subjective life of individuals, and the formists pointed to its great flexibility resulting in its ability to deal with purely formal issues. What is common to all these currents can easily be seen in the following example. Let us suppose that a portrait of a given person is to be made. It has already been said what would have been the behavior of primitive artists, realists, or impressionists, in this case. A man immersed in the reality of images would be far from attempting a study of the "characteristic features" of the model, nor would he even think of observing the model in the way a realist would choose, or of yielding to the effect of color patches in the manner of the impressionists. First of all he would try to become sufficiently acquainted with the model to be able to make out the model's image as one of the elements of the surrounding reality. The shape of the future image is unpredictable, and what the relation between this image and other images would be cannot be foreseen, either. As long as there is a constant and somewhat loose connection between the model and the artist's reality, no real subjective longing for creative activity arises. Such an impulse does not occur unless the image becomes so strong as to put off all other elements of reality. Then the artist may be able to achieve a perfect form more or less unconsciously, avoiding any destructive "cold" investigations of shapes and colors.

The problem of "likeness" will then be meaningless, but susceptible of being revived through the "force of suggestion" as a proper means of communication among men immersed in the reality of images.

As we have seen, it may be hoped that the "new art" will be able to become an equal partner with the traditional types of art, and, accordingly, we can consider as demonstrated our thesis concerning the equal theoretical rights of the fundamental types of painting and sculpture. On the other hand, we have just placed the reality of images within the scope of content of these arts, and will, therefore, be able to cope with an essential issue of the theory of art consisting of the following question: to what extent may the content be overcome in a work of art? This problem will be the subject matter of our discussion in the next paragraph.

4. As a general rule, artists of the past were not conscious of their aspirations toward a perfect form. What they formulated as being their aim was probably far more complicated. This can be seen best in poetry, which in the time of Homer had been teaching religion, philosophy, history, geography, and so on, and maintained this function until quite recently. And then, as the result of a differentiation of notions and interests, *modern artists became aware of themselves as deliberately aiming at the elaboration of a new style in art on the principle of overcoming its contents.* I shall refer to them as "formists." To be sure, the solution of this issue is equally possible within the framework of any reality, and, as has already been said, many primitive,

realistic, or impressionist artists have succeeded in their respective attempts in finding it. But the representatives of the above types achieved their objectives by treating content as something trivial, by pushing it to the background as a proper place for elements of interest, while the formists, owing to the reality of images, have at their disposal radically different means; they are in a position to take advantage of the lack of clear distinctions separating the objects within the reality from each other. Consequently, they necessarily face the issue of painting and sculpture *versus* ornamental art. The fact is generally known that there is no distinct demarcation line between these types of art, just as there are no clear criteria separating poetry from musical murmurs. Nevertheless, the theory stating that no essential difference exists between ornamental art, on the one hand, and painting and sculpture, on the other, should be rejected. That theory has been due merely to an erroneous idea in the old theory of art, consigning painting and sculpture to the imitation of reality while leaving ornamental art free from such an obligation. That idea had inevitably to be rejected; hence, the view identifying ornamental art with painting and sculpture was simply a temporary hypothesis indispensable for further development of these arts. A somewhat deeper insight into this issue will enable us to establish a new criterion, independent of the concept of content (or reality).

There is an essential difference between painting and sculpture, on the one hand, and ornamental art, on the other; paintings and sculptures should be composed in a way allowing them to be submitted, as given wholes, to a lasting contemplation, while the goal of the ornament consists in creating a background giving rise to a general artistic atmosphere.

The adoption of such a criterion provides a valuable indication as to a way of moving on this hardly noticeable border area where ornamental art meets with painting and sculpture. Not that this is all we need; a certain experience concerning some very simple problems will be necessary just the same; we shall have to know how to deal with the representation of shapes and their delimitations. These issues will be discussed in the following paragraph.

5. It is generally known that ornamental art involves the problem of distinguishing the motif from the background. If, for example, a white design is made on a black background, it might rightly be said that a black drawing has been made on a white background. Careful observation shows that neither of these two alternative possibilities could hold, for oscillations in both directions enable us to see either the first phenomenon or the other, alternatively. An attentive contemplation of Persian carpets or Moorish frescoes gives rise to even deeper oscillations deserving particular attention. They have been described by Leonardo da Vinci as follows:

> If you contemplate walls covered with various spots or stones composed of different ingredients, and if you want to imagine a landscape, then you will see on these objects various pictures: mountains, rivers, rocks, trees, plains, large valleys and hills of all sorts; you will also see battles and moving men with odd faces and clothes, and a multitude of other objects susceptible of being endowed with precise and proper shapes. For walls and stones are much like the sound of bells: in their ringing you might hear any name or word you can possibly imagine.

It can easily be seen that this phenomenon occurs, on a similar scale, practically everywhere. Let us draw on a scrap of paper a few lines in any possible combination, and we shall at once be able to perceive an object of some kind: it may be an eagle, a monk, a dog, a soldier's cap, or any other object we shall be inclined to accept as being "new." Moreover, what is curious is that we are able to perceive successively all these objects. The oscillations of visual impressions are quite distinct and independent of what we are willing to see. After a careful analysis of this phenomenon, the following facts can be established: the respective durations of the appearances of two given objects, *e.g.,* an eagle and a monk, are practically equal in time when freely perceived; when, on the other hand, we try to see an eagle, our perceiving the seeming monk continues but its picture has a relatively shorter duration. If certain new details were added to the drawing itself, suggesting the features of an eagle, even then the picture of the monk would not vanish, but it would last a shorter time, for the details featuring the eagle would grow in number. The same phenomenon will take place when the respective roles of the eagle and the monk are reversed.[8]

It must be borne in mind that no oscillations of words or notions (monk, eagle) occur in this experiment. These names were introduced merely as examples of two different shapes, one of them evoking an eagle, and the other a monk. The phenomenon of this kind appears with varying intensity in any field of vision, whether two- or three-dimensional, and might therefore be accepted as generally valid. Moreover, the same applies to spatial oscillations (cameo, intaglio, and the like), occurring, as above, in any field of vision.

A simple analysis of these types of oscillations leads to a fundamental distinction in the two main categories: *1*) even oscillations, and *2*) uneven oscillations.

With regard to *1*). Obviously, the former are, in principle, incompatible with an aesthetic impression, for they result in a feeling of boredom, and our attention is turned away from what is of essential value in a work of art. This explains the tendency in the theory of ornamental art to establish a univocal meaning of elements in an ornament.[9] This tendency, however, may be objected to on the ground that there is no ornament other than that submitted to even oscillations during prolonged observation. As a matter of fact, this feature of ornaments cannot be considered as their shortcoming from the standpoint of our assumptions. For, as already stated, the very nature of ornament does not assign it the task of focusing our attention on its limited space. In most cases ornaments are grouped in great quantities and are conceived so as to shift our sight with relatively high speed from one point to another. Such perception is capable only of providing visual impressions proper to ornament, and there can be no doubt that the case is analogous with music. Any systematic contemplation of a limited fragment of an ornament and the prolonged repetition of the first tunes of a song would be quite alike. The very problem of uneven oscillations is the proper concern of painting and sculpture, *i.e.,* of the arts that produce objects intended for long contemplation and confined within relatively small segments of space.[10] A picture consisting of a drawing made only for the purpose of experiments with the phenomenon of oscillations could never be considered a work of art. The same applies to "puzzle pictures": when carefully observed for some time and from two different distances they provoke periodical oscillations as well, and show two different pictures. This is also the case with any picture or drawing composed of elements undefined from the point of view we are concerned with. In this way we obtain an infallible criterion that enables us to exclude a great quantity of objects from the scope of painting and sculpture.

With regard to 2). Let us focus our attention on the above-mentioned fact that, when a contour made for experimental purposes has been filled with details featuring, *e.g.,* a monk, perceptive oscillations do not vanish but merely change in duration: as a general rule, we will see the monk, while the eagle will appear not so often and just for short moments. It is obvious that this phenomenon has no decisive influence upon the process of visual perception and does not occur except with persons properly trained in previous experiments. We can admit that in this case the field of vision is, in principle, immobile. It does not follow, of course, that a given picture *is* a work of art, but, at least, the fundamental obstacle consisting in the occurrence of even oscillations is removed. Now, if we try to "see," from this point of view, various paintings containing more or fewer details featuring the monk, we shall find it difficult to decide where the oscillations to be (practically) considered as even end, and where the uneven oscillations, pointing to a predominance of a single and determined shape, begin. This accounts for the main difficulty in distinguishing painting and sculpture from ornament: no great works of art were ever composed of objects distinctly modeled and clearly separated from each other. The so-called clumsiness of primitive artists, the glazes of the Renaissance, the techniques of modern realists in placing colors—let alone other kinds of painting —display a certain indeterminacy that frees the picture from a somewhat painfully rigid and "wooden" form. This factor proved inevitable even in photography, and was exemplified by the "artistic" type of this technique. There is no doubt, it seems, that the artistic value of undetermined shapes is directly linked with the phenomenon of uneven oscillations. It might be said that utterly periodical oscillations and exactly determined shapes are both to be avoided. The disturbances in the field of vision occurring temporarily and rarely, point to a strong predominance of one aspect and may become a decisive factor in the aesthetic impression. This also applies, even in a higher degree, to certain disturbances in the field of vision of a very complex nature, and so far undescribed, capable of intensifying considerably the impressions of vitality and movement, as well as the harmony of colors and shapes. To what extent the shapes may be loosened and still not give way to the dead areas of periodical changes, is not easy to say exactly, and nothing short of the intuition of an artist can define that limit. The more extensive the limits of his activity, the bolder his art and the greater his achievements. But he should not go too far and cross the border, thus reaching unconsciously the realm of ornament. This would necessarily provoke an impression of bad taste.

6. The results of the prior discussion might be briefly summarized in the following statement: *as a rule, painting and sculpture are constrained to construct their products with distinctly marked shapes*. It is obvious that it makes no difference what those shapes be like; they can be drawn from everyday life or be of an abstract nature (such as, *e.g.,* mathematical surfaces). The choice of a shape as substance for artistic performance is not a condition of the aesthetic value of a work of art, nor does it determine its belonging to a fundamental type or style. Thus, for instance, the photograph of a formistic sculpture is a realistic picture, and the plaster case of an exotic shell is a realistic sculpture,

while a figure of a man can be an element of any type of art. What is of essential importance is the way of representing a given shape and its relations to other shapes as elements of the same product. The manner of combining shapes may be governed, from the standpoint of pure form, by a few general principles, easily adaptable to the individual attitude. In modern painting, the following principles have been adopted:

1) *A work of art should form a self-contained whole.*

2) *The elements of a composition should be distributed according to a specified law (rhythmical composition).*

Curiously enough, any attempt at a more detailed formulation of these principles would be a failure. This can easily be seen in music, which has its theory developed to the highest degree. Its principles seem to have no other aim than that of encouraging artists to violate them all the more boldly if they are really talented. The unique value of this theory appears to be that of fixing such forms to which the human ear is best adjusted, and thus provides us with a starting point in our search for forms that are new but come sufficiently close to the old ones to be grasped.[11]

All endeavors to construct any such theory of visual arts have failed, the reason being that the readjustment of the eye to any new form is far easier and quicker than that of the ear, and thus a smooth evolution of visual forms is merely a fiction used for purposes of popularization. This state of things imposes on the representatives of visual arts the necessity of an extremely *arbitrary* choice of shapes and their composition. Obviously, that discretion is an illusion, and nobody but an ideologist could be deceived by it when considering that issue from a purely abstract viewpoint. Actually, the problem has quite a different aspect, for any genuine artist works under the influence of shapes that impose themselves upon him as an inevitable necessity. In this case, any "cold" considerations concerning the combination of shapes or deliberations as to how to fill a given part of the surface are out of the question, let alone the filling of the surface at random. In the process of creating his product, the artist is possessed by an ideal and he tends to attain it with perseverance and no other desire than its achievement on the canvas or in the stone. Artistic activity consists in *finding new shapes and new combinations of such within the chaos of data directly given by reality*. The representation of these combinations on the canvas or in the stone is something secondary, resulting from the degree of his technical skill. This is the only way for an artist to be able to avoid both the danger of imitating nature and equally perilous combinations of elements conceived "in cold blood." But the condition of such a performance is that of a new reality *in statu nascendi*. Owing to such an attitude toward reality (of images), modern formism has achieved its rigid criteria in spite of their being apparently quite loose. This is also the reason for the ruthlessness and fanaticism of adepts of new art in their struggle against anything that governed the art of the past.

In order to understand their psychological attitude it must be borne in mind that when the reality of images gradually comes to the fore, it becomes by this very fact an extremely interesting one. As a result of new combinations of shapes and colors involved in this reality, artists are overwhelmed by their power much more easily than realists or impressionists *blasés* from studying nature. Consequently, the artists belonging to the old schools easily abandon the application of the strict rules to which they were accustomed, while the formists firmly refuse to revise their own criteria, even those adopted temporarily and indiscriminately. As a rule, every formist elaborates his own style, more or less originally. The formation of a common and distinctly featured style might be the further result of a cooperation of artists and of mutual suggestions.

The above considerations provide us with the basis for a criterion of defining the principles of creative activity in visual arts; true, it will not be a final criterion, nor will it be a precise one, and yet it will help lay down these principles.

3) A necessary condition for a product to be considered as a work of art consists in its form's being drawn from a single reality.

This criterion, like the former ones, is not sufficient, for both masterpieces and daubs can be inspired by the same reality; it has, however, an undeniable negative value: it enables us to reject *a limine* the products that do not satisfy it. On the other hand, it should be applied only to cases of equal proportions of elements belonging to various realities—such as, for instance, a naturalistic head on an impressionist background (unfortunately, very popular with our acknowledged masters). It does not concern the imperceptible mutual penetration of various realities, which is typical of art at its best, such as results from the previously mentioned indeterminacy of certain notions. Such is the case, *e.g.,* of Tintoretto and Titian, and, by the way, of Greek sculpture, in which elements of primitivism can be found. The influence of realists on early impressionists (Manet, Renoir), and of impressionists on neo-impressionists, is quite obvious and not less than that of impressionists (and of primitive artists or realists) on modern formists. Elements of this kind function as *sui generis* dissonances, and, when properly used, do not depreciate a work of art, but, on the contrary, greatly add to its value.

7. The application of this theory to poetry proves rather difficult, for, as has already been said, the subject matter of propositions refers to relations occurring not only in the real, but also in the sphere of ideal objects, and the latter are linked somewhat loosely, if at all, with reality. This implies that it is not possible to classify poetry so precisely —as is the case of the visual arts—into four types corresponding respectively to the four types of reality. Yet, these main types—as belong to primitivism, realism, impressionism, and futurism (in the broad sense of the term)—may be distinguished just the same. But the actual task of the theory consists in the study of the relation of a sentence to its meaning, irrespective of whether this meaning refers to reality or to the realm of ideal objects. Since we are not concerned with this problem I shall only point briefly to some of its aspects.

Logic makes a distinction between meaningful sentences, or propositions, and meaningless sentences, and, in doing so, applies clearly formulated criteria constituting what is termed the theory of logical types. In this way it detaches from the class of all possible sentences a fixed class of propositions of a given type: first, second, third, and so on. Thus, all other sentences are left beyond the scope of logic, but some of them may be accepted as propositions of a higher type. However, a certain meaning can be, and often actually is, attributed even to sentences deprived of this property, for we use the concept of meaning not only in a strictly logical sense, but also in a larger sense, deprived of the scientific value, but possibly interesting from a different point of view. Now, the meaning of the term *meaning,* besides its strictly logical sense, may be defined in many different ways, and even a hierarchy of sentences may be established, corresponding to these various meanings of *meaning.* It goes without saying that in proceeding further on the scale we leave the scientific use farther and farther behind and with each step we come nearer to an empty sound of words, *i.e.,* to the "music of murmurs." In doing so, we successively abandon the problem of truth and falsehood to shift our interest toward purely formal questions. It is obvious that since poetry is inevitably inclined to stay away from science and other disciplines equally alien to itself, it tends toward that ephemeral area where pure music of murmurs does not yet exist, but problems of truth and falsehood are not to be found, either. This tendency could be named *formism* in poetry. Obviously, this problem, as previously conceived, cannot be solved merely by a theory or by formal experiments any more than it can in the visual arts: as in painting and sculpture, an essential genuineness of the artist, utterly obsessed by a given event or thought, is an inevitable condition. Events belonging to long-established realities, and ideas involved in scientific activity as well, prove useless as incentives of this kind, for they tend automatically to find their articulation in the form of clearly formulated propositions. On the contrary, events occurring in the reality of images and ideas belonging to the realm of vague notions are extremely complicated when it comes to their formulation, simply because the structure of language corresponds to the reality of things, *i.e.,* to what is radically opposed to the reality of images. Therefore, formistic poetry leads us to the problem of the broadening of the language used, and this is the case of each new poetry awakening to life. Moreover, there is one more relevant factor: the ephemeral nature of events themselves, as has been shown above in the quoted experience of Saint Theresa. These factors form an adequate basis to enhance the spontaneous artistic activity of the poets who will find their proper ground, irrespective of any theory.

8. The radical theory of aesthetics put forward in the prior discussion seems to consider any ideology concerned with literature or painting as of no value whatever. I insist, however, on the fact that such a conclusion would be erroneous. Unlike Spinoza, I do no believe determination to be negation, but, on the contrary, I think that the removal of elements external to a given object can only add to its value. The elimination of obscure notions from philosophy and a complete overcoming of content in art do not oppose, but promote, the rise of a new branch of theory: it should be mainly concerned with manipulating concepts in such a way as to evoke a specific feeling of depth and of metaphysical or religious concern, which means the broadening of our internal life. To this kind of activity belong the greatest products of the human mind, such as the holy scriptures of the East, the works of mystics and metaphysicians of all times and peoples, and particularly those of Hegel, Nietzsche, and Bergson, and mystic poetry in Poland. A few painters adhere to this group as well: Goya, Rops, Toulouse-Lautrec, and others. There is not, I think, a doctrinaire so obstinate as to deny the value of this kind of mental activity in the name of scientific accuracy or of pure art. But we have to bear in mind that an error of this kind might be possible. Generations in the past believed such an activity to be a synthesis of philosophy and art that grasped whatever the human intellect could produce in the realm of immaterial values. In our times the process resulting in the drifting apart of different disciplines from each other has been carried so far that any further search for this sort of synthesis is no longer possible. This is why we observe an

overwhelming tendency in science and art; both these disciplines are aiming at a complete separation from pure ideas, so powerful until recently and still trying to fill both science and art with its own content. It is only when the thinkers understand the value of their creative thought as such, inherent in any genuine endeavor of a creative character, that the danger of confusion in the realm of concepts will be removed.[12]

9. As we have seen, the theory of many realities in art permits both the justification of all main currents in art and the assignment of a specific place to the youngest art, conceived as an art preparing the formation of a new reality that is very specific and apparently paradoxical. It goes without saying that this result is by no means a decisive argument in the discussion concerned with the values of this reality. But, I think, this *is* a result that nevertheless deserves to be taken into account instead of being simply ignored. Since new art grows up constantly and gains new adherents every day, and thus will inevitably bring growing influence to bear upon the general features of life in the future, it seems worthwhile to insist on the fact that it does not contradict, in any respect, the results of scientific research, but, on the contrary, provides science with valuable material for new experiments and thus serves to justify them. . . .

NOTES

1. Cf., *e.g.*, L. Chwistek, *Zasada sprzeczności w świetle nowszych badań B. Russella* (The Principle of Contradiction in the Light of Recent Investigations of B. Russell) (Krakow, 1912).

2. *Nowe formy w malarstwie i płynące stąd nieporozumienia* (New Forms in Painting and Some Resulting Misunderstandings). Reprinted in S. I. Witkiewicz, *Nowe formy w malarstwie i inne pisma estetyczne* (New Forms in Painting and Other Writings on Aesthetics) (Warsaw, 1959).

3. Cf., for instance, the finish of birds' wings in Japanese paintings.

4. O. Spengler, *Der Untergang des Abendlandes* (15–22 unveränderte Auflage) (Munich, 1920).

5. *Expressionismus* (Munich, 1916).

6. Cf. especially Saint Theresa, *Castle of the Soul,* and Charles Baudelaire, *Les paradis artificiels.*

7. In *Castle of the Soul.*

8. Cf. "Sur les variations périodiques du contenu des images dans un contour donné:, in Full. de l'Academie des Sciences (Krakow, 1909).

9. Cf. K. Homolacs, *Podstawowe zasady budowy ornamentu plaskiego* (Main Principles of the Composition of Flat Ornaments) (Lvov-Warsaw, 1920), p. 89.

10. The notion of size is not clearly determined in this case. An ornament filling a whole page in a book may be huge in relation to its nature. On the other hand, the *Battle of Grunwald* (famous picture by Jan Matejko, of a very considerable size) is by no means particularly large.

11. Cf., e.g., A. Halm, *Harmonienlehre* (Berlin and Leipzig, 1916).

12. It should be emphasized that psychological literature and naturalistic or symbolic photography belong to separate branches and thus should be accounted for within our classification. The success of psychological novels in England, on the one hand, and the immense popularity of photography and science drawing, on the other, seem to testify to our being right in considering them as skills of much the same type as abilities applied in idiographic disciplines: history, zoology, and the like. The difference consists only in that in the former activities we are dealing not with actual, but with possible facts.

3

WHAT ARE AESTHETIC EXPERIENCES?*

by

Stanisław Ossowski

Translated from Polish by
OLGIERD WOJTASIEWICZ

Stanisław Ossowski was born in 1897 and died in 1963. He studied at the University of Warsaw and at the Sorbonne, and received his Ph.D. in 1926. He studied in England from 1933–1935, and was a docent at the University of Warsaw in 1933. He became Professor of Sociology at the University of Warsaw in 1945. He was Presi-dent of the Polish Sociological Association, and was elected Vice-President of the International Sociological Association in 1959. His most important books are: The Foundations of Aesthetics, *1933;* Social Ties and the Heritage of Blood, *1939;* Class Structure in Social Consciousness, *1957 (translated into English and other lan-guages) ; and* Special Features of the Social Sciences, *1962. Ossowski was author of many articles in Polish and foreign languages. His* Collected Works, *in six volumes, is now being published in Warsaw.*

The Sphere of Aesthetic Values

Now that various kinds of aesthetic values have been con-sidered [above, not reprinted], we have finally to determine

---

* Chapter 18 of *U podstaw estetyki* (*The Foundations of Aesthetics*), which forms vol. 1 of Ossowski's *Collected Works* (Warsaw, 1966).

what the concept of aesthetic value in general is. The question that arises first is: *In what respect do we evaluate objects when we formulate aesthetic judgments?* It has been assumed that aesthetic value is the value ascribed to objects with respect to a kind of experience evoked by those objects, namely, with respect to aesthetic experience. But in the question formulated above, the phrase "in what respect" does not refer to that. If all aesthetic value is in fact interpreted as dependent on aesthetic experiences, then the question above might include the word "respect" twice: in what respect do we evaluate objects when we evaluate them with respect to our aesthetic experiences? Or, to resort to a less complicated wording: *what categories of properties of the objects evaluated from the aesthetic point of view are taken into consideration in aesthetic judgments?* This question ought not to be confused with the problem of the criteria of beauty.

Attempts have often been made in aesthetic research to specify what is being evaluated in objects when aesthetic values are ascribed to those objects; this amounted to tentative demarcations of a specific sphere of aesthetic study among those phenomena which are external to man. There is a fairly common theory that aesthetic judgments always refer to the "appearance" of objects only, and that any aesthetic value is a value of appearance, the latter being interpreted, of course, not only as an optical aspect, but as an outward form perceived through the intermediary of sense data. Other theories, also quite common, state that an aesthetic value is a value of *form,* and that aesthetics is to be concerned solely with the forms of objects, the term "form" being not always used in one and the same sense.[1] There are also scholars who define the sphere of the objects subject to aesthetic valuations by referring to the function of reproduction, for instance, by interpreting beauty as self-delusion. This was done, *e.g.,* by Konrad Lange.[2] He tried to cover with that theory, which can apply to reproductive arts only, other spheres as well, as the promoters of socialist realism and of the "reflection theory" in gnosiology in their own way did after him. In justifying his theory Lange confused, for instance, the concept of reproduction with that of expression.[3]

All these opinions are untenable, unless the formulation that all aesthetic value always is a value of "appearance" is intended to mean just this: that all objects of aesthetic valuations are accessible to sensory perception and are evaluated *on the strength* of their form as perceived by the senses. But then, apart from certain reservations that would have to be made even in that case, such an opinion would not provide an answer to the problem raised above and would not assign to aesthetics any specific sphere of research in the world of external phenomena.

We have seen previously very different categories of objects and categories of properties with respect to which a given object belongs to the sphere of aesthetic study. In some cases aesthetic valuation pertained directly to the sensory form of such objects, in other cases we were solely interested in the reproductive function of those objects. In still other cases we used to ascribe an aesthetic value to an object with respect to expression, or with respect to purposefulness, or with respect to artistry. There were also such situations in which the aesthetic value was determined precisely by the lack of all effect of human activity. We have seen that even in the case of those objects which seemed to form a homogeneous class, for instance, those which owe their aesthetic value to the function of reproduction, aesthetic value may be an attribute with respect to widely varying categories of properties. True, it may be said that in all those cases the objects in question are assigned values with respect to the function of reproduction, but this relation between them would be merely verbal. The phrase "with respect to" is misleading again. When it is said that a work of art has an aesthetic value with respect to the function of reproduction, this simply means that a work of art, when subject to valuation, is interpreted semantically: this may mean both a valuation in which the function of reproduction is the *motive of appraisal* (for instance, appraisal with respect to the way in which the artist reproduces reality), and valuation with respect to certain factors for which the function of reproduction is merely an *indispensable condition*, without, however, being a motive of appraisal (for instance, appraisal with respect to the beauty of the persons reproduced).

It is not easy to decide where the analysis of those "respects" that determine aesthetic appraisal is to stop. We have seen the widely differing interpretations of appraisals with respect to the mode of reproduction and widely differing interpretations of the realism of a work of art. We have seen that illusionist realism, realism in the sense of grasping that which is the most essential in a given fragment of reality, and the realism of the subject matter (in the sense of a selection of objects that are characteristic enough) are all different things. In appraising various paintings with respect to their "realistic values," is it legitimate to compare and classify by the same scale both illusionistic paintings and those paintings in the case of which realism is conceived as a deliberate deformation of reality?

When we in turn start discussing the sense of "grasping that which is the most essential in a given fragment of reality," when an impressionist tells us that for him changing configurations of colored patches as direct sense data are the most important, while a painter of the old school brings out the contours of separate objects in the belief that that is the most essential thing, and an expressionist tries to bring out the "souls" of the objects he paints, we again can have doubts whether we may legitimately believe that in all these cases we have to do with appraisals of objects in the same respects, or whether all these appraisals are merely different ways of satisfying one and the same requirement. We may be rather inclined to assume that these types of appraisals *mean different things* and to conclude that a different category of properties is adopted as the basis of valuation in each case. Analogous doubts arise concerning valuation with respect to expression and valuation with respect to direct sensory form.

All analysis of types of aesthetic values is complicated still further by the difficulty of singling out the separate factors of appraisals. The same properties of objects may be subject to aesthetic appraisals from different points of view, but the *cooperation* of those different points of view may in itself be a completely new factor of appraisal. This is why I do not think that we might succeed in a consistent and exhaustive systematization of types of aesthetic values. At any rate, although the classification of such a vast and heterogeneous material leaves much room to arbitrariness, I do not see any possibility of finding a single category that would cover all those types from the point of view of objective properties, and hence a possibility of finding a universal answer to the question, with which aspect of phenomena aesthetics is concerned. When it comes to the problem *what is evaluated in aesthetic judgments,* only a pluralistic approach is possible.

Thus, if the links between the various types of aesthetic values are not to remain merely verbal, if the aesthetic values of a beautiful horse, a beautiful sonata, and a beautiful drama have something in common in addition to a common name, if all aesthetic values are to be treated as values belonging to one and the same category, then this is so not because of any objective reasons, but probably only with respect to the attitude toward the experiences of the person who evaluates. Then the only common characteristic of all objects that have aesthetic value would be the property of evoking aesthetic experiences, the property that, as it were by definition, has been considered above to be the criterion of aesthetic value.

This attitude toward experiences might suffice for aesthetics to be treated as the discipline the subject matter of which is a special and relative category of values, but on the condition that the concept of aesthetic experience proves to be homogeneous. But, although we have so far discussed the various kinds of emotions believed to be aesthetic experiences, we have not yet tried to suggest a *general* definition of aesthetic experiences. If we want to comprehend the concept of aesthetic value, we must now analyze the problem *whether all those types of experiences that are to be taken as correlates of aesthetic values can be subsumed under a single and adequate category.*

Types of Aesthetic Experiences

The types of experiences we have been concerned with so far included both simple sensory pleasures, such as the pleasure of perceiving color and sounds, and such complex processes as are sometimes evoked by symbolic art or by the contemplation of magnificent manifestations of nature, when we have the feeling of being in contact with issues much more important than those of everyday life. The *Adagio* in Beethoven's Piano Trio in D Major, with its septatonal motif that returns over and over again in the violin, may serve as an illustration of what is meant when one says that music includes "metaphysical" factors. The septatonal motif in several rising variations, with the last tune falling—a motif that is disquieting, like an ever-returning question, for which the Trio seems to provide only a background—wanders later, when the music is over, in the peripheries of one's consciousness like a visitor from the other world. Sometimes aesthetic experiences are cognitive in nature: they consist in the pleasure of acquiring knowledge of some facts, as, for instance, when one reads Balzac or Proust, or looks at a realistic painting, or takes pleasure in viewing facts from a new point of view or in discovering a new aspect of things known before. These arise from the feeling that one's knowledge of the world has become deeper. According to Woerman, an artist's sight is "either broader or subtler, or at least deeper and more penetrating, than the sight of ordinary mortals,"[4] and this is why an artist can teach us how to look at the phenomena of nature. "That which a worker will take from Shakespeare, Goethe, Pushkin, or Dostoevsky," Trotsky wrote, "will consist above all in a more complex idea of human personality, its passions and feelings; he will comprehend its mental powers, the role of the unconscious and other properties more deeply and clearly. He will accordingly become richer."[5]

We have seen experiences in which the listener or the spectator derived his satisfaction from having his intellectual powers stimulated to perform some ordering functions, *e.g.*, when he had to analyze step by step the intricacies of a configuration of sounds or lines, or a complex structure of a machine or an organism. In other cases, on the contrary, aesthetic contemplation was due to a complete passivity of of our intellect, or even a kind of stupor, such as results from a long listening to folk music or the music of certain exotic peoples, music consisting in an endless rhythmical repetition of one or two simple motifs, which sometimes are contained within the limits of one quintuple. A similar effect was, perhaps, intended by Ravel in his *Bolero*. The flow of traditional poems is a source of pleasure that differs entirely from the pleasure derived from the reading of some avant-garde poems that have no rhymes and no regular rhythm, and in which every word is intended to serve a special purpose and the sequence of words is semantically unpredictable. In the case of the former poems, the reader is enraptured by the music of rhythm and rhyme and the flow of images and the associations they evoke. Even if some metaphors are incomprehensible to the reader, he is not disturbed by that fact. In the case of the latter category of poems, the reader works together with the poet and senses his toil. To grasp the beauty of the poem he must unravel the meaning of each phrase, and in some cases, if the poem deserves such effort, he may experience something like the joy of solving an ingenious puzzle.

We have discussed in detail the experiences that involve empathy, whether it is directed to the mentality of other human beings and thus, as it were, contributes to a multiplication of our own existence, or to inanimate objects. Certain kinds of aesthetic experiences satisfy the desire for violent emotions combined with an intensification of our receptive powers (tragedy). Other experiences satisfy our need of perfection: I mean the pleasure derived from the contact with objects that we consider perfect from some point of view. A concert-goer expects different kinds of emotions when he is attracted by the programme as such, from those when he wants to listen to a virtuoso, even if the programme includes just works by Liszt and Paganini. Certain experiences evoked by those objects to which we ascribe an aesthetic value owe their intensity to the sex factor (the beauty of the human body, erotic novels and film, certain paintings). In still other cases aesthetic emotions are due to one's desire to free oneself from the problems of everyday life and the issues raised by civilized life.

In a word, when we approach the problem of aesthetic values from the angle of aesthetic experiences, we must state that such experiences are most varied in nature, that they correspond to different needs—some of them simply contradictory, and that they are conditioned by widely varying dispositions. We have to state that the variety of aesthetic experiences is probably not less than the variety of the objects of such experiences.

These experiences depend not only on the objects of aesthetic appraisals and individual mental dispositions, but also on the social milieu and one's social situation. Readers in present-day Poland cannot understand the hold that Przybyszewski's plays had on the public in the early twentieth century. The milieu shapes our sensitivity in different ways. It may also impose the "duty" to respond emotionally to certain works, and then it is difficult to realize where sincere responses end and a merely conformist behavior toward values accepted in certain circles begins. There is certainly a gamut of intermediate situations. Lefrancq wrote about certain modern compositions of still life: "Following an incessant repetition of statements that one is moved by the soul concealed in a roll or in a coffee jug it comes to this: that one really feels moved by them. These are *spiritual exercises,* extremely interesting to a sociologist."[6] I think that concert halls can often provide similar data.

Emotional Experiences Bordering on Aesthetics

Most factors supposed to characterize the various kinds of aesthetic experiences are not in the least the exclusive property of such experiences. Moreover, certain types of experiences that are reputed to be aesthetic in nature seem to be much closer to certain mental states that are usually placed outside the sphere of aesthetics, than to other types of aesthetic emotions.

Pleasant gustatory, tactile, and thermic experiences are not commonly believed to be aesthetic in nature, although we do not think much about why we should not include them in the same category as pleasant visual, auditory, and olfactory experiences, the aesthetic nature of which is usually not denied. A theater performance often provides the audience with emotions analogous to those they experience when watching sports events, if they are sufficiently interested in sport and/or become sufficiently excited by the fortunes of the competitors. On weekends many people hesitate over the question whether their emotional needs would be satisfied better by a theater show or a sport event. The famous actor Moissi could never vie with Dempsey when it came to the number of spectators, whose similar needs both satisfied. The latter probably also evoked stronger emotions in them, at least on the average. *Oedipus the King* will probably never drive the price paid for one seat to the level of the prices paid by those who came to watch the boxing match between Dempsey and Tunney. And even though the spectators could admire the finely built bodies of the boxers, the perfection of their movements and their skill in boxing, the majority—in all probability—went to see something else, and to experience stronger emotions, namely, those evoked when we anxiously wait for the outcome of the match. If the match were only a sham fight, with the outcome known in advance, then, even if the boxers displayed the same skill, they would never evoke in the spectators such strong emotions as those they develop when watching a genuine contest. Just consider how strong and dramatic are the emotions evoked in Spaniards by bullfights, where the watching of a violent struggle is accompanied by the sight of blood and by the consciousness of the danger of death that hovers over the arena. Burke claimed that the finest tragedy staged in the theater could never vie with the show consisting of the execution of a political criminal.[7]

The experiences of an average watcher of such performances come close to the emotions evoked by certain kinds of theater shows, not only because of the *dominant* emotion, but also because of the spectator attitude (one comes to watch a show) and because of various secondary circumstances. Yet, in the one case such emotions are considered to be aesthetic states, and in the other, usually not. It is true that in the theater we are dealing with an illusion, while during a sport event and during a bullfight we watch real events, that reality being an important factor in evoking emotions; but this would not make any decisive difference in our classifying those emotions, since not all kinds of emotions commonly believed to be aesthetic in nature are based on illusion.

The emotions experienced by a person who looks at artistically valueless personal souvenirs and/or national relics are usually not classified as aesthetic. And yet the delight with which a mother looks at a lock of the hair of her child whom she has not seen for a long time, and the delight with which a romantic lover looks at a dry branch of myrtle probably come close to the delight evoked by certain types of beautiful objects (we even often hear statements of this kind: this is more *beautiful* for me, because it is a souvenir).

It is still more difficult to draw even a vague demarcation line between a certain type of aesthetic experience and intellectual experiences not classified as aesthetic (the reading of an interesting work on a scholarly scientific subject), and between another type of aesthetic experience and the sphere of religious experiences. No less embarrassing is the task of defining the difference between aesthetic experiences and erotic emotions. The latter are sometimes tentatively characterized by a physiological substratum and the purely personal nature of sexual experiences. But a general formulation of such criteria would be difficult: experiences the aesthetic nature of which is not questioned also depend on the general condition of the organism of the person in question, and ecstasies evoked by music may be accompanied by glandular secretion. Erotic raptures often increase the general aesthetic sensitivity of the person involved, and erotic emotions are often described by the same words that are used with reference to one's aesthetic attitude toward music, poetry, visual arts, and/or nature: "beauty," "charm," "delight." When a distinction is made between erotic and aesthetic experiences, the vast scale of erotic emotions is usually disregarded; the same applies to the subtle forms of sexual intercourse which is striking in those situations in which a person brought up in a European urban milieu would expect elementary manifestations of physiological functions: I mean the erotic customs of the various primitive peoples. The tendency to exclude the sexual elements from the sphere of aesthetic emotions is certainly due to the disparagement of "the things of the flesh" in Christian culture. The Hindu books of wisdom subordinate the 64 fine arts (*kalas*) and a rich symbolism to the art of love (*kama kala*).

All such common, more or less traditional, distinctions are not psychologically justified. And we may not refer to the aesthetic value of the objects of experiences because, as we have seen before, we have to refer to the concept of aesthetic experience when we want to define aesthetic value.

This is why those authors who approach the problems of aesthetics from the psychological point of view, and not from that of the theory of art, often cover such varied dubious situations by the concept of aesthetic experiences. This was done, for instance, by the Polish psychologist W. Witwicki, who wrote that a gourmet who is a connoisseur of fine tastes and finds delight in them, also derives aesthetic satisfaction from them. Likewise, a good housewife finds pleasure in having her pantry full of fine food. He claimed that even the pleasure which a physician finds in examining a classic case of cancer or tuberculosis belongs in the same category of emotional states.

In defining psychological concepts we always have much trouble with doubts about their scope. This, however, is not a decisive obstacle in our analysis: doubts about the scope of aesthetic experiences may be left pending while we confine ourselves to those experiences whose aesthetic nature is not questioned. The basic issue is whether there are sufficient links between those various kinds of experiences which are universally considered to be aesthetic in character.

So far we have been noticing differences between the various types of aesthetic emotions rather than similarities they share. That which appears the most important, the most "essential," in some kinds of experiences does not occur at all in other types. But now we have to look for analogies between the mental states evoked by the reading of mystic poetry and those evoked by the view of a fine horse or fine arabesques. They are to be such analogies as will enable us to make a distinction between aesthetic experiences and other types of emotional states, and also be important enough to serve as a basis for a category of experiences that would in turn be a basis for the concept of aesthetic value.

The Concept of Aesthetic Attitude

In describing the various states with which we are concerned here people often refer to an *aesthetic attitude,* which is supposed to characterize all those experiences regardless of their object and regardless of the kind of shade of emotion. But the term "aesthetic attitude" happens to be interpreted in different ways: it may mean an attitude toward the objects perceived or imagined, but it may also mean an attitude toward experiences themselves; in the latter case, it may mean both an attitude toward actual, and an attitude toward expected, experiences. The term *attitude* itself accordingly changes its meaning: attitude as a relationship as against attitude as a disposition.

Let us begin with the last interpretation. In that sense, an aesthetic attitude would mean a momentary disposition to respond in a special way to perceptive ideas or their derivatives. In other words, it would be a *disposition toward aesthetic experiences.*

How much can this concept be used in defining aesthetic experiences? Should the previous adoption of such an attitude be an indispensable condition of an aesthetic experience, *i.e.,* should we be able to have aesthetic experiences only when we are in a state of readiness to experience them, then such a concept of aesthetic attitude would in fact be an essential factor in the description of such experiences. But no such attitude need precede aesthetic experiences, which may appear spontaneously. Certainly, readiness to have aesthetic experiences intensifies our aesthetic sensitivity. This is exactly the privilege of art: when we approach works of art we know that we can expect aesthetic experiences; when I go to the theater or to a concert I am prepared in advance to experience emotions of a certain type. But such a state of readiness is not necessary at all; in thousands of cases aesthetic experiences may take place quite unexpectedly.

In its second sense the aesthetic attitude would consist of *a special relationship to one's own states that are actually experienced.* Something like that is probably meant when it is said that the aesthetic attitude makes aesthetic experiences incommensurable with other kinds of emotions and that accordingly every type of mental state can become a substratum of an aesthetic experience. Aesthetic experiences would thus be "second level" states, states of split consciousness, when our attention is directed to our own experiences, as for instance, when I am looking at a realistic painting and I think of the illusion to which I am subjected.

But such an attitude does not in the least characterize all those varied emotions which are evoked by the beauty of objects. The most intense of such emotions are exactly free from such an self-observation. Should we consider it an indispensable condition of aesthetic states, we would have to deny aesthetic nature above all to all those experiences in which we are completely absorbed with a beautiful object. The delight derived from a complete immersion in music would not be an aesthetic experience. The states of consciousness split into the object of experience and the experience itself are encountered rather in self-observation made for psychological purposes, or sometimes in self-training, that is, outside the sphere of the phenomena with which aesthetics is especially concerned. We know from our experience that directing our attention to what we experience very often weakens the aesthetic emotion, if it does not destroy it altogether.

On the other hand, such "second level" aesthetic states in which a person's aesthetic experiences are due to his dramatizing his own mental states cannot in any way be taken as a rule, and it is not such situations that are meant by those who claim that the aesthetic attitude consists of a split consciousness.

If the phrase "to adopt an aesthetic attitude" means neither "to prepare oneself properly" nor "to adopt a certain relationship to one's own actual experiences," then the term "aesthetic attitude" can only be treated as an equivalent of the phrase *"an aesthetic relationship to objects."* But then the concept of aesthetic attitude does not contribute anything to our problem. It is merely a matter of wording: since no objective properties of the objects of experiences can be that factor which would characterize all aesthetic experiences, then instead of asking "what is common to all aesthetic experiences?" we may reformulate the problem by asking "In what does the aesthetic relationship to objects consist?" or "In what does the aesthetic attitude toward objects consist?"

The Aesthetic Attitude toward Objects

. . . There is an opinion that we adopt the aesthetic attitude toward an object if, when perceiving that object, we internally *isolate* it from surrounding reality and, according to some, also from the world of our thoughts.[8] This opinion is formulated in various ways, usually not clearly enough to let us know whether that isolation is to be a necessary or a sufficient condition of an aesthetic experience. According to another theory the aesthetic relationship consists of *nonintellectual contemplation,* that is, contemplation free from any mental effort and any organizing tendency, free—as far as possible—from conceptual thinking and verbalization. In such states the object of experience is supposed to reveal its face directly, free from the deformations imposed on it by our intellect. Numerous authors support the theory that the aesthetic relationship is one of *empathy* with respect to the objects perceived. Still others think that the aesthetic attitude means a *direct interest in the appearance of objects. . . .*

. . . we could state that as long as the term "empathy" has a definite meaning it is not possible to ascribe all aesthetic experiences to such an aesthetic attitude. The isolation theory finds special support in experiences in the sphere of those arts which reproduce reality. Outside the sphere of reproduction, the isolation of an object certainly plays an important role in aesthetic emotions, but only such as it plays in all other emotive states.

In Poland, the theory that reduced all aesthetic experiences to nonintellectual contemplation was advanced by Edward Abramowski (d. 1918). In his opinion, the aesthetic relationship between a person and a thing takes place when that person rejects the intellectual element, *i.e.,* stops at the threshold of thought.

This idea of the aesthetic relationship was probably suggested by those aesthetic experiences which we sometimes have when we are in a natural environment or when we listen to music. They are in fact nonintellectual, and they are sometimes so intense that they absorb all our consciousness. We might in this connection refer to certain trends in the visual arts (impressionism) and in poetry, which strive for a fresh look at reality and for a rejection of intellectual habits. The poet often tries to look at reality through a child's eyes.

Abramowski was right in defending the distinct nature of such nonintellectual states and in emphasizing their importance in mental life. But when he wanted to reduce all aesthetic experiences to nonintellectual contemplation, his generalization was contradicted by numerous facts. We know very well the charm that the world can have for a person who can look at it through a child's eyes, but we may not forget that there are aesthetic experiences that consist precisely in *intense intellectual activity.* It is only in a few cases that the goal of art is to bring a listener or a spectator to a nonintellectual state. In other cases a work of art specifically requires a rational interpretation. Even in the case of music, both nonintellectual contemplation, a passive surrender to a mood, and an intellectual analysis of a given work are possible. It seems that we have to admit that in both cases we have to do with an "aesthetic attitude."

Disinterested Contemplation

All these theories are too narrow. They are not contradictory, and in the works of certain theorists they are even combined in some ways. They probably have a substratum in certain common but vague intuitions, and it is only when it comes to a more precise formulation of such intuitions that different groups of facts are taken as the basis of generalization, and hence the aesthetic attitude comes to be defined in different ways. It seems that that common substratum consists above all in the sense of something that Kant called disinterestedness of aesthetic states. The concept of that "disinterestedness" is so difficult to formulate precisely and so embarrassing that today theorists are not willing to use it. But when we pass from the works of Kant to the recent theories of aesthetic attitude outlined above, we have the impression that they somehow depend on the concept of "disinterested contemplation." When we isolate an object from reality we thereby renounce all practical interest in it. He who is interested directly in the appearance of an object and concentrates all his attention on how that object looks, and not on what it is, also does not adopt a practical attitude. Nonintellectual relationship to an object is also supposed to be quite disinterested: in that respect too it is opposed to intellect, which is the guardian of interests.

Regardless of the degree to which the suspected connections between these opinions and Kant's approach are justified, the old Kantian idea has not become obsolete, even though its formulation is neither clear nor univocal, and the rigid forms of the Kantian conceptual framework in the sphere of psychology must seem unacceptable in aesthetics more than in any other sphere. The various categories: *jucundum, pulchrum, sublime, honestum,*[9] are by him opposed to one another as sharply as if they were chemical elements. But all this does not invalidate the pertinence of certain psychological interpretations.

It is not usually recognized that the extension of Kant's aesthetic categories is not identical with the extensions of the concepts used in various present-day papers and/or discussions on aesthetics. It must be borne in mind that not all of Kant's statements that have become widely known and that are supposed to represent his aesthetics refer to the entire sphere of aesthetic experiences. In addition to the concept of disinterested contemplation we can find in his works, though without any clear formulation, the concept of *aesthetic attitude toward beautiful objects*.[10] For Kant, that concept is narrower than that of "disinterested contemplation": it refers only to such experiences as are not disturbed by any strong emotion. Kantian beauty is confined to only one kind of aesthetic value as we understand it now: the cool beauty of form, a beauty that does not evoke emotions. The erroneous opinion has been spread that Kant did not accept other kinds of beauty, whereas in fact he merely termed them otherwise. He discussed the aesthetic value of *sublime* objects (*das Erhabene*) that, as opposed to what he termed beautiful objects, evoke strong emotions and can have their value intensified by chaos. In Kant, the disinterestedness of contemplation in the case of the beautiful differs from that in the case of the sublime. There are also experiences that we would classify as aesthetic which Kant does not cover by his concept of disinterestedness: this applies to experiences of *attractive* things (*der Reiz*).

In Kant's works, the various explanations concerned with the concept of disinterestedness do not coincide. On the strength of the statements to be found in *Kritik der Urteilskraft,* a disinterested liking might be interpreted as: *1*) a liking that is independent of one's belief that the object in question exists; *2*) a liking without any desire for the thing in question; *3*) a liking that is not due to any personal motives. Hence we find an ambiguity that paves the way for misunderstandings. W. Witwicki wrote in this connection that a disinterested liking is a paradox, a psychological impossibility, if it is assumed that the person concerned is sincere. This, of course, would be right in certain interpretations of disinterestedness, but the Kantians start from another interpretation of that concept, and "disinterestedness" does not in the least collide, for instance, with the desire to possess those objects which evoke such "disinterested" experiences.

However this may be, it seems certain that even in the case of the most well-intentioned interpretation of his text, Kant's concept of disinterestedness gives rise to various problems that we shall not discuss here. We have been concerned here only with certain intuitions of Kant that have survived and that are to be found in various recent theories, even though they are formulated and used in different ways.

Even today we are inclined to believe that in addition to a practical and gnosiological approach to reality there is still another somehow "disinterested" approach. We are inclined to believe that the characteristic feature of those specific emotions which we experience when facing beautiful objects consists in the independence of those emotions of any belief in the existence of such objects; in other words, our mental states of this kind are not based on existential judgments, although in the course of our analysis we have encountered certain types of experiences that are not marked by such an independence of existential judgments and that nevertheless are classified as aesthetic. Even today we are ready to treat aesthetic judgments as subjective judgments that pretend to be objective: judgments that are based on one's personal emotive response to the object in question, but at the same time independent of any personal considerations (*keine Personalbedingungen*). The trouble is that when we proceed to construct the category of aesthetic experiences, these various intuitions cannot be adequately brought into harmony with one another.

"Enjoying the Moment"

When we look for a general property characteristic of all those states in which we "experience beauty," "feel aesthetic satisfaction," "find delight (in something)," the best way is to approach these experiences in the same way as is done in recent psychological research: from the point of view of play. In this way it will, perhaps, be easier to explain why all those states somehow seem to be "disinterested."

Aesthetic experiences may in certain respects be treated together with what is termed "ludic experiences" (from Latin *ludus:* play). This holds when reference is made to the cathartic function of play, and when we point to the substitutive function of play (making life richer with fictions), and when we treat play as a mental rest from ordinary occupations. Above all, however, both all play and all aesthetic contemplation are marked by an important factor they have in common, a factor that may perhaps account for the feeling of disinterestedness that we associate with those states: in all those cases *we are enjoying the moment.*

When we start from the Aristotelian distinction between goal-directed activities (*e.g.,* the work of a craftsman) and activities performed for their own sake (*e.g.,* dancing), we can find two basically distinct orientations in our conscious life: orientation toward the future, and orientation toward the present. In the latter case we perform an action or we submit ourselves to certain experiences because we find them directly attractive, whereas in the former case we do so because we are concerned with something that is to take place in the future.

Future-oriented experiences are of various kinds. First of all, we include in this class those in which we are *directly* absorbed with the future, *i.e.,* the situations in which we are not concerned with what is actually happening to us and around us, because we are preoccupied with future events. Such are states of expectation and forecast-making, joyful or gloomy dreams about the future, states of hope and fear.

Next, we may speak of such future-oriented states in which we are absorbed with the present but wish to free ourselves from such present experiences because they are unpleasant (toothache, boring company). The intentions that accompany those experiences are projected into the future.

Finally, to come back to the starting point, a very important sphere of future-oriented experiences is that of experiences that accompany all goal-directed activities, *i.e.,* activities whose total value in the eyes of the agent is due to their relation to certain future facts. Our consciousness may then be absorbed with the present, *i.e.,* the very activity performed: our activity may be goal-directed even though we do not think of the goal. This is why in many cases it would be difficult to ascertain by way of introspection that our activity is future-oriented, although the goal has not ceased to be the subconscious motive of action. Sometimes, when we carry out a goal-directed action in which we are not directly interested, another motive may come to the fore: the intention to carry out what has been undertaken. But then, too, our activity is future-oriented: we are moving toward the moment in which we shall be free from the obligations assumed and in which we shall feel the satisfaction of discharged duty.

Most of our conscious life is organized so that the present moment is subordinated to the future. Clearly, this is so not only when we are carrying out far-reaching plans, but also when we discharge our everyday duties, when we plan future actions, when we make forecasts, when we expect something, when we fear something, when we feel sorry or happy about something that is to happen. Till Eulenspiegel, who, when walking down the slope, was concerned about the future climb uphill but enjoyed the prospect of the remainder of the walk downhill, is not just a fabulous person: I think that many a ski fan experiences something like that. Remote unpleasantness, which may not materialize at all, poisons our present day. We are then experiencing something that has not yet happened. The future devours the present moment.

All this can be opposed to those moments in which we enjoy the present regardless of what is going to happen later. These are activities and experiences which we find attractive by themselves and which are as it were gaps in our "serious" life, for when we live "seriously" we look into the future.

The distinction between those moments in which we are future-oriented and those in which we are absorbed with the present is, however, not so easy to make as it might seem. When a farmer goes to the fields in the spring, his goal-directed activities do not prevent him from enjoying the fresh morning air, the clear blue of the sky, and the singing of the lark. And his work as such may also prove attractive and be a direct source of pleasure. The attitude with which an action *is being undertaken* need not accompany the *performance* of that action. An action undertaken for the sake of a distant goal may prove so interesting in itself that the goal becomes superfluous: we would feel disappointed if the goal were achieved immediately and thus deprive us of the motive for further action; or perhaps we might even be ready to go on with that work, even though it has ceased to be goal-directed any longer. This is the case, for instance, of a professional dancer who earns her living by dancing, but finds dancing such a rapture that she forgets all financial considerations. In such situations we have to do with the coexistence, or even the rivalry, of two attitudes: the original, oriented to the future, and the secondary, oriented to the present. Sometimes that secondary attitude may triumph over the original one.

There are also cases in which from the very outset we want to find a direct interest in an action undertaken with a goal in view; that interest is to be independent of the goal, yet without that direct interest the action in question could not be goal-oriented. For instance: the recreations in which a person who is overworked or has had depressing experiences engages in order to regain his nervous balance; or aesthetic experiences that a person seeks for self-educating purposes, being convinced that such experiences will make him a better man. In such cases the activity in question serves its purpose better if its purposiveness is forgotten.

Since in the various types of experiences there are various relationships between these two attitudes, it is not easy to define them precisely, the more so because when we make sure that a person is future-oriented we sometimes have to refer to subconsciousness, and this may always raise doubts. Nevertheless, I think that the concept of "enjoying the moment" can easily be grasped by our intuition and that we can avoid misunderstandings if we agree to apply the term "enjoying the moment" to all those periods in our conscious life which are marked by a lack of a clear orientation to the future, or at least by a clear domination of an orientation to the present. These two types of orientation can also be found in our approach to the past: one's attitude toward past events may be either future-oriented (when we want to make good some ill-effects of the past, or when we reflect on the consequences of past events), or present-oriented (when we passively review the past).

In some cases the orientation of experiences may give rise to misunderstandings in connection with our definition of enjoying the moment. Those states which we classify as enjoying the moment in its purest form would also include the experiences in which we consciously strive for a future moment and in which the thinking about that future moment is to a large extent the condition of the intensity of our experiences. There are numerous plays in which the player strives for a given goal: one who plays chess strives to checkmate his opponent; one who plays tennis strives to win the match. The same applies to future moments in reading a crime story or watching an interesting play: we are anxious to know what will happen next, or we are anxious about the outcome of the plot; our fear rivals our hope.

Yet, contrary to all appearances, these examples do not contradict our interpretation of enjoying the moment. In all such situations the future situation for which we strive is also covered by enjoying the moment and as such is excluded from our serious life. A play may have its own distinct goal, such as defeating the adversary, but if it is really only a play, and not something "decisive," then in fact *the goal is subordinated to the play, and not the play to its goal:* we set ourselves a task in order to play. The same applies to reading a crime story or watching an interesting performance: we are anxiously waiting for the end in order to be able to experience a number of emotions before that end comes. Here too the main value of that final moment consists in evoking the process that leads to it: the art of reading is not principally conceived as the means to reading the book to the very end.

We have here to do with a dynamic type of enjoying the moment, as opposed to such nonoriented types of enjoying the moment as the pleasures of riding a see-saw, of playing tennis without keeping score, of contemplating fine paintings, and of taking delight in the beauty of nature. In such "dynamic" experiences there is orientation, but—as in the case of nonoriented experiences—there is no subordination of the present to any future moments: although we move toward the future, it is the present that is important. This is why we consider such processes to be pure forms of enjoying the moment. In the case of a theater performance, we shall ascribe the orientation toward the present to the spectator who is feverishly waiting for the denouement; on the other hand, we shall ascribe the orientation toward the future to the bored critic who is watching the same performance without any anxiety about what is to happen next, who is watching it merely because he has to write a review of the play.

In the lives of various people these two attitudes are to be found in different proportions, which is finely illustrated by the fable of the ant and the grasshopper. Some people subordinate all their interests to wealth in old age; others are totally concerned with the afterlife; still others show incessant fear of disease: all their lives they are concerned with their health, of which they are unable to make any good use. But this constant orientation toward the future is also typical of men of action, such as social workers, dedicated to a given cause. We also know other people in whose life enjoying the moment takes the place of pride. These may include a born tramp, a Petronius, a jovial, good-companion personality. In children, enjoying the moment is, as is known, the dominant attitude, which the various educational measures on the part of the older generation strive to restrain.

The formation and scope of the two attitudes depend on living and working conditions, and the amount of leisure time is a factor of primary importance.[11] The resulting associations point not only to the opposition between the privileged and the underprivileged classes, but also to the opposition between the highlanders, engaged mainly in animal breeding and agriculture, and the industrial workers in the same country and in the same epoch. Other social factors also come in question: personality patterns and scales of values propagated in the various milieus (e.g., bohemians versus businessmen) and in the various cultures. In earlier cultures, play and all those activities which, as Aristotle put it, are performed for their own sake, are appraised positively, while work that does not cause satisfaction is appraised negatively; even the very concept of work may in some cases be considered negative, as the etymology of the term *negotium* (*nec-otium*) would indicate. The role of ludic elements in magic and in religious ceremonies is well known. The same applies to early trade.[12] Huizinga collected numerous data bringing out the ludic nature of old trials and ordeals and also the ludic elements in military art.[13] He also drew attention to the fact that in all cultures poetry preceded prose. It was not long ago that prose drove out verse from novels, and in Poland, even as late as the turn of the eighteenth century, Staszic, following Parmenides, Empedocles, and Lucretius, wrote his treatise on the evolution of the human race in verse, while Bishop Załuski compiled the catalogue of his library also in verse. It is said that in Japan documents of state used to have poetic form up to the Meiji reform in 1868.[14]

William Morris, a craftsman, artist, poet, and socialist, considered the sharp distinction between the production of objects for practical use and the creative activity in which man finds direct satisfaction, to be one of the characteristics that marks the difference between rational capitalistic culture and the earlier, less commercialized, form of economy. That was why he thought that in all social classes in his society, happiness could be attained only by artists and by thieves.[15]

An attitude hostile to enjoying the moment found expression in the late eighteenth century in Franklin's famous advice to a young man. A few decades later (in 1844) the young Marx pointed to the connection between that attitude, as represented in our culture, and that which Max Weber later would term the spirit of capitalism. In his notes to *The Holy Family,* Marx wrote ironically that political economy was the most moral of all disciplines. Its principal rule was renunciation of the self, renunciation of life and all human needs. The less you ate, drank, bought books, went to the theater, balls, and cafés, thought, loved, theorized, sang, and painted, the greater would be your treasure that neither the worms nor rust would destroy—that is, your capital.[16]

"Enjoying the Moment" and Aesthetic Contemplation

That attitude toward reality which I have termed "enjoying the moment" has the properties that might have affected the formation of certain opinions about aesthetic experiences; I mean above all the isolation theory and the concept of disinterestedness. I think that it is not a coincidence that they were formulated in the classical period of capitalism. We have said above that the theory of the isolation of the objects of aesthetic experiences from the surrounding world is too narrow to serve as a basis for a general concept of aesthetic attitude. But where there is isolation of objects there is also usually isolation of those experiences which refer to those objects. And in that theory it is the reference to isolation of experiences that is probably the most important. Now always, when we are enjoying the moment, we are concerned with such an isolation, isolation in *time* and not in space. Everything that we experience then is, subjectively, not connected with the future; it is excluded from our "serious" life, and takes place as it were on the margin of our life.

When we come to *disinterestedness,* enjoying the moment suggests to us one more meaning of that term. From a certain point of view we may say that we are interested in an object, not when we want to possess it, but when we see it as *a means to some of our ends*. Such an interpretation of interest in something is not at variance with common intuitions: we can easily concede that all interest in something always projects into the future. Hence from that point of view, enjoying the moment is a disinterested attitude toward reality.

This concept of disinterestedness differs from those encountered in the theories of aesthetics discussed before, but I think that if all aesthetic experiences are classified as disinterested, then an analysis in depth would disclose just such a broad concept, interconnected with the other interpretations of disinterestedness, as would cover all kinds of enjoying the moment. The fact is that the concept of disinterestedness in aesthetic experiences is associated with the belief that beauty is a value that is appraised as such, regardless of any *consequences,* apart from the pleasure of contemplating that very value.

Enjoying the moment is a very broad category, incomparably broader than the subject matter of our analysis here. It covers both *active* and *contemplative* experiences: a dance or a contest makes it possible for both the actors and the spectators to enjoy the moment: the former experience active states, the latter, contemplative ones.

This distinction seems to bring us closer to an adequate description of aesthetic experiences: contemplative enjoying the moment is a very important characteristic of aesthetic experiences, and its scope covers all types of such experiences. Yet this category too is only the *genus proximum* for them, since it also covers various kinds of experiences that are not usually classified as aesthetic, namely all kinds of sensual pleasures (including the pleasures provided by the lower senses), religious ecstasies, erotic raptures of all kinds, the joy of seeing one's friend, a "disinterested" inebriation with success, and so on.

We would extend the concept of aesthetic experience so as to cover those emotions too, and from the psychological point of view such a step would be well substantiated. Should we do so, however, we would unfortunately destroy all possibility of establishing a correlation between aesthetic experiences and a concept of aesthetic values the extension of which would more or less agree with the ways of valuation adopted in our culture.

If we want to avoid such a discrepancy, we have to assume that the sphere of experiences in question, namely, disinterested enjoying of the moment, is a category superior to that of aesthetic experience. But it seems that this is in fact the *closest* category superior to all types of aesthetic experiences. But it seems also that within that *genus proximum* we cannot find for them any general *differentia specifica:* we cannot find any specific property that would draw a demarcation line between all aesthetic experiences and those contemplative forms of enjoying the moment which we would not be inclined to term aesthetic experiences.

Such an adequate distinction could be made only by means of a number of separate provisos. For instance, the pleasure derived from meeting a friend or looking at souvenirs and/or relics could be eliminated by the Kantian requirement that aesthetic experiences may not be determined by any personal circumstances, *i.e.,* that only those experiences are classified as aesthetic in which the person in question ascribes his pleasure to the objective values of the object perceived, and is convinced that that object is pleasant *not only to him* for certain special reasons, but that every person having analogous tastes could experience a similar pleasure when viewing that object. Experiences involving the lower senses would be eliminated by the requirement that the object of an aesthetic experience should be characterized by a certain complexity (which would, however, eliminate simple visual and auditory impressions: beautiful sounds and beautiful colors), or by some other requirement that would restrict aesthetic experiences to those based on the senses of vision and hearing. Still other requirements would make it possible to eliminate those emotions which, because of their object, are not considered noble enough (such as the pleasure derived by some people in watching a street row).

In this way we could ultimately arrive at a category whose extension would more or less comply with current intuitions and linguistic usages. But such a concept, based on different and mutually independent assumptions concerning either the experiences themselves or the objects of such experiences, would be too artificial. The singling out of such a category is motivated in historical terms only, not in psychological ones. The extension into which we would like to make it fit is characteristic of cultured Europeans and is thus demarcated by purely accidental circumstances.

If we therefore do not want to abandon the psychological ground, we either have to admit that there exist different categories of mental phenomena that are considered aesthetic experiences—categories that are somehow interrelated, but that do not lend themselves to being covered by a single common and adequate concept—or have to adopt a category with a broader extension: either by admitting that the aesthetic attitude is manifested in all forms of enjoying the moment, or by introducing some other criterion.

NOTES

1. In his *Studies on the Form and Content of Works of Art* (in Polish), *Przegląd Filozoficzny* (1949) Ingarden analyzes nine meanings of the term *form*. [References to texts available only in Polish have been omitted or abridged.—Trans.]

2. K. Lange, "Der Zweck der Kunst", *Zeitschr. fuer Aesth. und allg. Kunstwissenschaft* (1912).

3. *Ibid.*, pp. 178 ff.

4. Quoted by S. Ossowski from a Polish translation of K. Woerman's book on the History of Art.

5. Quoted from N. Yefimov's *Sociology of Literature* (in Russian), (Smolensk, 1927), p. 166.

6. J. Lefrancq, "L'esthétique et la sociologie", *Revue de l'Institut de Sociologie* (Brussels, 1928).

7. *Essay on the Sublime and Beautiful* (1756).

8. Theodor Lipps, *Die aesthetische Betrachtung und die bildende Kunst* (1903–1906), p. 60.

9. *Kritik der Urteilskraft* (Leipzig, 1902), p. 10.

10. *"Das reine Geschmacksurteil,"* pp. 41, 65, et passim.

11. Following his long comparative anthropological studies, F. Boas came to the conclusion that the scope of artistic activity in the various people

depends on the amount of leisure time they have at their disposal. Cf. *Primitive Art* (Oslo, 1927), p. 300.

12. Cf. M. Mauss, "Essai sur le don, forme archaique de l'échange," *Année Sociologique* (1925); B. Malinowski, *Argonauts of the Western Pacific* (London, 1922); P. Freuchen, *Arctic Adventure* (1935).

13. J. Huizinga, *Homo Ludens* (London, 1949).

14. *Ibid.*, p. 127.

15. W. Morris, *The Socialist Ideal in Art* (London, 1897).

16. K. Marx and F. Engels, *Gesamtausgabe,* vol. 1, part B, p. 130.

4

ABSTRACT ART AND PHILOSOPHY*

by

Władysław Tatarkiewicz

Władysław Tatarkiewicz was born in Warsaw in 1886. He received his Ph.D. at the University of Marburg, and an honorary Ph.D. from Jagiellonian University in Cracow. He has been Professor of Philosophy at the University of Warsaw since 1915, and Professor of Aesthetics since 1957. He is a member of the Polish Academy of Sciences and Letters, an honorary member of the International Institute of Philosophy, and a member of the Board of the International Committee of Aesthetics and the International Federation of Philosophical Societies. He was editor of the Polish Philosophical Review *from 1925–1948, and of* Estetyka *from 1960–1963. He was Visiting Mills Professor at the University of California, Berkeley, in 1967. His books are:* History of Philosophy, *1931, 7th ed., 1968;* On Happiness, *1947, 4th ed., 1968;* History of Aesthetics, *vols. 1 and 2, 1960, 2nd ed., 1962, vol. 3, 1967;* Concentration and Reverie, Essays on Aesthetics, *1951; and several volumes on the History of Art, in particular on Polish architecture and sculpture of the seventeenth and eighteenth centuries.*

---

* This essay is a revised version by the author of the essay that appeared in the *British Journal of Aesthetics* 2 (1962), translated by Adam Czerniawski. The original essay appeared in Polish in *Estetyka* 1 (1960), and in German in *Jahrbuch für Aesthetik* 6B (1961).

I

Art produces objects of use: houses to live in, chairs to sit on, plates to eat from. This is a natural function and is not puzzling in any way. Art also embellishes and decorates these useful objects—houses, chairs, plates; in this too there is no mystery.

But there exist certain types of art, such as painting and sculpture, that are neither functional nor decorative, do not produce objects of utility, and do not decorate such objects. What then is their purpose? A very widespread theory answers that they create things of beauty. We are so accustomed to this answer that we are astonished when the historian tells us that it is comparatively new. The older answer, the one that was more common in the past, was different: it was to the effect that the purpose of these arts is not so much beauty as the representation of reality. This answer comes from Greece and may be found in Plato and Aristotle. According to them such arts as painting and sculpture are imitative or representational in their essence. There are, however, various ways of imitating, or representing, reality, and at least four of these will be distinguished in this paper. They appear most prominently in painting but also *mutatis mutandis* in sculpture.

1. Often enough painting and sculpture have confined themselves to portraying the outward *appearance* of things. Dutch painting is a classic example of this.

2. Or they have portrayed things not in order to reproduce their appearance but their *structure,* as do the paintings of Poussin and Cézanne, or their essence, as the Byzantine icons do.

3. Yet other works portrayed the material forms of things not for their own sake but in order to convey psychological facts, that is, character, *feelings,* experiences of people. Instances of this are discernible particularly in Baroque and Romantic works, in the paintings of El Greco or Delacroix.

4. Still other works portrayed things in order to display

their beauties of line or color: the objects portrayed are utilized on account of their possibilities for ornament, as can be observed in the paintings of Botticelli and Carlo Crivelli.

Imitative art thus had *four* avenues that it could explore: it presented either the *appearance* of things, or their structure and *essence,* or *psychological meaning,* or the *beauties* of their form.

Of these four types of representational art, two have accepted names. The art that portrays the appearance of things is known as *naturalism,* but the term has been used so often and so inaccurately that it has lost its sharpness of significance. The art that emphasizes the psychological meaning of things is known as *expressionism.* It is easy to find suitable terms for the remaining ones: art that attempts to present the essence of things could well be called *essentialism,* while art that approximates things to beautiful shapes could be called *formalism* or *calligraphism.* Innovation in terminology might be pushed even further. Since the term *naturalism* has been overworked, one could in accordance with the custom of coining terms from Latin roots, use the word *aspectus,* that is, appearance, and call *aspectism* that art whose aspirations are limited to representing the outward appearance of things. Similarly, art that reaches for the essence of things could be called *prospectism.* This term is suggested by the great painter Poussin, who distinguished two methods of seeing: the ordinary way and that when we observe objects closely, with our minds as well as our eyes.[1] The second way of seeing he called "prospect" from the Latin *prospectus*—a distant view. In the long run it is immaterial what terms we choose so long as they are understandable and in current use. However, the terminology *aspectism-prospectism* seems to be a proper one. And though the modes of representational art are fourfold, the opposition of aspectism and prospectism is essential. Prospectism may stand in our times for all nonaspectist art, being its most important variation.

My first point is, then, that there are different types of imitative or representational art. They all have this in common, that they represent real objects. And they do so with the help of real shapes and not abstract signs. Reality is to them both a means and an end. That is why they are sometimes known as *realism*. But this word carries other implications, and it is better to say that they are all ways of "representing reality."

In the course of 2500 years of European history, from the Greeks to our times, all four types of representational, imitative art have been cultivated; but at some periods the aspective art accounted for almost the whole of European art, especially in the nineteenth century.

II

At the turn of the nineteenth century a change took place in the "imitative" arts, particularly the art of painting. First and foremost, artists began to abandon aspective art. In which direction did they proceed? Toward expressionism and what has just been called prospectism. The new prospectism originated with Cézanne and culminated in cubism. It certainly gave new forms of art but it did *not* create a new principle of art; even cubism, together with all the work of Picasso,[2] belongs to imitative art understood in the broadest sense. Art continued to be representational.

But the swift course of evolution swept beyond the bounds of imitative art to *abstract* art. Under various names such as Suprematism, Tachisme, and so on, art broke away from its traditional role of imitating real things. It was no longer imitative in any of the four ways described above. It created abstract forms.

Abstract art had from the very beginning, and still has, various facets.

1. One school depicts abstract forms for their own sake, simply because they are beautiful or pleasing. For them form is both a means and an end and there is no concern for anything beyond form. It is an embodi-

ment of abstractionism, but of formalism as well. It is the *formalistic* mode of abstractionism.

2. The second type of abstract art employs forms because they are emotive, because they convey feeling and move us. This is the *expressionistic* variety, which Kandinsky had in mind when he wrote that "each form is an expression of inner meaning" and "the artist is a hand which with the aid of one form or another is capable of rousing the human soul." He also said: "In art is no form that is wholly material." "Every method is good [hallowed] if it arises from inner compulsion." "Beauty of color and form are not a sufficient aim for art." "A thing is beautiful if it has inner beauty."[3] Similarly Ben Nicholson: "A square and a circle in art are nothing in themselves and are alive only in the instinctive and inspirational use an artist can make of them in expressing a poetic idea."[4] The expressionist version of abstract art is also represented by the French painter Bissière when he says that he wants to create paintings in front of which "everyone can dream his own dreams."[5]

3. And there is still a third type of abstractionism. The forms that it uses may appear similar, yet the underlying intention is different. They are not an end in themselves, as in the first type, nor a means of expressing and arousing emotion, as in the second. Here the artist uses abstract forms to state an attitude toward the world, to express his *understanding* of the universe. This school claims that abstract line and color are capable of containing the nature of things— not their appearance but, precisely, their nature—because paradoxically this can be achieved more successfully with abstract lines and colors than by the representation of appearance, which is external, fortuitous, and superficial. This is the way in which Piet Mondrian understood art: in his paintings he made use of horizontal and vertical lines, not because of their intrinsic beauty, but because they are "the ex-

pression of two opposing forces of the universe."
Clive Bell, one of the first theorists of formalism,
maintained that in art everything is form, but "significant form," denoting the essence of being.[6] The
French abstract painter Alfred Manessier, who combines both cognitive and expressive aspirations, writes
about his art that "it enables the contemporary painter
to catch the *inner* truth and endows him with an awareness of the *essence of things*."

Some abstract artists make theoretical statements that
leave no doubt that in their works they wish to express the
essence of the cosmos.[7] For this reason this type of abstract
art has come to be called *cosmism*. Such art has cognitive
ambitions: without imitating nature it aims, nevertheless,
at rendering the essence of nature through abstract line
and color, and, what is more, tries to function *like nature*.
Hans Arp writes: "Art is a fruit on a plant and a child in
the womb."[8] And Mondrian: "We have no wish to copy
nature . . . we do not wish to reproduce but to produce
in the way plants produce fruit."[9] This type of abstract
art is cognitive in its aim in a more profound and metaphysical sense than the four types of representational in
the means it employs.

What has been said above shows that there is a parallel-
ism between the types of representational and abstract art.
By definition abstract art cannot include a type that portrays
the external appearances of things—it cannot exist in the
mode of aspectism. Its categories, however, correspond to
the three remaining types: the one seeking beautiful forms,
the one seeking expressive forms, and the one seeking true
forms. This is my second general proposition: abstract art
has a variety of modes and this variety corresponds with
the variety of representational art.

III

Representational art may be considered as the natural

expression of human activity; yet it was stimulated as well by philosophy. The imitative theory was the first general European theory of the arts; it was voiced by the great Greeks, Socrates, Plato, and Aristotle, no less than by the great modern thinkers, Alberti, Leonardo, and the followers. It led directly to aspective art, allowing that nature is perfect and that art can achieve perfection only by imitating her. Therefore imitation, "mimesis," was supposed to be the essence of painting and sculpture; and the arts that we call "fine arts" were for centuries called "imitative arts."

The connection of other modes of representational art with philosophy is no less clear. No less than aspective art, prospective art was dependent on philosophy; this was so either unconsciously or consciously. A major instance of conscious dependence is Byzantine painting, which expressed in visual form the doctrine of Neoplatonic philosophy. Plotinus maintained that the arts do not imitate things in nature but ascend to their prime causes out of which natural things have grown.[10] Drawing on him, Pseudo-Dionysius said that "through sensual images we ascend to the contemplation of things divine,"[11] and his followers, the Byzantine theologians and philosophers John of Damascus and Theodore of Studion,[12] maintained that "painting leads man to the sight of celestial things." And indeed, the Byzantine paintings attempted to grasp in their works "things divine" and "celestial things" and therefore were not confined to the aspect of earthly things.

IV

Now our problem is: has contemporary abstract art also been *stimulated* by science, and, in particular, by philosophy? The answer is positive: it has been so stimulated by both science and philosophy.

    A. Let us consider first the influence of *science* and *letters:* of new physics, new psychology, and new history of art.

1. The *new physics* has been a stimulus to art, both through its general conceptions and also by the models and photographs of wave motions and vibrations. These give a new picture of the real world, a picture to some extent more regular than the world we see, and often spellbinding in its beauty.[13] Artists have had far too many opportunities of seeing the new models and photographs to be able to remain immune to their influence. The similarity between the forms they have created and patterns of the new physics is in some cases too strong to be coincidence. We know that certain artists, like Paul Klee, had a good knowledge of natural sciences and of the latest developments in it. And the philosophy of Whitehead took the step from physics and philosophy to aesthetics and tried to link the "abstractions of physical science" with "the principle of aesthetic experience."[14]

   In his *Ruckblicke* Kandinsky wrote: "I felt the splitting of the atom as equivalent to the breaking up of the whole world. Suddenly the most impregnable walls crashed. Everything became uncertain, wavering, soft."[15] The news of the splitting of the atom, by making everything that had been known until then "uncertain, wavering, soft" gave rise to the conviction that the ordinary forms of the world had lost their dominance, that the artist must and could seek new ones. That was in 1911, when abstractionism was in its infancy.

2. At least one theory of twentieth-century *psychology* might have a bearing here. Just as psychoanalysis contributed to the rise of Surrealism, *Gestalt psychology* performed a similar function for abstractionism.[16] It claimed that we see and think about the world in terms of defined forms, that each appearance must be subjected to them, and that these forms are more general and more permanent than their content. On reaching the artists, this

theory encouraged them to represent forms *per se* as the general and permanent features of the world.

3. *Historians of art,* especially Worringer since 1908, encourage abstract art in demonstrating that abstraction is by no means an impossible and never-used form of art.[17] On the contrary, they showed that abstract art made its appearance earlier than imitative art, that for many centuries it was the natural form, that these early cultures, even when they represented natural objects, deformed and approximated them to abstract forms. This we can see in Egyptian and Near Eastern art as well as in Irish illuminated manuscripts and old Scandinavian carvings. This early abstract art was, in most cases, religious or was understood in terms of magic, and was much closer to cosmic than to pure formalistic art.

B. Did *philosophers* also stimulate our abstract art?

1. Certain theorists of abstract art maintain that the stream of *irrational* philosophy at the beginning of the twentieth century known as Bergsonism has contributed to its creation. There is no doubt that the influence of this school upon intellectual life has been considerable and widespread; its influence on poetry has often been demonstrated, but it has also affected the plastic arts. As late as 1955, that is, at a time when the influence of Bergson's philosophy had already begun to wane, Herbert Read, the chief exponent of abstractionist theory, wrote: "I must acknowledge the inspiration I continue to receive from the only metaphysics that is based on biological science—the metaphysics of Henri Bergson."[18] This inspiration concerns not so much the abstract character of modern art as its metaphysical claims.

Bergson[19] was of the opinion that reality cannot be apprehended by reason alone: only intuition is capable of that. Intuition relies in turn on images. Metaphysical truth "cannot be contained in a sys-

tem of concepts" but "may be given us directly
through intuition" and "indirectly suggested by
images." Bergson was thinking of images in the
human mind, but images painted by an artist are
born from images in his mind and represent a
selection from such images. The meaning of Bergson's deduction was as follows: cognition through
images is not only possible but has more importance than cognition through concepts. It reaches
deeper into the nature of being. This means that
art may serve cognition even better than science
does.

2. It is striking that some *rationalist* trends reached
an analogous conclusion. In his *Essay on Man,*
Cassirer[20] wrote that artistic forms participate in
building and organizing human experience and that
humanity derives its view of the world not only
from scientists but from artists as well. This means
that he too supported the cognitive-cosmic aspirations of art. Also Münsterberg[21] maintained that
true knowledge is not acquired through science,
but through aesthetic contemplation, because science studies causes and effects whereas contemplation concerns things themselves.

3. These theories were known primarily to specialists
and enjoyed less popularity in artistic circles. They
could not, therefore, exercise very much influence
over the artists' aspirations and their understanding of art. Such an influence was exercised, however, by the general situation in philosophy. I mean
the disagreement among the various schools, the
fragmentation of philosophy, and the oft-repeated
saying among philosophers that an outlook on the
world cannot have a scientific basis and therefore
everyone can think as he pleases. Knowledge of
this state of affairs reached beyond professional
circles. If there is no philosophy that is authoritative, men thought that everyone, the artist included,
could philosophize in his own way. Artists sought

this, not through words and concepts, but with their proper tools, that is, through forms and colors. They tried to reveal the forces operative in the world—creation and destruction, durability and transitoriness, law and accident. And abstract forms seemed better suited to this task than real forms, which show only tiny segments of the world. It is not enough to say that modern art with its cosmic pretensions is inspired by philosophy; it wants, itself, to be a philosophy. "What artist," wrote Paul Klee,[22] "would not wish to be in the great temporal and spatial changes, in what one might possibly call the brain or heart of creation in the womb of nature, where a mysterious key of the universe is safely stored?" This is no longer a philosophy of philosophers taken over by artists, but a philosophy of artists. The irrationalism of the twentieth century produced a suitable atmosphere for it to thrive. Philosophy is like war: when the professional army capitulates, partisans take to arms. Art has also taken over those obligations which according to traditional division of functions were the domain of philosophy.

The third major proposition of this paper is: scientists and philosophers *have stimulated* modern abstract art. And the fourth proposition will be: earlier philosophers have also *foreseen* the possibility and advantages of abstract art.

V

A. Let us go back to the eighteenth and nineteenth centuries. It will appear that ideas favoring the abstract art were being propounded even in the epoch of neoclassicism, which rather subscribed to the representational idea of art. Winckelmann wrote: "Beauty must be like clear water drawn from a pure spring; the less taste it has, the healthier it is."[23] By this he meant

that the more general and abstract a work of art is,
the more beautiful it will be. Even more emphatic
was the voice of his French counterpart, Quatremère
de Quincy,[24] who wrote that beauty is the greater the
less it is particularized and that it then acquires the
characteristics of geometry—"il y a en elle du géomé-
trique." And elsewhere he maintained that true representational art "reduces the particular existence of
things to an *abstract* existence of space and genus."
We find similar ideas in Goethe, who maintained that
fine arts never began with nature[25] and that the highest
art is that in which the subject matter is indifferent.[26]

Winckelmann, de Quincy, and to some extent
Goethe were classicists. But Baudelaire, a man from
another camp, had similar ideas on art. He wrote:[27]
"A good way of proving to oneself whether a painting
is melodious is to look at it from a considerable distance, so that neither the object nor the line is distinguishable." This implies that the fact that a painting represents something real has no bearing on its
aesthetic impact.

In all these opinions a definite philosophical influence, that of Platonism, is discernible. If, without
pausing at the various stages of its history, we go back
to Plato, its founder, we shall find in his writings a
pure and radical theory of abstract beauty.

B. In "Philebus" Plato[28] has written, in a curious and
memorable way, that when he speaks about beauty
he has in mind not the beauty of living creatures but
such beauty as that of the straight line and the circle.
And he justifies this by saying that this beauty alone
is not relative, that only such beauty is permanent and
beautiful by itself, and that it alone is capable of giving the greatest pleasure—which the beauty of sensible objects cannot give.

But the beauty of straight lines and circles did not
for Plato signify formal beauty alone; on the contrary, geometrical beauty was cosmic beauty. He was
convinced that the world was created in accordance

with geometrical forms. He denounced the art of his day for representing the external appearance of things, which is merely a figment, an outer shell, and a pretense. The essence of the world is more regular and more geometrical than this outer cover. Thus Plato was the spokesman not only of the abstract, but also of the cosmic, approach to beauty. Whenever this appeared in later centuries it could be traced back to him; but none has formulated it in bolder terms than he. He anticipated the two essential characteristics of modern art, which is abstract as well as cosmic; and his words in "Philebus" might serve as its motto.

This is the fifth purpose of the present paper: to recall an idea of Plato that is less well known than it deserves to be. It must, however, be kept in mind that there is a difference between Plato and modern thought: Plato was convinced that geometrical beauty is the perfect beauty of the universe, but it had not occurred to him that *art* could take upon itself the task of representing this beauty.

VI

Three final remarks may be added. First: the ideas of modern philosophers concerning the cognitive faculties of nonaspective arts are not a novelty. Particularly in Hellenistic philosophy the idea was current that the meaning of the universe may be more readily expressed in images than in concepts of a philosopher. It has been written about Phidias that before carving his Zeus he had to spend a long while contemplating the cosmos because his work contained so profound an understanding of it. And Dio of Prusa wrote as follows:[29] "There are three sources of man's idea of God: nature, poetry and law; but as a fourth one may add the plastic and sculpting art of painters, sculptors, stonemasons and in fact of everybody who has undertaken to imitate divine nature."

Second remark: both antagonistic theories of art, aspectism as well as prospectism, derive in some way from the same philosopher, from Plato. He defined painting as "mimesis," *i.e.,* as imitation of the aspect of things; and at the same time he advocated cognitive cosmic art.[30] How was the duality possible? Plato supposed that *existing* art in his times was aspective, but *good* art should be prospective, and this good had formerly existed, particularly in Egypt. What is more, Plato not only formulated both aspectist and prospectist theories, but in "Philebus," as we have seen, he also cleared a way for abstract art.

Last remark: In the history of European philosophy it is possible to extract two tendencies, two *streams.* One, the stream of empiricism and materialism, did not favor abstract forms and metaphysical pretensions in art. But this support was given by the other stream, beginning with the Pythagoreans and Plato, embracing thinkers of a metaphysical bent in late antiquity, and continuing with Neoplatonists, Pseudo-Dionysius, the Byzantine theologians, St. Augustine, and the medieval Augustinians, the Neoplatonists of the seventeenth century, until we reach the theorists of Neoclassicism and Romanticism. Some of these thinkers laid greater stress on the abstract form of art, others on its metaphysical content; many emphasized both. After a break during the nineteenth century, this ancient stream has again found an echo among artists of the twentieth century, who for the most part do not realize how old their lineage is.

NOTES

1. N. Poussin, Letter to Fr. de Noyers, 1642, in P. du Colombier, *Lettres de Poussin* (1929), p. 74.

2. P. Picasso did not admit the possibility of an abstract art: "Il n'y a pas d'art abstrait. Il faut toujours commencer par quelque chose. L'homme est l'instrument de la nature; elle lui impose son caractère, son apparence." Quoted by B. Dorival, *Les étapes de la peinture française contemporaine,* vol. 2 (1944), and by M. Brion, *Art abstrait* (1956).

3. W. Kandinsky, *Über das Geistige in der Kunsta,* 5 Aufl. (1956).

4. *B. Nicholson,* with an Introduction of H. Read (1958).

5. Another spokesman of expressive abstract art was the painter K. Male-wicz, *Gegenstandslose Welt* (1927). Many quotations stressing the expressive faculties of abstract art are in M. Seuphor, *A Dictionary of Abstract Painting* (1958), and G. Habasque, *Au delà de l'informel,* in *Oeil,* no. 59 (1959).

6. C. Bell, *Art* (1914).

7. One of the earliest representatives of a metaphysical interpretation of "Pure Form" was S. I. Witkiewicz, *Nowe formy w malarstwie* (1919), and *Szkice estetyczne* (1922). For a view on art that may also be considered as metaphysical, see H. Read, *Art and Society* (1937), p. 260.

8. H. Arp, *On my Way* (1948).

9. P. Mondrian, "The new plastic Approach to Painting," in *De Stijl* (1917).

10. Plotinus, *Enneads* 2. 8. 7.

11. Pseudo-Dionysius, *Hierarchia Coelestis* 3, *Patrologia Graeca,* vol. 3, col. 121.

12. John of Damascus, *Oratio Apologetica* 9, *Patrologia Graeca,* vol. 94, col. 1360. Theodore of Studion, *Antirrheticus, Patrologia Graeca,* vol. 99, cols. 444 and 344.

13. H. W. Franke, *Kunst und Konstruktion, Physik und Mathematik als fotografisches Experiment* (1957).

14. A. N. Whitehead, *Religion in the Making* (1926), p. 116, and *Adventures of Ideas* (1956), p. 341: "The teleology of the Universe is directed to the production of beauty."

15. W. Kandinsky, *Rückblicke* (1955), in particular in M. Bill's Introduction to this book.

16. W. Tatarkiewicz, *Historia Filozofii,* 6th ed. (1968), vol. 3, pp. 301–5.

17. W. Worringer, *Abstraktion und Einfuhlung* (1908). Earlier Analogous ideas are found in A. Riegl, *Stilfragen* (1899).

18. H. Read, *Icon and Idea* (1955), p. 19.

19. W. Tatarkiewicz, "L'esthétique de Bergson et l'art de son temps," in *Actes du X Congrès des Sociétés de Philosophie de langue française* (1959), p. 197.

20. E. Cassirer, *Essay on Man* (1953), p. 212.

21. H. Münsterberg, *The Principles of Art Education* (1905).

22. P. Klee, *Über moderne Kunst* (1947), p. 47.

23. J. J. Winckelmann, *Geschichte der Kunst des Altertums* (1764), vol. 4, p. 20.

24. Quatremère de Quincy, *Considérations sur l'art du dessin* (1791), p. 66. Cf. R. Schneider, *L'esthétique chez Qu. de Quincy* (1910).

25. J. W. Goethe, *Neue Untersuchungen über verschiedene Gegenstände der Kunst.* Cf. H. v. Einem, *Beiträge zu Goethes Kunstauffassung* (1956).

26. Firmenich Richartz, *Die Brüder Boisserée,* 1916, vol. 1, p. 316. Cf. H. v. Einem, p. 171.

27. J. P. Hodin, "Art and Modern Science," in *The Proceedings of the Third International Congress for Aesthetics* (1956).

28. Plato, *Philebus,* 51 C.

29. Dio of Prusa, *Oratio* XII. 4.

30. Plato, *Republ.* 597 D ; *Leges* 798 D ; *Sophist.* 235 D–236 C ; on the other hand, *Republ.* 472 D. Cf. W. Tatarkiewicz, *History of Aesthetics,* vol. 1 *passim.*

5

HUSSERL AND PICASSO*

by

Ksawery Piwocki

Translated from Polish by
K. OŁDAKOWSKA

Ksawery Piwocki was born in Lvov in 1901. He received a Doctor of Arts degree from the University of Lvov in 1931, and is a historian, critic, and theoretician of art. He was conservator of relics in Vilnius from 1935 to 1938, and from 1938 to 1939 was Director of the Museum of Industrial Art in Lvov. Since 1946 he has been Professor of the Warsaw Academy of Art. From 1954 to 1960, he was Professor of the History of Art at Poznan University, and since 1957 has been Director of the National Museum of Ethnography in Warsaw. The following are among his most important publications: "The Problem of Research Methods in Folk Art" (Zagadnienie metody w badaniach nad sztuką ludową) *printed in* "LUD" ("The Folk") (1930); Folk Woodcut in Poland (Drzeworyt ludowy w Polsce) (Warsaw, 1934); "On the Historical Origin of Polish Folk Art" (O historycznej genezie polskiej sztuki ludowej) (Wroclaw, 1953); *The Development of Research Work on National Art and the Problem of Antiquarianism* (Rozwój badań nad sztuką narodową i zagadnienie starożytnictwa) (Warsaw, 1955); *The History of the Academy of Art in Warsaw* (Historia Akademii Sztuk Pięknych w Warszawie) (Wroclaw, 1965); "The Lvov Center of Historians

* This essay was originally published under the title "Husserl i Picasso," in *Estetyka* 3 (1962).

of Art" (Lwowskie środowisko historyków sztuki), printed in Krakow in Folia historiae artium (1967); Living Art (Sztuka żywa); a selection of papers and articles published in Polish and foreign periodicals from 1928–1968.

The title of this article is a contraction of thought. It suggests some relationship between Husserl and Picasso, although at the time that cubism was developing and its theory was being codified there was no such relationship. Everything seems to indicate that at that time the two men knew nothing about each other. Moreover, the type of cubist theory here described is not represented by Picasso who, as is known, always deprecated the formulation of any artistic programmes. Thus here the great name of Picasso is but a symbol. This permits one to avoid in the title a too-lengthy allusion to the problems broached in this article.

We are, however, compelled at the outset to present the *structure* of these considerations. We will begin by listing the basic assertions given in 1901 by Husserl in his *Logische Untersuchungen,*[1] completed by some remarks on eidetic cognition in *Ideen zu einer reinen Phänomenologie . . .*[2] of 1913 (subsequently, these dates will appear to be of the utmost importance) and also some formulations of the theoreticians of cubism at the time of its development before the First World War. Also, some further statements by the artists and historians of cubism may add to the explanation of the theoretical bases of this artistic movement. We purposely say *"some"* remarks and formulations, which indicates an arbitrary choice. The very numerous inconsistencies and even contradictions found in the declarations of artists, in articles written by critics and historians of cubism that were so well derided by Fosca[3] (but so unjustly from the methodological point of view), do not allow me to compare the attitude of Husserl and of the cubists without giving a great deal of thought to the choice. It should be here emphasized that this does not seem to be an error in method. Fortunately, art is not univocal. It is multiform, multivalent, and multivocal, and this is the secret of its importance all through the ages. Art makes it possible for every generation to seek in it new content and new knowledge. But it is extremely important to the historian of artistic movements to realize fully the basic elements of the artist's attitude typical of the given time. And the historian chooses his material from this point of view. The intention is to investigate the intellectual climate in which the given movement was started. The last part of this article endeavors to give a short methodological justification of the comparisons given, determining within what limits they are scientifically allowable and when they seem to be absolutely necessary.

First, let us consider with whom Husserl fights.[4] His main enemy is psychologism. Some time ago positivism deleted psychology from the system of sciences, because psychological assertions based on interior experience do not have any objective or intersubjective character. Further research, however, on cognitive action, especially those made by empiriocritics, led to the assertion that experience consists in perceiving facts, therefore in the psychic experience of them. The flow of changing impressions goes through the centralized psychic system of the person who perceives, that is, through his brain, if it conditions his experience. Consequently, psychology is the basis of the science of cognition. Thus, at the end of the nineteenth century cognitive psychologists dominated various branches of knowledge, from Wundt's ethnography to Dilthey's historiosophy. Psychological research should be borne in mind too, as well as research on the meaning of the sense of touch or sight (*Tast und Seebild*) in the history of art by Riegl, Wickhoff, Schmarsov, and Wölfflin. This is just what is contradicted by Husserl in defining the fundamental aim of his work: "In order to criticize psychologism we must first explain the notion of relativism or subjectivism. . . . It is originally defined by the Protagorean formula that man is the measure of everything, if we interpret this in the sense that the individual man is the measure of every truth. The truth for each individual is what seems true to him. . . . We can, therefore, choose also the following formula: every truth and every cognition is relative—relative for every subject accidentally giving his opinion. . . .[5] The subject is the final source of cognition."⁶ And further: "When we attack relativism, we naturally think of psychologism. In fact psychologism in all its branches and forms is nothing more than relativism . . . and it does not matter whether it is based on a transcendental psychology or on an empiric psychology. Every psychologism draws the necessity of laws from the casualness of facts."⁷ And finally Husserl expresses his position as follows: "It is not our problem how experience originates, whether naive or scientific, but what its content should be to make it an experience of objective value. The problem is: what are the ideal laws which confirm such an objective importance of real cognition and how should their action be understood? In other words, we are not interested in how the ideas in the world originate or change, but we are interested in objective law according to which the scientific ideas contrast with all other ideas in the world.⁸ The tendency to identify a possibly accurate rationalism with the tendency of biological adaptation (to the stream of impressions), or to draw this tendency from rationalism, and finally the considering of this tendency as the main psychic force—all these are a sum of errors which can be compared only to the psychologists' falsification of the laws of logics."⁹ Thus, for Husserl, the worst enemy of knowledge is psychologism in all its forms.

Let us now consider whom the originators of cubism opposed. In the catalogue of Braque's exhibition in 1908, Apollinaire defines impressionism as a period of ignorance and madness. "The frantic storm of various temperaments, more or less noble, tries to manifest warmly, rapidly, irrationally and with as little art as possible, their astonishment in the face of nature: these features are typical of impressionism."¹⁰ In 1912, Gleizes and Metzinger in their *Du Cubisme* state that the retina of the impressionists dominates their brains. The impressionists were only "practical servants of purely sensory petty needs."¹¹ We know that the cubists have drawn the final consequences of the criticism of impressionism from Cézanne, whose exhibitions in 1904 and 1908 shattered the originators of cubism. For the great recluse at Aix—and similarly for Seurat, Van Gogh, and even Gauguin—Monet was not only a great eye but also a great master; but for the generation of cubists the passive, perceptive attitude toward nature was something quite foreign and almost revolting. It is not necessary here to repeat well-known things; it is enough to state that the stream of purely sensuous, visual experiences that were the inspiration of the impressionists, the platform of their experiences of reality and what defined their attitude toward phenomena, has an unambiguous analogy with the psychological attitude of the empiriocritics, Husserl's antagonists. The fight against subjective vision and subjective cognition, the fight against grounding knowledge on sensory experience alone and against the one-sided image of the subject—that is, of the variable excitation of the sense of sight—indicate clearly connected views of this scientist and the group of young, rebellious painters.

If the two parties are united only by a similar criticism of the past, we must first draw attention to another aspect of this matter. Before Husserl, Bergson fought extensively against empiricists of all types. But this attempt had begun in common attitudes. Psychology played an important role in Bergson's analyses by investigating the spiritual specificities or psychic forces, which the postpositivist thinkers disregarded. But Husserl was much more radical. He was not satisfied with the flashes of intuition with which Bergson illuminated the darkness of the unknown. He wanted to reach the sacrosanct, from which even the thought of Kant recoiled. He wanted to know the essence of phenomena, the thing itself, "das Ding an sich." He expressed this aim only in his *Ideen zu einer reinen Phänomenologie,* but in *Logische Untersuchungen* he had already prepared the way and cleared the path to the sacrosanct. Similarly, in the field of art, the above-mentioned great painters criticized impressionism, but they did not have such radical aims as the cubists. The experienced sense image was still their starting point, but they struggled for the right to transform the material submitted by the eye. "Art is man added to nature," cried Van Gogh.[12] "Nature, reality, truth, yes! but with a significance, with a conception, with character. . . ." "We must paint what we see," wrote Cézanne, "forgetting everything that was done previously."[13]

Naturally we do not wish here to lecture on Husserl's philosophy. It is sufficient to quote a number of the statements of this originator of phenomenology that explain his attitude toward research and his aims. We are not concerned with all of his ideas, but only with thoughts and remarks that can be compared with quotations from the theoreticians of cubism.

In the introduction to the second volume of *Logische Untersuchungen,* Husserl wrote: "Phenomenological analysis tends to experience pure being excluding any empirical factology. . . . It is therefore essentially different from empirical and psychic experiences. Psychology describes individual experiences and it opposes, in a fallacious manner, interior and exterior observations. The difficulty of phenomenological analysis consists in the fact that it demands an unnatural direction of perception and thought. . . . We have to "reflect," that is, to make acts of perception and their sensuous content the subject of our investigation. While the objects seen, thought of, theoretically investigated . . . are considered as real, we must direct our theoretical interest not to these objects. We must not regard them as real . . . but on the contrary, just these acts of cognition . . . are to be the object of our conceptions and theoretical investigations. We must view them as new deeds of thinking and imagining, analyse their essence, describe them and make them the subject of our thoughts. . . ."[14] The essence is to approach in a pure description the pure relations of the phenomenon. This purity requires one to withdraw from and to reject psychological realism. . . . Phenomenology does not speak about any circumstance of the animal type. It describes perceptions, judgments, feelings, and the like, as such, what is peculiar to them, *a priori,* in an absolute generalization as pure units of purity, what can be perceived only with a pure intuitive conception (*Wesenschau*) of the essence (*ejdos*) of the phenomenon, just as pure arithmetic speaks of numbers and geometry speaks of volumes on the basis of a pure view in an idealized generalization."[15]

The phenomenon is not only the experience in which the given object appears (*e.g.,* a concrete experience of observation), but also the appearing object itself that is included in our consciousness. Phenomenological cognition consists in the direction of looking that turns away from the actual observed objects and is directed to their specificity in being perceived.[16] And further: "In this sense, what I experience, or what my consciousness experiences is just the experience of the object. There is no difference in phenomenology between the experienced, realized content of consciousness and the experience of the object. . . ."[17] The essence of the content that is phenomenologically felt is something quite different from the perceived being of the object which is represented in the content of consciousness."[18]

Here Husserl gives the famous example of the box revolved in the hand. We have continually different impressions, different images of the object, but continually the same content of consciousness. The impressions are different but the object is the same. The essential experience and the content of consciousness is the consciousness of the existence of the box. Similarly we have another image, that of a tree in the wind. We can change its image by coming nearer to the window or retreating, changing the accommodation of the eye. The color of the leaves changes as they are turned by the wind, and the color of the trunk changes in the light shaded by the clouds. We must therefore differentiate the color of the changing impressions (the noetic moment) and the essential color (Noematic).[19] "Noematic is the field of unity (that is, of the object); noetic is the field of changing variations."[20] Husserl repeats a similar argument several times, for instance in the example of the table around which we are walking.[21] The act of consciousness consists of multiple intentions, partly purely perceptive, sensuous, and partly imaginative and even sign-like (that is, abstractive). "Thus a pure phenomenological perception is fully adequate to all "sides" of the perceived object. The object is to be seen in the phenomenologic act of perception from one side, then from the other, from nearby and from a distance. But it is always the same phenomenon, the same object. Sensuous perception is made in one act. Phenomenological cognition is based on many acts, both psychic and sensuous perceptions."[22]

Husserl in 1913 emphasized the part played by the imagination when thinking, in eidetic cognition; he did this in a remarkable way and in a way very close to contemporary methods of artistic creation. "There are reasons for which, in phenomenology, as in every eidetic science, realizations (*Vergegenwartigungen*) and, strictly speaking, imaginary creations (*Phantasien*) take priority over perceptions."[23] To prove this thesis, Husserl describes the work of a "pure geometrician": "In his fantasy he has the incomparable freedom to change and transform at will the imagined forms, to see in his imagination the continually modified possible creations, and thus to create an infinite number of new forms —the freedom which gives him access to distant fields of the possibilities of being (*Wesensmöglichkeiten*) and infinite possibilities of discovering their essence. Therefore usually designs follow the constructions of fantasy . . . and they serve mainly to fix and thus to reveal the stages of an already accomplished process. When one thinks, in looking at (*im Hinblick*) a form, the newly appearing processes of thought are . . . processes of the imagination which establish new lines of form. This matter is not different for a phenomenologist who has to deal with "reduced" experiences and their essential correlates. Also the phenomenological shapings of the "ejdos" (*Wesensgestaltungen*) are innumerable. . . . Anyhow here too, the freedom to investigate the essence of the matter absolutely requests one to operate with imagination. . . .[24] Thus, actually, if one likes paradoxes and understands the ambiguous sense of these words, one can say truly that "fiction" is an essential element of phenomenology, as well as of every eidetic science and that it is the source of 'eternal truth.' "[25] In a remark in his notes Husserl says: "This is a sentence which, given as a quotation, would be quite suitable for a naturalistic derision of the eidetic method of cognition."

It is worth while to note the words characteristic of Husserl's searching attitude, words that are continually repeated in the course of his considerations, namely: the "description," the "view," and the "image" of the phenomenon, rather than the "notion," or the "definition," of the notion as used by the classicists and the neopositivists. Husserl's attempts tend to visualize the image of the essence of the object. According to the quoted texts, this does not concern the image corresponding to sensuous perception, but the integral, or as Husserl says, "pure" image, free of every fortuitous element of sense experience.

Declarations of the cubists, and of the theoreticians and historians in explaining their attitude are, of course, innumerable. A selection of them, which is necessary for comparison with quotations from Husserl, is grouped here according to four principal problems: first, the scientific and rational ambitions of cubism; second, the transition from being interested in the sensuous phenomenon only to attempt to give an account of the content of consciousness, to analyze this content and to transpose it into an image of the object; third, the problem of simultaneity; fourth, the ambition to cognize and represent the essence of the object, or, using the language of phenomenologists, the ambition of eidetic cognition. Finally, I want to draw attention to the part played by the imagination in modern art.

Apollinaire, who was very close to the young cubists, wrote the following about the scientific attitude of their artistic research: "Picasso investigates the object like a surgeon making a post mortem. . . .[26] Wanting to attain the proportions of the ideal, not limiting themselves to human models only, these young painters give us works that are more intellectual than sensuous. . . .[27] What makes cubism different from earlier painting is the fact that it is not an imitative art, but an art of conception, tending to achieve the level of creation."[28] Many years later Picasso himself was to use a similar definition in his conversation with Marius de Zayas: "We express our conception through art, which is not nature."[29] Coming back to Apollinaire, we find the well-known, often-quoted thesis: "One of . . . the tendencies (of cubism) is scientific cubism. It is the art of painting new entities consisting of elements that are not taken from visual reality, but from the reality of cognition. Everybody has this sense of interior reality."[30] A year later (1912) Albert Gleizes and Jean Metzinger had defined their attitude as follows: "The visible world does not become the real world exclusively by sense operation but also by the operation of thought. . . . The objects which are spread with the greatest force before our eyes, are not always those whose existence is richest in its artistic truth."[31] Speaking of earlier days, André Lothe notes: "Cubism was, above all, a way of feeling; it was an aspiration toward ordered impressions; it was the experience felt by many ancient masters who had sufficiently proved that impressions themselves do not attain anything if they are reconveyed in a chaotic manner, without previous judgment and concentration."[32]

The chief historian of cubism, Maurice Raynal, who wrote a monograph on Picasso, defines the scientific aspiration of the art of our century as follows: ". . . it is inspired by the only faith, the faith in philosophical and scientific truth." And also: "Modern painting cannot be regarded as the expression of purely sensuous pleasures. It is penetrated by science and philosophy and it has become an instrument of cognitive discoveries."[33] The above-mentioned opponent of cubism, Fosca, deplores that "cubism is responsible for the fact that the painting of today has to be justified by philosophical consideration, expressed in a philosophical jargon. Today, those who think that they can paint, or write about painting or delight in it, are absolutely bound to acquire a powerful philosophical culture."[34] Clearly, our painters were very anxious to compete with contemporary thought in discovering the truth about the world through their art.

Husserl endeavored to obtain the true image of reality by his method of analyzing the content of our consciousness, by not trusting the testimony of the senses alone. Let us see what the cubists say on this subject. In *Du Cubisme* by Gleizes and Metzinger, we find astonishingly similar thoughts, though they are formulated somewhat differently. "There is nothing real outside of us, there is nothing real outside the point where impression intersects with the direction of individual thought. We are by no means doubting the actual existence of objects that act on our senses. But rationally we cannot have any surety except the image that our mind evokes."[35] And finally: "Separating that which we regard as inseparable, let us study through color and shape the integration of artistic consciousness. . . ."[36] In order to arrange painting space, all impressions of touch and movement and all our intellectual faculties should be utilized."[37] Therefore, it is not only the eye, not only the senses, that build up our knowledge of objects. Integral analyses of all the elements of our consciousness are needed, too.

Cooperating with the cubists, Severini wrote: "A work of art should be started by analysis not of the effect but of the cause, and it cannot be constructed without a method relying on the eye and on good taste only. . . . The forms that we see are replaced by the forms of which we think."[38] And Braque adds, in his often-quoted aphorism: "The senses deform and the mind forms."[39]

It is worth while quoting Raynal as a historian of art: "[Cubism] wanted to show nature in all planes, that is, to construct the image of the object not only on the basis of a vulgar view given by our senses, but of the true reality that our mind constructs on the screen of our thought. It has become the rule to construct new compositions from elements of reality but outside their sensuous, decorative, psychological, or other expression."[40] Mieczyslaw Porębski describes the cubists' attitude as follows: "What is the object? Not that which we see. Our knowledge of the object is wider than that of our senses. It is also shared by thought as by imagination detached from sense impressions. All this must be depicted. And then, even if the real content of being is not finally penetrated, the reality achieved will prove to be greater, more powerful than our thoughts, our feelings, our imagination, and so then we will at any rate have taken a step forward, we will have achieved a more penetrating instrument of artistic perception, one that is more universal than ever before."[41] Abandoning the external view of the object for an analysis of what is going on in the mind at the moment of cognition of reality by integrating all elements in the act of cognition of the phenomenon, seems in the light of the above quotations to be very close to Husserl's attitude.

One of the methods of such an analysis applied by the cubists was simultaneity, that is, the simultaneous realization of the view of the object from its various aspects. In 1925, explaining this method, Gleizes began by analyzing older art. "If Renaissance painting considered the surface of a picture as a mirror, then the person who looks into the mirror and sees the picture as a reflection cannot consider the picture to be the real object. The post-Renaissance picture does not agree with nature, perhaps only inasmuch as a mirror reflects the sky and trees. . . . In spite of the painters' knowledge, that is, their conscious organization of the picture, this art was not life; it was only organizing shows and appearances in the lustre of the mirror. The reflection of the object is an abstraction if the object itself is concrete. The Renaissance, in resolving the problem of space, found only an imitative resolution, the illusion of a third dimension kept the painters 'aloof' from the objects. . . ."[42] The authors of *Du Cubisme* found salvation in applying the following method: "We are sure that even those less thoughtful will recognize that the wish to shape bodies . . . by enumerating various aspects, is just as justified as imitating daylight by using blue and orange. Therefore, we turn the object around so as to control its various sections, which, set in one picture, will reproduce this object in its essential duration."[43] Pronaszko expressed it more clearly, though perhaps not so subtly: "Observing the object, that is, thinking about it, I do not see only its frontal part; on the contrary, my imagination is struck by its various planes and, reassimilating them into the picture, I attain its expression, its essence. Thus, I attain the third dimension, which has nothing in common with the traditional perspective."[44] Similarly Jacques Villon: "In its heroic period cubism analyzed the relations and proportions . . . [qualities that] made it possible to represent as a unity . . . many aspects of one object."[45] The methods of uniting in one view various aspects of the investigated phenomenon, as in Husserl's example with a box of matches, was reflected also in poetry, at the end of G. Apollinaire's poem "The Victory": "Look—Victory will be foremost—To see well from far—To see everything—from near—And that everything should have a new name."[46]

Simultaneity was naturally only one of the forms applied by the cubists to reach the full, as they judged, picture of the object or phenomenon. As for Husserl the method of phenomenological description and pure view (*Wesenschau*) was but the road leading to eidetic cognition—to the cognition of the essence of the phenomenon, so for the cubists the integral analysis of the view of the object and simultaneity, which was sometimes but not always applied, were stages leading to aims defined as follows: "The cubist picture is simplicity itself, because it is true. . . . Inclining towards eternity, it detaches the forms surrounding us of their temporary reality. . . . It clothes them in their geometric purity, equalizing them in their mathematical truth."[47] After the First World War Gleizes realized still more clearly the efforts of the prewar cubism: "A new conception of naturalism arose. A tendency was established that came closer to the essence of the matter: to realize more precisely that which we call life. . . . One must be completely deprived of judgment or be a complete ignoramus . . . not to understand that the changes in the methods of cognition have corresponding changes in aesthetic methods. . . .[48] When I say that a new conception of naturalism has arisen, it is because a new type of artist is being formed who is convinced that the cognition of nature is attained not only by an intellectual perception from a distance, but by penetrating into the object."[49] And to attain the aims of cubism: "We look for the essence of things, but we look for it in our own personality."[50]

Juan Gris, in the poll of the "Bulletin de la Vie Artistique" in 1925, admits: "Cubists put under visual phenomena that which they considered as the essence of the form. But this assumed a purely descriptive and analytical representation. Yes, I am well aware that the beginning of cubism was analysis, which was no more painting than the description of physical phenomena is physics."[51] In his letter quoted in 1919 by Kahnweller, Gris wrote similarly: "I think that I will achieve a precise expression of imaginary reality consisting of intellectually pure elements."[52] This purity of approach to the content of consciousness was the greatest concern of the originator of phenomenology.

The desire to attain the essence of phenomena is emphasized in agreement by critics and historians of cubism. Kahnweller states: "These painters attempted to grasp the essence of things and not their appearance."[53] Roger Fry, in his article published by the "Burlington Magazine" in 1918/19, wrote that Picasso ". . . shapes his forms by induction, eliminating in turn all incidentals so as to draw out the pure substance."[54] Let us end this paragraph on the essence of the cognitive tendencies of cubism by quoting the beautiful fragment of Apollinaire's poem "The Hills":

Unknown depths of consciousness
Will be searched through tomorrow
Who can know what creatures
Will be drawn out of these depths
And the whole universe with them

.   .   .   .

I have investigated everything that until now
Could not be even imagined
I have weighed in my hand a thousand times
Life which has no weight
I will be able to die with a smile[55]

It is possible, of course, to find in the declarations of artists of that time many analogies with the astonishing avowal of Husserl, who attached such importance to imagination in his method of cognition. It will suffice, perhaps, to recall as an example the words of Chwistek in his reminiscences of the time very close to cubism when Polish formism was beginning: "To paint the world as I want it to be. To paint the reality of imagination. To look into the life of colors and light in nature, but not to paint from nature. . . ."[56] It is also worth while to draw attention to the evolution of cubism from the analytical cubism of the years 1910-1912 to the synthetic cubism of the years 1913-1914, in which free imagination begins to play a growing part. Picasso says of this part: ". . . the artist . . . is often astonished by results he has never anticipated. . . . Sometimes the drawing engenders the object, or the color suggests the shapes defining the object. . . ."[57]

It seems that even in such a condensed form, the comparison of Husserl's definitions of 1901-1913 with the declarations of cubists, their theoreticians, and their historians, has yielded an astonishing concurrence of thoughts and notions. What scientific sense can it have? In what conditions will such a comparison be of cognitive value? I want to consider these questions.

Of course it is no discovery to mention philosophical formulations in an attempt to explain different trends of modern art or the work of different artists. Thus, for example, Charles Gauss devoted his whole book to considerations of this kind,[58] and Christopher Gray applies similar considerations to cubism.[59] He compares cubist analysis to Kant's analysis. I must add here that Fritz Novotny compares Cézanne with the same philosopher.[60] Though Gauss is probably more correct in comparing Cézanne with Poincaré's theory, which introduces subjectivism into the exact sciences, Gauss's remarks connecting Renoir with Bergson should also be favorably mentioned. In justifying the cubists' attitude, Leonce Rosenberg mentions Plato.[61] Many more examples could be found. I do not think all of them are correct and scientifically justified. At the end we shall once more revert to this problem. I would like to consider the possibility of such endeavors according to opinions in classics of the history of art.

Schnaase, in 1843, had already discovered that the nations' feelings, thoughts, and customs were manifested in art, because art is the center of their intellectual activity.[62]

But only the theory of creative will, submitted by Aloisius Riegl in 1901,[63] opened the way for investigating the entire cultural phenomenon (that is, including philosophical ones) and its justification. For the moment it was only a general formulation and it was made in order to justify the need of positive evaluation of all the arts of every period after the classical canons of evaluation had been eliminated. It was also to help in finding objective criteria of historical development. According to the definition given by Tatarkiewicz, the creative will is above the individual; it is a style-creating tendency of the period.[64] Therefore, it necessarily defines these tendencies in every particular case. The task of defining more precisely the meaning of the term (creative will) used by Riegl is taken up in the next generation of the Vienna school by Max Dvorak, in *Kunstgeschichte als Geistesgeschichte* in 1924. He sees in works of art (this is expressed in scathing terms by Lionello Venturi)[65] only philosophical documents, above all, religious ones; and he ascribes intellectual and religious values to works of art with such force that he forgets about their aesthetic values. A more important objection is that definitions of the "creative will" spread over schemas embracing too long periods of time and immense numbers of artistic facts. As a result Dvorak explains the spirit of the epoch without deigning to explain the different trends or the individual artistic attitudes. A further step was made by Erwin Panofsky. "A work of art is an object made by man and is destined (besides other functions) to provoke an aesthetic experience. Most often it is also a group of signs that possess a definite meaning and whose function is to convey this to the observer. The interpretation of the content of a work of art must be a semantic interpretation. It goes in three layers. . . . The last of them, the iconological, does not concern the senses only, but explains the work of art as a historical phenomenon, a document and a symptom. It discovers its interior meaning, its symbolic form."[66] Though in practice iconology concerns chiefly and almost exclusively symbolic motifs established by tradition, which are therefore rather allegoric (that is why its supporters become helpless when they are dealing with works of art operating with individual symbols), nevertheless possible comparisons that I have made here are justified by understanding the necessity of confronting a work of art with various disciplines in order to find out its meaning. This seems to me to be especially correct and important with regard to the works of contemporary art, the semantic meaning of which has nothing in common with any traditional symbolic motif and about which the iconographic tradition has absolutely nothing to say. It is rather the form itself that carries the content and much more seldom is the content expressed by an individual, metaphoric, ambiguous, and symbolic motif. It is the direct equivalent of feelings and thoughts, as has been noticed by Theodore Lipps.[67] Under these conditions the meaning of the work of art, or of an artistic trend, can be found only in analyzing the form and, in no less degree, in investigating the attitude of the author or authors toward reality in its widest sense. Their works do not speak of particular facts; they do not formulate univocal, semantic definitions, but show the attitude of the artist toward the world and toward human beings, and these are clearly problems connected with philosophy. Thus, if in our investigations we do not concentrate on aesthetic elements and want to interpret the meaning of a work of art as a reflection of the attitude of contemporary man, we must look for analogies first of all in contemporary philosophical thought.[68]

Such investigations can be valuable only if we look for analogies among really contemporary trends. For this reason we pay extensive attention to dates. Husserl expressed the thoughts here considered in 1901-1913, Lipps in 1903-1908, cubism in 1908-1914. One might add the declaration of Benedetto Croce of 1907,[69] but that would lead us too far. Refuting Pinder's mystical "Wurfe der Natur" in his theory of generation, it is impossible not to observe in the contemporary world—albeit within comparatively narrow sections of time and only in this case—a unity of atmosphere, of spirit not of the period but of the day, which favors the appearance of similar cultural and creative phenomena in various branches of human activity. The unity of contemporary civilization; the universality of information and the speed with which we gather it from various fields, consciously and unconsciously; the identity of perspectives that surprise us; the terror of dangers threatening us; the delighting in the same products of culture and casting away of similar bonds and remnants of traditions; and surely many other things, create this atmosphere of similar attitudes. The most sensitive seismographs of changes occurring in the world are the young artists, that is, persons with a special sensitivity and—in the same period of time—much older thinkers who are perhaps less sensitive but who instead are better and more fully informed and have a wider view of the whole. Though the philosophers' opinions usually do not reach the consciousness of the artists and their groups, the attitudes of these two groups are comparable and can throw an interesting light on the essential sense of artistic research and on the astonishing realization of thoughts of many philosophers who seem to be abstracted from life. They can explain the deepest semantic layer of a group of contemporary works of art and at the same time give an artistic illustration of apparently completely abstract deductions of a philosopher.

The comparison of deductions made by Husserl and by the cubists was chosen here because, in this case, there was no possibility of conscious repetition. Certainly it would be possible to find comparable declarations of this artistic group, for example, Bergson, Poincaré, and so on, but they belong to an older generation; they formulated their ideas in the nineteenth century and they should be compared with their contemporary art. Besides, the paradoxical lack of contact between Husserl and Picasso proves better and more evidently the thesis of this article. Another analogy can also be pointed out. As cubism was the basis of the whole development of twentieth-century art and without it the further development could not be even thought of, similarly phenomenology became the ferment of the most widespread contemporary philosophical ideas. In a certain sense Sartre can be considered the continuator of Husserl.

NOTES

1. According to the 3d ed. (Halle, 1922).

2. *Ideen zu einer reinen Phänomenologie und phänomenologischen Philosophie* (1913).

3. F. Fosca, *Bilan du Cubisme* (La Bibliothèque des Arts, 1956).

4. W. Tatarkiewicz, *Historia filozofii,* vol. 3 (1950), p. 302.

5. *Logische Untersuchungen,* vol. 1, p. 114.

6. *Ibid.,* p. 116.

7. *Ibid.,* p. 123.

8. *Ibid.,* p. 205.

9. *Ibid.,* p. 207.

10. G. Apollinaire, "Introduction to the catalogue of Braque's Exhibition" (1908), p. 3.

11. A. Gleizes and J. Metzinger, *Du Cubisme* (1912), p. 28.

12. P. Eluard, *Anthologie des écrits sur l'art. Les frères vagants* (1952), p. 16.

13. From the letters to Emile Bernard. Letter of October 23, 1905, translated in the *Głos Plastyków* (Krakow: Związek Plastyków, 1937, p. 26.

14. Vol. 2, p. 9.

15. *Ibid.,* p. 11.

16. W. Tatarkiewicz, p. 304.

17. Vol. 2, p. 352.

18. *Ibid.,* p. 383.

19. *Ideen zu einer reinen Phänomenologie,* vol. 1, pp. 201–3.

20. *Ibid.,* p. 207.

21. *Ibid.,* pp. 73–74.

22. *Logische Untersuchungen,* vol. 2, p. 383.

23. *Ideen zu einer reinen Phänomenologie,* vol. 1, p. 130.

24. *Ibid.,* p. 131.

25. *Ibid.,* p. 132.

26. G. Apollinaire, *Les peintres cubistes* (1913). I am quoting from the Polish text: *O kubizmie,* p. 19.

27. *Ibid.,* p. 23.

28. *Ibid.,* p. 31.

29. "Conversation avec Picasso," *Cahiers d'art,* Nr. 10 (1935).

30. Apollinaire, p. 32.

31. Gleizes and Metzinger, p. 6.

32. A. Lothe, *De la palette à l'écritoire* (1946), p. 3.

33. F. Fosca, pp. 80, 118.

34. *Ibid.,* p. 141.

35. Gleizes and Metzinger, p. 30.

36. *Ibid.,* p. 13.

37. *Ibid.,* p. 18.

38. G. Severini, *Esthétique du compas et de la nombre* (1921).

39. Quoted by Brion *L'Art abstrait* (1956), p. 17.

40. M. Raynal, *Pablo Picasso* (1922). According to F. Fosca, p. 117.

41. M. Porębski, *U początków sztuki współczesnej, materiały do studiów i dyskusji z zakresu teorii i historii sztuki oraz badań nad sztuką.* (At the beginning of modern art. Materials for studies and discussions on the theory and historical investigations of art) (Państwowy Instytut Sztuki, Warsaw, 1955), p. 179.

42. A. Gleizes, "La Peinture et ses lois. Ce qui devait sortir du Cubisme," *Bulletin de l'Effort Moderne,* no. 11 (1921), p. 9.

43. Gleizes and Metzinger, p. 36.

44. Z. Pronaszko, "Wstęp do katalogu Wystawy Formistów i Ekspresjonistów Polskich. ("Introduction to the catalogue of the exhibition of Polish formists and expressionists") (Krakow, 1917).

45. J. Villon, *Bulletin de la Vie Artistique* (1924).

46. G. Apollinaire, *Chosen Poems* trans. A. Stern (1957), p. 132.

47. Gleizes and Metzinger, p. 13.

48. A. Gleizes, p. 9.

49. *Ibid.,* p. 10.

50. Gleizes and Metzinger, p. 31.

51. F. Fosca, p. 65.

52. *Ibid.,* p. 124.

53. *Les années héroiques du Cubisme* (1950).

54. Fosca, p. 121.

55. *Chosen Poems,* trans. J. Kott, pp. 80–81.

56. L. Chwistek, "O sobie" ("About myself"), *Głos Plastyków* (1935), p. 61.

57. *Propos des artistes* (1925). Conversation with Florent Fels.

58. Ch. Gauss, *Aesthetic Theories of French Artists* (1949).

59. Ch. Gray, *Cubist Aesthetic Theories* (1953).

60. F. Novotny, "Das Problem des Menschen Cézannes im Verhaltniss zu seiner Kunst," *Zeitschrift für Aesthetik und Allgemeine Kunstwissenschaft* (1932).

61. L. Rosenberg, *Cubisme et tradition* (1920).

62. K. Schnaase, *Geschichte der bildenden Künste* (1843).

63. A. Riegl, *Spätrömische Kunstindustrie in Oesterrich-Ungarn* (1901).

64. W. Tatarkiewicz, "Rozwój w sztuce" ("Development in Art"), *Świat i Człowiek* (The World and the Man), vol. 4, pp. 228–81.

65. L. Venturi, *L'histoire de la critique d'art* (1938), p. 206.

66. J. Białostocki, "Metoda ikonologiczna w badaniach nad sztuką" ("The Iconologic Method in Investigations of Art"), *Przegląd Humanistyczny* (Humanistic Review), nr. 2/3, (1957).

67. Th. Lipps, *Aesthetische Psychologie* (1903), and more clearly in *Raumaesthetik und geometrische Raumtäuschung* (1908).

68. W. Tatarkiewicz drew attention to this in his article "Nowa sztuka a filozofia" ("New Art and Philosophy"), *Estetyka* 1 (1960):139.

69. *Estetica come scienza dell' espressione e linguistica generale.*

6

ON SO-CALLED TRUTH IN
LITERATURE*

by

Roman Ingarden

Translated from Polish by
ADAM CZERNIAWSKI

*Roman Ingarden was born in Krakow in 1893 and died in 1970.
He studied philosophy under Kazimierz Twardowski at Lvov and
under Edmund Husserl at Göttingen. At Göttingen he also studied
mathematics under David Hilbert and psychology under G. E.
Müller. He received his Ph.D. under Husserl at Freiburg. In 1921
he was appointed Privatodozent in philosophy at the University of
Lvov. He received the chair of philosophy at Jagellonian University
at Krakow in 1945, but was barred from teaching philosophy during
the early 1950s by the Polish government. During this time he
translated Kant's* Critique of Pure Reason *into Polish. He regained
his chair in 1956 and retired in 1963. Ingarden's works in aesthetics
include:* Das literarische Kunstwerk. Eine Untersuchung aus dem
Granzgebiet der Ontologie, Logik und Literaturwissenschaft *(Halle,
1931);* O poznawaniu dzieła literackiego *(On Comprehending the
Work of Literature)* (Lvov, 1937); *Studia z estetyki, (Studies in
Aesthetics), 3 vols. (Warsaw, 1957–58). Ingarden has also written
major works in epistemology and ontology. Among these is* The con-

* This translation is a slightly abridged version of the Conclusion of
vol. 1 (pp. 415–64) of *Studies in Esthetics* (*Studia z estetyki*) (Warsaw,
1966).

troversy over the existence of the world, 2 vols. (Krakow, 1947–48). Vol. 1 has been partially translated by Helen R. Michejda as Time and Modes of Being (Springfield, Ill., 1964). A more complete bibliography may be found in The Encyclopedia of Philosophy, vol. 4.

Are declarative sentences in a literary work judgments in the strict sense of the word?

I

In my book *Das literarische Kunstwerk* I argued that declarative sentences, and especially predicating sentences, in literary works are not strictly judgments but quasi-assertive sentences, and that all other types of sentence, like, say, the interrogative sentence, undergo an analogous modification. I then said that in quasi-assertive sentences "nothing is seriously asserted." As a result of this, objects presented in a literary work acquire the character of reality, but this is merely an external apparel which has no pretension to be taken quite seriously by the reader, although in practice literary works are often read improperly and readers think that they are joining the author in judgments and seriously but mistakenly regard the presented object as real.

The question is whether my position is correct and whether, assuming that quasi-assertive sentences appear in literary works, judgments in the strict sense also appear.

In practice we are well aware of the quasi-assertive, quasi-interrogatory nature of sentences in a literary work and of the resulting veil of reality covering the object presented in the literary work. We are thus all ready to laugh at the peasant who, during his first visit to the theater, started looking for his umbrella when rain began to "fall" on the stage. And yet the nature of these sentences is not easy to describe precisely. It is connected with the aesthetic attitude with which we read literary works and specifically with the special way in which as a result the reader regards predicating sentences. As I once tried to maintain, sentences are not ideal objects that are totally independent of subjective acts in their existence and their properties. They are the product of these acts. Their meaning and their function in literary, scientific, and other works depend on the course these acts take. In order, therefore, to get a clear idea of the meaning and function of a sentence, it is advisable to refer to these acts, and in particular to the sentence-forming act, to analyze the aesthetic attitude and the various features of the aesthetic experience. It has long been felt that this experience, especially the aesthetic experience of literature, gives rise to a peculiar variant of the function of judging. The history of European aesthetics, beginning at least with Kant and his *interesseloses Gefallen,* through various theories of empathy and their corresponding theories of aesthetic reality, the theory of aesthetic experience as a game or amusement, the illusionistic theory of art, on to Husserl and Odebrecht, who regard aesthetic experiences as "neutralized" experiences, is a long series of attempts at explaining that specific modification of the belief regarding the existence of the presented object, an object which, generally speaking, either reveals itself in the aesthetic object or which is specifically designated in a literary work by quasi-assertive sentences. It can be shown that none of these theories is satisfactory, although each one of them is close to the truth. However, Husserl's view that the aesthetic experience is a neutralized experience, that is, one in which the belief in the reality of the object of experience is deprived of all force, seems to me remarkably far from the truth. His theory would turn predicating sentences in a literary work into pure "assumptions" (*Annahme*), in Meinong's sense. But no less mistaken is the opposite view that such sentences are judgments. We must therefore seek a compromise account of sentences appearing in literary works and of suitably modified acts or thoughts. And third, we must give an account of the specific existential mode of objects designated in such sentences, that is, of variants of purely intentional objects. Thus the whole problem is complex and involves three related questions: logical, epistemological, and ontological. All attempts at simplification lead to false and grotesque results.

I shall confine myself to the epistemological question, and in particular to remarks concerning acts of judgment and their modification, in order to decide whether my view about "serious" judging is correct.

What happens when a doctor judges that his patient has typhoid fever? What happens when I judge that my interlocutor does not understand a certain problem? When I judge I do not just perform a special act of knowing culminating in the formulation of the given sentence. It is not just that in judging I arrive at the conclusion that what I judge is really so, but also that having this belief I do so in all "seriousness." But what does this mean? It is a matter of how the acts of judgment are performed and this is most difficult to describe. Judging "seriously" is the primary and proper sense of judging performed with full conviction when the judging subject discharges himself fully in the act of judgment without any reflective distance from himself (assuming of course that the judgment is not about the subject's own personality) and without any reservation regarding either the judging itself or the object of this judgment. When I judge seriously I do so in good faith and take full responsibility. I am prepared to defend the rightness of the assertion either by producing suitable argument or by actions conforming to the content of the judgment, and I am also prepared to abandon such an assertion if either I myself or someone else with the help of suitable and seriously proposed arguments were to convince me that this assertion is false. When I judge I engage myself personally: the act of judgment issuing from the center of my consciousness constrains me to accept responsibility for the given assertion, for contending that things are as the assertion proclaims. This is not a game from which I can always withdraw by simply declaring that the assertion in question was expressed as a joke without an act of judgment entering into it and without that specific solidarity with one's own judging which is so characteristic of judgments. If there is anything at all that forces me to withdraw from the position I have taken up it can only be a serious counter-argument. If, then, I notice that my opponent does not produce his arguments in all seriousness but simply in order to show off his dialectical skill or in order to enjoy my embarrassment, I simply ignore such "arguments." But if the arguments force me to abandon a previously held assertion, I feel a burden of guilt for having uttered a false judgment.

It is true that we are not always fully conscious of our responsibility for the judgments we make and for the "serious" nature of such judgments. Nor are we always ready *ex post* to draw practical consequences from our responsibility for the uttered judgment. All the same, the act of "seriously" declaring about a given state of affairs in reality designated by the content of that judgment is the essential and proper way of judging, without which there would not be any judging in the strict sense. But neither the evaluation of the asserted state of affairs nor any accompanying emotion is part of judging. On the contrary, realizing the negative influence of *a priori* views and emotions on the cognitive value of our judgment, we attempt, precisely in order to assume the full responsibility for that judgment, to free our judging from these factors.

Judging gives rise to the presumption of truth, that is, the judgment proclaims that in a realm of reality independent of it just that particular state of affairs intentionally designated by the judgment-content exists. A predicating sentence that does not imply this presumption of truth cannot be called a judgment in the logical sense. In speech this feature of judgment is marked by a special inflection in the voice; in print we do not on the whole use any signs to mark this and the assertive character has to be inferred from the context. And this leads to uncertainty as to whether a particular printed sentence is a judgment, whether, say, it is an assumption in Meinong's sense or whether it is still something else, especially when the sentence is torn out of context. To avoid this confusion Bertrand Russell has, as we know, proposed that an assertion sign should precede every judgment. In scientific works we normally take declarative sentences as judgments, which we either accept or reject.

The only other possibility is to suspend judgment altogether. But in any case we know that their character as judgment demands that the reader either accept or reject them.

But how different it all is when we read in, hay, *Pan Tadeusz:*

> Such were the fields where once beside a rill
> Among the birch trees on a little hill
> There stood a manor house, wood-built on stone;
> From far away the walls with whitewash shone,
> The whiter as relieved by the dark green
> Of poplars, that the autumn winds would screen.*

Here, for reasons that we may for the moment ignore, these sentences were not stated by me as judgments, nor do I assume that the author was asserting them in this way. But neither are they assumptions, but what I call apparent assertions. By coming to understand them I perform the sentence-forming act, but at the same time I behave as though I were judging that I was not doing this seriously. As a result I do not engage myself openly, I take no responsibility, I do not intend to submit what I am reading to an examination, I do not look for arguments for and against the assumption that what the sentences say is or was true. I do not for a moment assume that they claim a right to truth or even that they designate a certain state of affairs in the real world. I know in advance that they do not say that there really was such a nobleman's manor in Lithuania. On the contrary, I know that these sentences, because of their assertive apparel, designate and set up an object in some quasi-real world, which unfolds before our eyes through the twelve books of *Pan Tadeusz,* in a world which, thanks to specific descriptions and intentional references to the real world, is quite artificially placed in the real world (precisely because of the function of quasi-assertions) in such a way as if it really belonged to it, so that it acquires a character of reality. But this very nature of apparent assertions means

---

* A. Mickiewicz, *Pan Tadeusz.* From a translation by Kenneth Mac-Kenzie (London, 1966).

that the objects that are the referents of sentences in a literary work, cannot really belong to the real world, that, unlike the objects of judgments, they are not simply picked out of the real world, but rather are created mentally, and artificially (this artificiality having been skillfully disguised) placed in the real world (but only apparently), or are themselves designated as real (but only apparently).

It is not just that subjective acts which bring about such quasi-assertive sentences are not serious judgments: there is a quite different basis that gives rise to them. Judgments are caused by receptive cognition of objects that the subject finds impose themselves upon him. But quasi-judgment arises from acts that are either deliberately or involuntarily created, from acts of poetic fantasy whose ultimate goal is not a straightforward faithful accommodation to what already exists before these acts have been performed but rather progress beyond the world already given, and sometimes even liberation from it and the creation of an apparently new world.[1] These acts somewhat resemble the deceits of born liars, who enter fully into the story they are making up, who are on the point of believing the reality of their lies, and yet never lose certainty that all this is untrue. The objects of this new poetic world, although they are sometimes created "in the image and likeness" of objects in the real world, are not on the whole meant to copy that world in the way that photographs and newsreels ultimately enable us to be in commerce with real objects. On the contrary, endowed by creative acts with such and such beauty, charm, and appearance of liveliness and a stamp of reality, they are themselves to become the chief objects of our interest, they are to take such coloring from reality that we might be seduced by these appearances and at least temporarily and half-seriously see in them a separate reality. "Art" is nothing but the technical means used to impose upon the consumer the products of those creative acts arising from and molded by the poetic fantasy. These methods differ in the various arts and in literature; one of them is the quasi-judgment, which appears to make an assertion. By formulating quasi-judgments on the basis of creative acts, the author not only ultimately shapes the created objects by linguistic means, "fixing" them with regard to at least some of their properties, but he also adopts an attitude of regarding these objects that he has created as though they were precisely such as the quasi-assertive sentences say they are. Because it has emerged from acts of creative poetic fantasy, this quasi-judging seems to be addressing these objects like this: be such and such, have those particular properties, exist as though you were real. Quasi-assertive sentences are in the nature of axioms *vis-à-vis* the objects they determine. It is these axioms which the reader has to join the author in judging, precisely by adopting both a judging and a creative attitude while at the same time submitting to the suggestiveness of the apparently assertive sentences to such an extent that it should seem to him that he is really judging about certain objects. He may allow himself to succumb to such an extent as to think that he is really judging in all seriousness, but he will in fact not be judging in this way because his experiences will lack that "serious" aspect. This will happen even where he is most deeply involved in what is happening in a given literary work.

All this assumes that we are reading the work as an example of literary art and not as a scientific thesis, a factual report, or a psychological document about the author's experiences. We may read Sienkiewicz's *Trilogy* improperly as a straightforward account of historical events, and then, naturally enough, we judge and formulate a number of false judgments. But what is more important here is that we thereby falsify the literary work, because we see in it what is not intended in its structure and purpose.

Finally, the question whether a declarative sentence (and especially a predicating sentence) is a judgment, an assumption, or an apparent assertion, does not form part of its material content, always assuming that the content is meaningful.[2] Even a sentence that predicates something unlikely or strange may function as a judgment and, on the other hand, a sentence that predicates something that we know to be true in reality may function as an assumption or quasi-judgment. But if we read in Sienkiewicz's *Trilogy* that King

John made vows in Lwów cathedral, a fact that is confirmed by historical sources, we have no right on the basis of the content of this sentence to assert that this, in its role as part of the *Trilogy*'s text, is a judgment. Whether a particular sentence is or is not a judgment depends on a variety of circumstances in which it appears in a totality of a higher type, and in a literary work this specifically depends on the context and a number of other factors that I shall discuss below. It is, however, true that a reader faced with sentences predicating something quite unlikely is inclined to interpret them as quasi-judgments or assumptions, while when he reads a sentence like the one in the *Trilogy* he is inclined to treat it as a judgment. But these inclinations do not by themselves solve anything, for very often they have to be overcome if the work is to be read in accordance with the author's intention.

II

Before I consider the question whether judgments as well as quasi-judgments appear in works of literature, I have to introduce certain reservations that will tighten up the formulation of this problem.

We must not forget that not all works that are classified as literature by the common reader and even by scholars should be so classified and even if they happen to be works of literature, they are not all in this category to the same extent. This is not because they are not all of equal artistic accomplishment but because there are some that are *par excellence* pure works of art and others that have a dual, mixed character and form borderline cases. Apart from distinctively literary and artistic qualities, such works also possess elements that may not only be artistically neutral but may even be foreign to all literary art. There are various types of these borderline cases. Some are on the borderline between literature and sculpture, others on the borderline between literature and music, while others stand on the borderline between literary art proper and writings whose purpose is science, popularization, politics, propaganda, factual reporting, and so on.

Realizing that this is quite a natural phenomenon, I drew two methodological conclusions from it when writing *Das literarische Kunstwerk*. 1) Literary structure must be analyzed in examples of pure literature; only then can various types of borderline cases be considered, and 2) one should not present an *a priori* definition of a literary work of art that would schematically draw a sharp distinction between it and nonartistic forms of writing, because no such sharp distinction exists, and if we are to attempt a definition of literary work at all we can do so only after exhaustive and wide-ranging investigations and not just by starting off with a conceptual model that ignores the facts.

The existence of many different borderline examples has a bearing on whether strict judgments appear in a literary work, because otherwise even the diagnosis that in a given work judgments as well as quasi-judgments appear cannot be settled until from a further separate analysis it becomes clear whether the given work is an instance of pure literary work or whether it belongs among the borderline cases. Thus, only those examples which are instances of pure literature will be relevant to our problem. In propaganda and various types of persuasive literature we shall undoubtedly come across many judgments, especially in the shoddier examples of the genre, which we shall be clearly compelled to accept as coming directly from the author and as being intertwined with the whole of the work in such a way that its strictly artistic elements will be shown up as an obvious pretext enabling the author to present the judgment to the reader's attention as a judgment. But from this fact nothing follows about the justice or otherwise of the thesis that a pure literary work contains only quasi-judgments.

Secondly, the mere fact that in a pure literary work there appears a judgment in the strict sense cannot decide the issue. For we must in addition consider the role that that judgment plays in the work, and in particular whether its appearance is not an indication that the author has slipped up or that he harbors intentions that have nothing to do with literary art. Only an instance where the appearance of a judgment in a literary work does not constitute a blemish and is not a clear deviation from the character of the work as a work of art would be evidence forcing us to accept the thesis about the existence and artistic role of judgments in this type of work.

Thirdly, we have to consider that a literary work contains declarative sentences, and in particular predicating sentences of different types, and that they perform various functions in the structure of the work as a work of art. These are usually singular statements describing the properties or circumstances of objects presented in the work. Sometimes they refer to particulars of the lowest type, such as individual persons, particular houses, trees, rivers, mountains, and so on. Sometimes, however, they predicate particulars of a higher type, such as regiments and companies. The function that singular statements perform in a literary work is the construction of the quasi-real world presented in the work. They appear in two forms: *a*) impersonal sentences that seem to be uttered by someone only because every sentence as such is the product of someone's sentence-forming operation. Sometimes these may even be sentences uttered by the narrator who, although he himself belongs among the characters presented in the work (cf. the novels of Karl May, Conrad, and some of Plato's Dialogues), he utters them so impersonally that in the course of the narration he vanishes from our field of vision; *b*) as sentences clearly uttered or even only thought by one of the characters presented in the work. There are plenty of such sentences in epic poems and novels, whereas in drama what in *Das literarische Kunstwerk* I call the "main text" consists of sentences uttered by the presented characters and quoted within the work's text. These quoted sentences uttered by a character presented in the work themselves form one of such objects and they normally refer to other objects that belong to that same presented world. They thus contribute to the construction of the presented quasi-reality although they themselves do not belong to it.

Apart from the singular and plural predicating sentences,

we also have singular statements of the type "Some S are P" and general statements of the type "Every S is a P," but the objects that are the referents of such sentences are always particulars of either a higher or a lower type. Their function in a literary work is, in principle, the same as that of singular statements.

Finally, the literary work contains predicating sentences that are "general" in a special sense. These are gnomic generalizations that do not refer directly to any particulars presented in the work and can be said to refer to them only indirectly, for example:

> 'Tis hard not to love and to love
> Is poor consolation when thoughts
> By desire deceived sweeten too much
> the things which alter must and which must rot . . .
>
> (Szarzyński)

or

> To love and to lose, to want and regret,
> To fall in pain and to rise again,
> To banish longing and long for its lead,
> This is life: nothing and more than enough . . .
>
> To search a desert for the only jewel,
> To dive in the deep for a dazzling pearl,
> Leaving behind us nothing save
> Marks in the sand and ripples on the sea.
>
> (Leopold Staff)

The sentences of this first category may belong either to the basic text or they can be sentences uttered by one of the characters presented in the work. Both the sense of such gnomic generalizations and their function relative to the world presented in the work is quite different from that of the other types of sentences. It is not at all easy to realize what this function is and I shall make some attempt to bring this out with the help of examples. But we must remember that the functions of this type of sentence may vary, depending on the type of work in which they appear. We must

also guard against hasty generalizations and confine ourselves to the discussion of specific instances.

But there is another matter that we ought to consider
while analyzing the examples. The function or character of
a sentence, that is, whether it is, say, a judgment, is defined
not only by the sentence structure but also by its context
together with the work's title and other elements. Apart
from the exclamation and question mark, we have no separate signs with which to define it; so that when we have a
sentence taken out of context it is impossible to decide
whether it is or is not a judgment. We must therefore take
as our examples, not individual sentences, but either the
total work or at least the given sentence with its background
and the function it plays in the totality.

The examples that we have to consider fall into separate
groups:

a) sentences clearly quoted in the text and uttered by
one of the characters presented in the work.

b) sentences appearing in lyrical works like du Bellay's
"Heureux qui comme Ulysse a fait un beau voy-
age. . . ," Szarzyński's "'Tis hard not to love and
to love Is poor consolation" and Shakespeare's "Love
is not love Which alters when it alteration finds. . . ."

c) sentences appearing in works of a borderline character. We may include here Goethe's "Doch Homeride
zu sein, auch nur als letzter, ist schön. . . ."

With regard to *a*): we may select a text from Virgil that
consists of part of a speech made by Aeneas at the moment
when, having just arrived at Carthage, he examines the
bas-reliefs on the walls of Juno's temple portraying the
Trojan war:

> constitit, et lacrimans;—quis iam locus—inquit—Achate,
> quae regio in terra nostri non plena laboris?
> en Priamus, sunt etiam sua praemia laudi,
> sunt lacrimae rerum et mentem mortalem tangunt,
> solve metus; feret haec aliquam tibi fama salutem—
> sic ait. . . .

The sentence "sunt lacrimae rerum . . ." in particular is

expressed by Aeneas as a general judgment, although it refers to Troy's past and the Trojan war, which he vividly recollects while examining the bas-reliefs. On Aeneas's lips and certainly in his own mind this is undoubtedly a judgment, which in the guise of a poetic simile expresses an aspect of the past belonging to Aeneas and his companions, but because of its general formulation the sentence also casts light on human destiny in general as it is understood by Aeneas. The reference to Aeneas's past dominates the sentence while the generalization about human destiny is only an accompaniment that enriches the work as a whole. But let us not worry about details: what is essential to our problem is that this is a judgment uttered by one of the characters presented in the *Aeneid* and refers to that same presented world to which Aeneas also belongs. As a judgment uttered by Aeneas, it also expresses his mental state; when examining the bas-reliefs he recollects earlier experiences. In this way his judgment helps us to a better understanding of his character.

Now, my contention that predicating sentences in literary works are quasi-judgments applies primarily to singular statements that are neither quoted in the text nor uttered by a person presented in the work. One is inclined to say that these singular statements that determine facts, events, and the properties of individual objects within the presented world are uttered directly by the author. But here caution is needed, because the expression "directly by the author" is ambiguous. Although we are to some extent saved from likely misunderstandings by the proviso that the sentences are to establish facts within the presented world, the difficulty is caused precisely by the question as to when the author speaks as the author-poet about objects of the presented world, and when he abandons this role and in an extra-artistic attitude speaks of a world that is independent of his act of consciousness. Or, to put the matter more rigorously: Is it that, when the author utters directly within the realm of his poetic work certain judgments in the strict sense of the word about some extra-artistic reality, he abandons his poetic role, or is it that, by uttering them, he not only retains his role but such utterance also constitutes the effective fulfillment of his role?

This it seems to me is the crux of the matter. But before I turn to deal with it, I must emphasize that my thesis that predicating singular statements that are neither quoted nor uttered by any of the characters presented in the work and that apply to objects presented in the work, are not judgments in the strict sense of the word, is not a thesis that excludes the possibility that sentences uttered by a presented character were intended by that character as judgments concerning matters in the realm of the presented world. Judgments of this type appear quite often in a great many works of literature and the only question is whether, like unquoted assertions that form part of the work's basic text, they undergo a similar contextual modification.

Although as far as the character is concerned he is undoubtedly uttering judgments, the fact that these are judgments uttered by a person presented in the work means they can only refer to things belonging to the same presented world as the speaker himself. Being himself the product of poetic fantasy, his horizon is limited to the world in which, thanks to that fantasy, he has found himself. And for the reader who necessarily remains outside the realm of that world, all judgments made by presented characters cannot be regarded as anything but presented judgments, just as much as the speaker is a presented character. They cannot be regarded as true and real, and even if within the realm of the presented world they claim the right to assert something about a world that is, in relation to them, autonomous, they cannot in fact fulfill the function of effectively grasping anything that exists autonomously. Thus, when a work is read properly as a work of art, such sentences are taken as only the opinion of the presented character (that is, Aeneas in our example) and not as sentences that can and ought to be referred to an extra-artistic reality and either accepted or rejected as false. In other words, these sentences are relative to the character who is uttering them and they are not judgments that can be truth-claiming irrespective of who utters them and when they are uttered. When we read Rutherford's paper that gives an account of the splitting of the hydrogen atom, the fact that this statement is signed by the author of the paper does not lead us to conclude that this is an expression of a private opinion about a realm of purely intentional objects belonging to his own theories. On the contrary, the statement is of interest to us only because it is a judgment in the strict sense of the word. What it asserts, namely the splitting of the atom under specified conditions, either does or does not take place in a world independent of Rutherford's experience. Judgment arises only where a sentence predicating a certain state of affairs "places" that state of affairs in the real world or in some other world existentially independent of the act of judgment.

All the same, judgments uttered by characters presented in a literary work do have an aspect of truth within the work itself. It is relative to the world presented in that work. In relation to the particular world that is presented in certain books of the *Aeneid,* the sentence "sunt lacrimae rerum . . ." seems to be true and its truth plays a certain role, perhaps an aesthetic role as well, in the structure of the work. In any case, it illuminates the world of Aeneas in a particular way by, among other things, creating the impression that it is not an imagined but a real world. It also illuminates Aeneas himself in that by uttering that judgment he appears before our eyes as someone judging the world around him.

But if this aspect of the truth of the sentence "sunt lacrimae rerum" is to be preserved and is to play a cognitive role in relation to the presented world by giving that world not only an existential but also a qualitative stamp, this world must be exactly as it is in the *Aeneid.* For if we assume that the fates of Aeneas and of Troy were quite different from those "factually" presented in the *Aeneid,* so that they would not allow the kind of illumination that flows from the sentence under consideration, that sentence would lose its truth aspect; it would appear "unconvincing" and in conflict with that world, and moreover it would emerge as a source of an aesthetically negative disharmony.

What then does this aspect of truth and the consequent

aesthetic value of this sentence come down to in relation to the *Aeneid*'s other elements? It contributes to the maintenance of thematic consequence within the work and to its strengthening by capturing a portion of the presented world in a gnomic statement or maxim. And since this sentence includes poetic metaphor, which must not be taken in the strict sense of the word, but which, as a metaphor, not only imposes upon the presented world a certain stamp, but also allows to shine through what corresponds to these "tears of things" (and thus reveals a tragic glimpse of the presented world and of man's fate in it), the sentence and the phenomena both acquire an aesthetic value. We may also say that this sentence performs a special artistic function just because it appears in this precise manner in the presented world. Would it have performed that role if it were strictly a true or false judgment independent of the conditions of its utterance?

This seems to me very doubtful. Even ignoring the fact that when we judge strictly about reality, we on the whole avoid metaphor and try to achieve judgments as true to reality as possible, a strict judgment brings us too close to the reality with which it is concerned, and this direct intercourse which brings us happiness or unhappiness, which reveals the beauty or ugliness of an object in the real world, is too overwhelming and moving for us to succumb to a charm characteristic of true art. Even where we learn of events that bring us happiness or unhappiness by means of certain judgments (that is, not directly), the belief that things are just so in reality moves us too directly and strongly for us to have an aesthetic experience in the strict sense of the word. The bodily beauty of the beloved person or the splendor of someone's heroism may be the object of our admiration in life, yet these experiences are not like those we have in commerce with a work of art. Only an aesthetic experience contains that specific distance in relation to what we admire or dislike, so that even our most profound involvement in what the work of art presents does not move us with that absolute seriousness with which we are affected by facts of real life. This distance is possible only where we do not have a straightforward unshakable conviction about the reality of what is either directly given or conveyed in a judgment. We might think it a defect in art, for it is unable to invoke in us such a naïve total conviction that is evoked by every experience derived from the real world. But it is this apparent lack that makes possible the development of a whole gamut of specific experiences that no experience of real facts can provide us, because the latter is accompanied by that naïve total belief in the reality of the facts acquired either in sensible perception or in a conscious act of judgment that results in judging in the logical sense.

If, therefore, I am right in my analysis of the aesthetic experience, then a sentence like "sunt lacrimae rerum" could not have performed the artistic function in the *Aeneid* that it does in fact perform had it been a judgment in the strict sense of the word. Only by weakening the assertiveness and the belief in the reality of its referents can the sentence develop its artistic function, can it compel the reader to develop an aesthetic experience and take up a proper distancing attitude.

Therefore, critics who tear such a sentence out of context and submit it to special treatment seem to me to be wrong. They regard it as a self-contained unit, but they have at some stage to replace it in its proper context. At the same time they regard it as a judgment about the real world and place it for no obvious reason in the author's mouth, where it is made to appear as the author's own judgment about the real world and not, say, Aeneas's judgment about the presented world.

There are two problems. *1*) What right have we to regard judgments of this type as the author's views on reality? *2*) What right have we to alter its meaning by taking it out of context (for now the judgment is made to refer to something different) and then quietly to replace it in context as though within the context of the whole work that sentence carried its new meaning given it *ex post?*

It is undoubtedly true that in the context of a poetic work the author utters judgments that it is clear are expressions of the author's own views. But these are sentences uttered directly by the author and not by one of the presented characters. But there may be other clues that would lead us to believe that the author merely put his own views into the mouth of the hero while in fact he is uttering them in his own capacity as an expression of his own belief. And the question arises whether, from the fact that this is sometimes the case, it follows that wherever we come across gnomic utterances or maxims we have the right to treat them as the author's own convictions (as the views of a real person irrespective of his poetic function), which he is expressing in just the way that views are expressed in scientific works. Were we to ask the interpreters how they can discover that the author is in fact expressing his own views, we would receive unsatisfactory and conflicting replies showing how arbitrary such interpretations are. The correct methodological procedure is surely to keep faithfully to the text, and to search for the author's hidden intention only where there is clear evidence for this either in the text of the work itself or in some extraneous evidence in the form of instructions from the author that he wished certain sentences in the work to be interpreted as his own views. But then the work of art ceases to embody the author's true intentions and becomes merely a pretext for the expression of certain views that should have been expressed in a proper and unambiguous way in a written work like a diary, a scientific treatise, or a political article, and not in a work of literary art.

This has, I think, also given us the answer to the second question. Altering the meanings of individual sentences by tearing them out of context and saturating them with a content taken from other sources is not an acceptable way of analyzing a literary work if the analysis is to be faithful and accurate, and this indeed applies to any other written word, be it scientific or otherwise. Precisely because sentences are only to a certain extent units of meaning, their meaning being filled out in various ways by content and by the position of the particular sentence in that context, individual sentences must be taken with the whole context in mind. The context also defines the function that the sentence is to play in the work. In particular, if it is clear that a given general statement is uttered by one of the presented characters, it is admittedly a judgment in that character's mouth but refers to the presented world and accordingly has its assertive function clearly modified as being the expression of a merely imagined person. It is not permissible to consider its truth or falsity in relation to any extra-artistic world, the real world especially, and to do this in the belief that one is merely conducting a literary analysis.

But all this is not to deny that we can formulate a sentence that is either similar to or identical with "sunt lacrimae rerum," to take it as a self-contained totality, to reflect what true meaning is hidden behind the poetic metaphor (for if we take it as a literally true judgment it is a grotesquely false sentence), and, having thus arrived at a reformulation of that sentence, to consider it as a judgment whose truth or falsity in relation to the real world can be settled. We might then also consider whether this new judgment would have been acceptable to Virgil and even to attempt, assuming we have sufficient basis for this in historical sources, to construct upon such judgment a new system of assertions about the real world that would add up to a philosophy acceptable to Virgil or anyone else. Such reflection may be quite interesting and even quite significant for the study of the history of ideas. But we must remember that doing this we cease to study the *Aeneid* as a work of art and move beyond it. Doing this we use the work as a springboard for reflections that have little to do with the interpretation of a literary work.

With regard to *b*): before we discuss the second group of examples we have to make some general observations about some properties of lyrical works.

The lyrical work, or rather the sentences forming its text and understood in its dynamic development from the beginning to the end of the work, form an utterance and therefore a mode of behavior by the lyrical subject. That is, someone whose mental make-up is defined solely by the fact that he utters or thinks the words of the text. But the full description of his behavior must go beyond the utterance of these words to include the elements of his life and mental make-up (say, his mental state in a given situation, his emotional reaction to the facts expressed in the content of the sentences) which are not stated in those sentences but which nevertheless the sentences express.

The person who talks or thinks in a lyric work is commonly called "the author." If this is merely a shorthand expression, there is nothing wrong with it, but if it is meant to refer to the real author of the poem, such expression must be avoided even though in certain cases it might be correct. Simple accuracy as well as methodological considerations demand that we distinguish between the lyrical subject and the work's author. The lyrical subject is a purely intentional object designated by the work's text and belongs to the world presented in the given work, whereas the author is a certain real person who has written the work, who might have but need not have expressed himself in the work. We do not learn about authorship from the context of the poem but from circumstantial evidence showing that such and such a person has written a work under such and such conditions. In certain cases the identification of the lyrical subject with the author may be justified, but we must have independent evidence for this, as when a lyrical work forms part of a letter that expresses the author's feelings and state, and that is as a matter of fact addressed to someone he knows. But this need not be the case, and the lyrical subject may equally well be a fictitious person toward whom the author shows an emotional sympathy or who acts as a mask behind which the author consciously hides. It is therefore advisable always to distinguish between the lyrical subject and the author, and only in certain cases after proper enquiries should one try to establish the relationship between the lyrical subject and the author. Even if we are treating the work not as a work of art but as a psychological document that serves as material for the psychological analysis of the author's life and mental make-up, we have no right automatically to identify the author with the lyrical subject. In many cases we would be in great difficulty if we had to decide whether and to what extent the author is expressing himself and is not merely someone whom, on the basis of a specific selection of properties found in the work, one could infer to be the author. In order to be able to deduce this with absolute certainty we must have at our command criteria that would enable us to distinguish cases where the author is expressing himself from those where the lyrical subject and its utterances constitute an artistic fantasy.

Thus the world presented in a lyrical work comprises a) sentences uttered by the lyrical subjects that constitute the work's text, or more accurately, that are quoted in the text, b) the lyrical subject, c) the referents of the sentences constituting the work, and d) what the sentences express regarding the lyrical subject's life and mental make-up. Sometimes the meaning of sentences constituting the text is so constructed that this whole presented world performs the function of either symbolizing a necessary connection between a metaphysical quality and a certain mental state or of showing a certain metaphysical quality.

That sentences appearing in the text of a lyrical work are really the utterance of the lyrical subject is borne out by the fact, with which everyone agrees, that for adequate determination a lyrical poem demands an actual or imagined recitation, that is, it requires a molding of the auditory stratum and method of delivery consonant with the mental state of the lyrical subject and which therefore, considering his mental state, appear "natural." This is particularly true of works written in the first person.

Although it is necessary for the lyrical subject to express himself in the work, this is not, however, in itself a sufficient condition for the work's being a lyric. Words uttered by a character presented in a play also form part of that character's behavior, and yet they do not thereby constitute a lyrical work. In order to arrive at a distinction between poetry and drama, we must note that the behavior of the lyrical subject differs from that of a character in drama. The lyrical subject is passive in relation to his environment; he takes up the attitude of a spectator rather than that of an actor, and even when he does talk of action his words apply to the past or the future. His activity in the present consists either of a straightforward emotional reaction or an outburst of feeling arising from the conscious contemplation of either the past or the present. The lyrical subject is too much preoccupied with himself, too much at the mercy of his current emotional state, for his behavior to be classed as action that affects the world in which he finds himself. In reflective lyrics, the overwhelming emotion does not allow the formation of a cool object-directed, cognitive act referring to the subject's environment.

The objects referred to in the sentences of a lyrical work and the state of affairs designated by such sentences embrace either the life and mental make-up of the lyrical subject or his environment. But as regards the existential mode of that environment, it is in fact only an intentional equivalent of the lyrical subject's attitude and life, even though the lyrical subject regards this world as real. But the subject does not describe this world in an "objective" way as something that is quite independent of him and his emotional state. This contrasts with epic works, where, although the world is also merely presented, as indeed it must be, the intention behind the description is to show it as something quite independent of the narrator, as something that he finds given. But the lyrical subject, by finding a complete expression in what he is saying or thinking, employs such phrases, metaphors, and sentences as designate only a certain aspect of his environment relative to his actual mental state. To use the common but inaccurate expression, we may say that a lyric gives us a merely "subjective" picture of reality.

The lyrical subject's special mode of behavior means that that aspect of his environment has a specific *gestalt* differentiating it from the *gestalten* under which the presented world appears in an epic or a dramatic work. This is shown not only in the fact that things, people, and events referred to in lyrical works are usually sketched in the simplest manner, with all detail left out, but also in that the feature chosen to describe the particular object is not so much characteristic of the object in its own purely objective existence as it is, rather, a feature of an emotional relationship between the lyrical subject and that object, a relationship that is of importance to the lyrical subject. Engrossed in his own experiences, the lyrical subject talks about the objects in just the way he sees and feels them. Seen in this way, the objects in the lyrical subject's environment play merely a background role in the totality of the lyrical subject's object stratum. The lyrical subject's emotions play their part and usually they are not even verbally defined, but reveal themselves spontaneously through the expressive function of the sentences that are being uttered. Hence, although the lyrical subject regards an aspect of his "reality" as his reality, nevertheless he never in fact responsibly judges either about his environment or about anything else.

The lyrical subject is too closely bound up with his environment upon which he has projected his own emotion to be able to stand back from it and, having apprehended its objective properties, to express a judgment about it. If he does utter sentences that on the face of it have the appearance of assertions, this is only an expression of a revelation born of his direct emotional relationship with his environment.

The discussion of these two fundamental features of a lyrical work provides us with a basis for the solution of our problem. Predicating sentences that appear in a lyrical work must be regarded as quoted statements, irrespective of whether they are singular or general. These sentences belong to the lyrical subject, although we do not use quotation and the narrator is normally not described in the text, as he often would be in an epic poem. Predicating sentences uttered by the lyrical subject are not strictly judgments, but neither do they refer to objects that in relation to the work are transcendental. They are quasi-assertions referring to the lyrical subject's environment in a subjective and relative manner. The maxims or gnomic utterances I discussed earlier are an expression of the lyrical subject's awareness born of the state in which he finds himself in the world. The belief engendered by this emotion endows these expressions of emotion and awareness with an appearance of judgments. This belief, however, belongs to the lyrical subject, that is, to one of the objects presented in the object stratum of the work, and is expressed in sentences that refer to the intentional equivalents of his experiences. Moreover, the function that these sentences perform in the totality of the work and in the work's effect upon the reader in his capacity as an aesthetic recipient is different from the function of judgments in, say, scientific papers. These sentences normally appear to sum up the lyrical work, and thereby emerge on the basis of the lyrical subject's state, which reveals to the reader a certain qualitative harmony with a specific emotional emphasis, or metaphysical qualities that, as we know, are also saturated with specific emotional features, or of some relation between the lyrical subject's state and a certain metaphysical quality. Arising on such foundations, these sentences provide a conceptual grasp of this harmony or metaphysical quality, and through this conceptual definition name what in other circumstances it would not have been possible to conceptualize at all. Even where the tone of the whole work is extremely irrational, they constitute an element of rational awareness and of an understanding of what we usually experience only emotionally. It is here that these sentences' specific role of discovery lies, a role that, however, can become actualized only through an imposed concrete mental state and the emotion expressed in the work that imposes itself upon the reader. To treat such sentences as strict judgments is not so much to grant the lyrical work a place in the realm of human cognition, as is thought by those who support this view, or to recognize that here lies the work's "idea"; it is, rather, to weaken the suggestive role of poetry. Worse, it amounts to a fundamental disruption of the balance of forces in the work in favor of a shallow intellectualism and leads to the view that man has no need for poetry in his deepest spiritual needs, that it is merely a plaything that could profitably be replaced by a theoretical discussion between critics and interpreters of literature. And precisely because, despite all efforts of interpretation, despite quite extraordinary ingenuity shown in discovering not only judgments but complete philosophical systems in lyrical works and in poetry in general by those who are determined to see judgments in poetry (and who thereby themselves turn their scholarship into second-rate poeticizing), it is impossible to replace a truly poetic lyrical work with a thesis. A fully poetic work that *inter alia* contains general statements or implies them is unsurpassable in its role of discovering the most essential links between the ultimate qualities present in the deepest layers of the human psyche and in functioning as a palpable understanding of these connections. These are the best reasons against seeking judgments and theories in poetry and the best reasons for coming to understand the uniqueness of its methods and achievements.

Sometimes the opposite happens, that is, general thoughts appearing in a literary work serve to fill in the background against which the lyrical subject's experiences evolve. The presence of this background influences the course of these experiences or makes it possible to underline some of their aspects, which are imposed upon the reader, rather than directly named or described, and which may reach the reader's consciousness and enrich his life only through an emotional experience.

Let us put this a little differently. Through its conceptual apprehension of a certain metaphysical quality, a poem includes a certain idea that takes it beyond the strictly particular concrete situation that it embodies. What is presented in the poem acquires the character of a paradigm of what occurs not only in this but in all other similar instances. But if, when perceiving the work aesthetically, we are faithful to its structure and function, this element which outgrows the poem opens up a perspective on to what, given certain conditions, manifests itself generally. This "something" enhances the work, adding to its charm and weight, but could not in itself form a totality and could not without the work as such be expressed in judgments. Were we to detach this "idea" from the totality of the work and, with the help of certain rigorously formulated judgments, attempt to spell it out for the reader, it would not only have lost its essential function in the totality of the work, but, ceasing to be a feature that harmonizes with the full polyphony of the work, it would turn into an amputated limb. We would be left with one or several empty and blind judgments that would be incomprehensible without reference to the specific mode of experience that poetry can give us. The whole value and purpose of general statements in lyrical poems is precisely that, since they emerge on the basis of a vision of a certain quasi-reality that has been irrationally imposed upon us by artistic means, they enrich the polyphony of the totality of the work with an element of understanding.

Thus, although lyrical poems may serve as a point of departure for general reflections on the subject of, say, a certain metaphysical quality or of certain aesthetically valuable qualitative clusters that ultimately lead to judgments in the strict sense of the word, nevertheless we must not forget that in conducting these reflections, *1*) we use the work of literature as but a starting point, moving on to what is no longer a literary work, *2*) we formulate new judgments that do not appear in the work itself, and *3*) we bypass an essential function of the work, whose task is, not to offer the reader a selection of general judgments about extra-artistic reality, but to supply him, through the concretion of the aesthetic object, with a vision and an emotion as well as an understanding. Their role in life is just as significant as that of pure rational cognition, even though it is quite different.

In support of my thesis I shall analyze Alfred de Vigny's "La mort du loup." I confine my quotation to part III, but would like my readers to read the whole of this poem:

1. Hélas! ai-je pensé, malgré ce grand nom d'Hommes,
   Que j'ai honte de nous, débiles que nous sommes.
   Comment on doit quitter la vie et tous ses maux
   C'est vous qui le savez, sublimes animaux.

5. A voir ce que l'on fut sur terre et ce qu'on laisse.
   Seul le silence est grand; tout le reste est faiblesse,
   —Ah, je t'ai bien compris, sauvage voyageur,
   Et ton dernier regard m'est allé jusqu'au coeur.
   Il disait: si tu peux, fais que ton âme arrive,

10. A force de rester studieuse et pensive,
    Jusqu'à ce haut degré de stoïque fierté

Où, naissant dans les bois, j'ai tout d'abord montée.
Gémir, pleurer, prier, est également lâche.
Faire energiquement ta longue et lourde tâche

15. Dans la voie où le sort a voulu t'appeler,
    Puis, après, comme moi, souffre et meurs sans parler.

This quotation includes in lines 5-6 and line 13 two general statements or maxims, and both offer a clear interpretation of an event that had been previously shown in the poem and directly imposed upon the reader. Both the narrating subject in part I of the work, which contains few lyrical moments, and the lyrical subject of part III are one and the same, so that both sentences are uttered by the lyrical subject and quoted in the text. Both are also a clear discharge of emotion by the lyrical subject in the face of certain facts presented in the work, and especially in the face of a metaphysical moment including the metaphysical quality of a heroic endurance of fate, which is revealed on the basis of these facts. These sentences have the task of isolating this moment in a conceptual interpretation. The utterance of these sentences expresses something that has not been mentioned in some many words: the lyrical subject's humble admiration for mute heroism in the endurance of fate.

I realize that my attempt to recreate the content of the quoted work is inadequate and imperfect. But this is not due solely to my incompetence as a writer. The main reason lies elsewhere. There is an essential difference between a poetic and a theoretical presentation, between quasi-judgments in which the lyrical subject discharges his mental state and a theoretical account expressed in judgments. In this case the quasi-judgments are more effective, the poetic presentation giving more than a nonpoetic interpretation. The "more" is precisely what cannot be ascribed to purely rational concepts. The poetic work shows, reveals, and uncovers the palpable *gestalt* of qualities with which it affects the reader directly. A theoretical account describes, names, and judges what is being named only in a conceptual way, so that our emotional response too is different in both the situations. If we uproot the sentence from the totality of

the work, if we remove it from the presented web of facts,
if we deprive it of melody, rhythm, tone, and other contextual factors, if we deprive it of what this sentence expresses in the psyche of the lyrical subject, we shall be left
with a sentence that, naturally enough, we would be able to
regard as a judgment in the strict sense of the word, but
then the whole dynamism of poetic charm would have vanished, leaving only, as Charles Lalo remarks: ". . . la
valeur prosaïque de vérité, et non lyrique de beauté."

The same, I think, is the case with the sentence in Shakespeare's Sonnet 116, which I quoted earlier. We must also
remember that it is part of a cycle, and in order to be understood the remaining sonnets must also be read. The same
is also true of Szarzyński's sonnet, and indeed of all reflective or "symbolic" lyrics, assuming that these are truly poetic
works and not just paper-thin observations on various topics.
The works of Baudelaire and Verlaine, the lyrics in Rilke's
Book of Hours, Goethe's youthful short lyrics, and several
poems by Staff are all examples that may be used to test
the validity of my thesis. All we have to do is to be able to
submit ourselves to the workings of the poems and to comprehend them without introducing extraneous elements.

Rilke's Schlusstück:

> Der Tod is gross,
> Wir sind Seinen
> lachenden Munds.
> Wenn wir uns mitten in Leben meinen,
> wagt er zu weinen
> mitten in uns.

Like Szarzyński's sonnet and like the poem by Staff that I
quoted earlier, all at first glance give the impression that
they consisted of maxims and nothing else, as though they
lacked the background of a presented world, especially the
background of an expressed mental state of the lyrical subject. Because of the sentence structures (the use of infinitives
in Staff and Szarzyński), they all appear very impersonal
and the lyrical subject seems to dissolve. This might therefore lead us to assume that in these instances we have judg-

ments in the strict sense and not exclusively apparent assertions.

On closer consideration however we see that this is not so. Here too, of course, we can use the text to construct certain judgments but this is not the point. The question we have to answer is whether these sentences taken exactly in context (including their sounds, ordering, rhythm, and metaphorical use) are judgments. Do they demand to be read as judgments in the strict sense or as fulfilling a different function? A closer analysis shows that Staff's and Rilke's poems do contain a lyrical subject, although in each case he is discreetly hidden. In both poems we hear the subject's emotion expressed in the uttered sentences and the only thing that distinguishes these poems from, say, the work by de Vigny is that they do not project a concrete particular object situation that brings about the emotion of the lyrical subject discharging itself in the uttered sentences.

Many defenders of the thesis that judgments do appear in literary works would feel that, if they were to agree with me, then the gnomic statements I have just been considering would completely lose their significance as components in the structure of the whole work. This is a false view, because for a number of reasons the meaning of a gnomic statement or maxim conceptually designating the idea of the work plays a significant role in reflective poetic works. They have a structural role and are the ultimate element in the construction that binds the whole work and introduces a rational element subduing the work's irrational elements. Next, the meaning of such maxims may have various aesthetic values. The so-called thought which they carry may be distinguished by simplicity, ingenuity, depth, and finesse, not to mention such rather subtle qualities as perspicuity, clarity, and complexity. They may also have the specifically aesthetic value of aptness, the thought being apt in relation to what appears in the object-stratum of the work and especially in relation to the lyrical subject's environment and the mental state that arises in that environment. This aptness, which often strikes us in reading, is doubtless one among many of those "truths" which defenders of judgments in literary works talk about in an ambiguous way. All these features appear in literary works and sometimes even play a leading role enriching the works' qualitative harmony. And there are works that seem specifically constructed to impose on the reader the "thought" that crystallizes the works' idea. But in order for these values to emerge in the aesthetic perception of the work, we cannot seriously judge such "thoughts," which form either parts or wholes of such works; we must make the sentences the objects of aesthetic perception, we have to maintain a certain reflective distance from them. And this would be impossible if we were to take such sentences simply as judgments.

But how can we tell that certain sentences in a lyrical work demand that when we take up an aesthetic attitude they should be construed as quasi-judgments? The decisive moment is primarily the tone in which they are uttered, the tone born of the lyrical subject's emotion, which also expresses that emotion. Closely connected with this tone is the choice of words and their ordering, the auditory properties of words, and, as in the second verse of Staff's poem, various poetic images. All this together, assuming that the selection is well made, leads to the formation in the reader of an initial aesthetic emotion, developing into subsequent phases of the aesthetic experience, and then the modification of assertive sentences into quasi-judgments is merely one of the elements in the evolving experience. If someone wished to communicate his theoretically grounded judgment on life he would not, like Staff, employ verse form, he would not use such poetic images, and he would not express all this in a tone suffused with emotion. He would wish to convince us about a certain state of affairs and to this end he would use suitable arguments and justifications; he would not wish to move or delight us with the charm of his work, nor would he reveal the emotion to which he himself is subject.

This supports what I have said at the beginning, namely, that whether a sentence is a judgment or a quasi-assertion depends very much on the other elements of the work and the basic function of its totality. And the reverse is also true: the question whether the work belongs to the art of literature and is not rather a scientific thesis or a straight-forward report, is not decided solely by the fact that it contains quasi-assertions, but also by the fact that it contains a great many other elements and features and that their selection leads to a polyphonic harmonization of all the strata and phases, to an aesthetically valuable harmony. Where we are concerned with judgments, all the other elements of the work, apart from the meanings of sentences and their relationship to a reality that is transcendental in relation to the work, are of no consequence to the value of the given sentence or the whole work. Such a work may be written in any natural language, in a scientific terminology or even in logical symbolism, and so long as its meaning is preserved it is always one and the same work whose value depends solely *1*) on the truth of the judgment and *2*) on the significance of the issues raised. But where we have quasi-judgments as elements in a literary work, there all the remaining elements and features of the work must be suitably selected to fit in with the meaning of the quasi-judgments so that upon their base a polyphonic harmony of aesthetically valuable qualities may be constructed without which the work would not qualify as a literary work of art. Within such a harmony the meanings of sentences, having performed their constitutive function *vis-à-vis* other strata of the literary work, play the role of an element possessing its own specific qualities.

With regard to *c*) : finally, we have to discuss the example taken from Goethe: *Doch Homeride zu sein, auch nur als letzter, ist schön* . . .

In this case I admit it is true to say that this is a judgment in the strict sense of the word. But then, it is taken from the so-called Preface to *Herman and Dorothea*, which is in any case often printed separately as an elegy. It functions in fact as the author's preface addressed to his readers; it is a kind of open letter. It is admittedly written in hexameters and employs various strictly literary technical means, and this is why it is marginally a literary work, but considering its function as a preface it should have been written in prose and the author should have spoken directly and cast aside his poetic mask. The poet's object was to present a number of judgments in which he dealt with his critics. The form he chose may therefore appear unsuitable to this task. But in those days there was a fashion for all sorts of prologues in which the author, half seriously and half in jest, would appear to address the reader directly while he was already draped in his poetic toga and hardly a real human being at all. But this specific form, which places this work on the borderline of literary art, cannot change the judgments it contains into quasi-assertive sentences. Apart from judgments, the work does, of course, also include quasi-judgments in conformity with the mixed borderline character of the totality.

Generalizing this instance, I would be inclined to say that wherever a work contains judgments as well as quasi-judgments, where, that is, other elements and features of the totality cannot change these judgments into quasi-judgments or vice versa, we are dealing with borderline works of one among many possible types, which may be more or less far removed from a pure literary work.

There are many such types of borderline literary works, which may impinge on scientific papers, newspaper articles, political pamphlets, and letters. They all characteristically have a double aspect and demand a similar duality in the reader's attitude. But irrespective of what type they happen to represent, they may all be divided into those whose duality or marginality stems from faults in construction perpetrated by their creators, who often are either simply lacking in talent or do not understand either what art is about or that there are types of writing whose functions are essentially different from those of literary art, who write rhymed catalogues of books or kitchen recipes; while on the other hand we have works that, despite their marginality, are excellent examples of artistic excellence and power, as, for example, Słowacki's "Beniowski," or, to choose a quite different instance of a marginal work, Plato's philosophical dialogues. I shall not waste time in considering the first category, representing artistic failures, but I would like to say a few words about this second category of marginal works. I shall consider only two out of all the possible types.

One of the types is represented by such works as Plato's "Symposium" and the "Phaedrus." Although they are homogeneous in their construction, they may be read in two different ways. Two different concretions may be derived from the same work, which can be read either as *a*) a work of literary art, or *b*) a learned treatise. Only a detailed analysis would reveal the weakness of this type of work, but here it is enough to observe that when we read the "Symposium" as a work of literary art, the singular and general statements become quoted sentences uttered by characters presented in the work and are expressions of these characters' views. They are then quasi-judgments, and this becomes especially clear when we consider that the "Symposium" as a whole is a story told by Apollodorus. When, however, we read the "Symposium" as a special type of learned treatise, then the various views become contributions to the problem under discussion. They are complementary or contradictory, but possible solutions of the same problems and then assertions uttered by individual characters become judgments in the strict sense of the word. It is then irrelevant which of the characters actually utters them and all that matters is that they are truth-claiming sentences. In the first instance, we cannot consider the merits of, say, a certain view expressed by Socrates; we must simply accept this as either an artistic or even a historical fact, for the work may also be read as a historical account. Regarding it as an artistic fact, we may concentrate on the aesthetically significant details of the idea, its simplicity or its clarity, its originality or its superficiality and banality, its tortuousness and clumsiness. Certain views, like the myth concerning the division of a formerly complete man into two halves to form man and woman, may from a scientific point of view appear to us naïve and unjustified. But when we read the "Symposium" as a work of art, these same views may, for this or that reason, appear to us beautiful. Truth and falsity do not play any part here, and the reverse is also true: such aesthetic charms as the "Symposium" might possess do not play any real part when we study it as a philosophical treatise. Nothing apart from the truth or falsity of its statements is at stake, and no aesthetic charm can save it if its most important statements are false or even if they are merely unsupported or improbable.

Let us now move on to Słowacki's "Beniowski," which, unlike the "Symposium," does not allow different interpretations, but instead forces the reader to change his attitude during the reading of specific phases of the work. The story of Beniowski is told half seriously and half in jest, partly as pure fantasy and partly as a narration of real facts, and is punctuated by lengthy digressions, that is, various episodes which, although they are also composed in *ottava rima* stanzas and have a poetic style, refer not to Beniowski and his more or less fictitious escapades, but to various issues that preoccupied Polish emigrés in Paris during Słowacki's lifetime and to his various personal and literary skirmishes with his friends and enemies. Some of these digressions can be fully understood only if we know certain facts about Słowacki, but their character as intrusions is obvious from the fragmentation of the poem's themes and their intermixture. The unity of the whole is maintained thanks only to the presence throughout of the same narrator, the homogeneous style, and the general half-mocking, half-serious style. Those to whom this poem was addressed could see the distinction between the actual narration and the digressions (although one may dispute as to what the "actual" theme of the poem really is), for when the narration is about Beniowski, the singular statements forming part of that story create a separate poetic reality, even though Beniowski's adventures have a specified geographical locality, whereas the singular predicating statements in the digressions refer to specific persons and states of affairs, even though in most cases these persons' true names do not actually appear. Thus the assertive sentences that refer to such real characters and events not only transcend the sphere of purely intentional objects presented in the work and reach out to an extra-artistic reality, but they also clearly have the character of judgments, even if we do not identify Słowacki with the narrator. But readers contemporary with Słowacki were in no doubt that it was the poet who was expressing those judgments, and this was so, irrespective of any poetic elements present in the work. If, however, a reader who knew nothing of Słowacki's life and environment were to read the poem, he would at least be struck by the fact that the narrator (who is identified as one of the characters presented in those parts of the work which are exclusively concerned with Beniowski) takes time off to talk of himself and his friends, who, although they are not clearly seen as living in a world that is different from Beniowski's, are nevertheless not in any spatio-temporal relation with Beniowski. What is more, the narrator clearly regards himself, not as a historian who is telling us about a real Beniowski, but as a poet who is spinning a fantastic tale. This absence of any connection between the two groups of persons and events, together with the contrast between Beniowski and the people in his environment as characters in a poem and persons who are the poet's own contemporaries, is bound to lead a reader not possessing extraneous information to conclude from the text itself that some of the predicating sentences ought to be read as judgments and others as quasi-judgments. It therefore seems to me that both types of reader will be struck by a dual character of the whole work, although for readers acquainted with the poet's biographical material this contrast will be sharper. Thus, in contrast with the "Symposium," the poem cannot be read in only one way in the course of a single reading, because if the reader is to do justice to its properties he must keep switching his attitude. In some phases of the work he must be prepared for a purely poetic reality, which is intentionally created by means of the sentences belonging to the text, and in others, to adjust himself to Słowacki's real environment.

I have no wish to deny that "Beniowski" is a poetical work, that it is a work of great value with a variety of good qualities. Even this oscillation between the real and the poetic world constitutes a merit of the work as a whole, but this is entirely due to Słowacki's great poetic skill, because today we would not bother reading those digressions if their interest were purely factual. And today this factual element becomes less and less important, while the purely artistic value of the digressions comes to the fore, with the consequence that the sentences as judgments begin to lose their significance and begin to appear as another aspect of the artistic pretense, and the unity of the work as a whole is thereby enhanced.

Finally, let us ask why we include this type of work which, though it stands on the borderline between the poetic and the nonpoetic, is yet accepted as coming within the limits of poetry and not outside it. Why do we regard "Beniowski" as one of Słowacki's masterpieces, and, indeed, as one of the masterpieces of Polish literature? Is it because it contains judgments in the strict sense of the word? Or is it despite the fact that it contains judgments? It seems to me that there is no doubt as to how these questions ought to be answered. The presence of judgments in even such a borderline work as *"Beniowski"* is not an element that decides whether *"Beniowski"* is a work of art or not. If these judgments were presented, not in a strictly artistic form, but in a faithful adjustment to reality, the work as a whole would become so nonhomogeneous that it would not be possible to retain its artistic unity. Whereas if, on the other hand, the work were to consist entirely of judgments, then, despite its "beautiful form," it would not be classed as a work of literary art and its "form" would shock us as being peculiar. There is thus no question as to how we are to draw the distinction betwewen works of literary art and literary works that do not belong to art. That is, we have to do it in such a way as to leave within the limits of literary art works that do not contain any judgments in the strict sense, or, if such judgments do occur, such works ought to be placed on the periphery of the area, with various other considerations playing a part in the decision as to which borderline type the given work is to be allocated. But if the judgments not only take up a considerable part of the work but play such a significant role in the total composition that they are central to the whole work, while at the same time other

sentences, especially quasi-judgments, serve merely as a pretext for the utterance of judgments, with the various elements of the artistic form being but a means for the more
effective fulfillment of judgments in a certain extra-artistic
reality, then such a work would fall outside the limit of
literary art, although it would tend strongly to resemble
such works. And we must not forget that within literary
works we find various types of quasi-judgments and numerous variations of their "truth." From this point of view
we may construct various kinds of division within the realm
of literary art as such, but all this emerges only once we
are agreed that primarily or exclusively literary works of
art include only quasi-judgments and not judgments in the
strict sense.

In conclusion I would like to make two further observations.

1) The distinction that I have just drawn amounts to a
diagnosis based on observation of actual works of art and
it is not a value judgment or a statement of principles according to which literary works of art ought to be composed.

2) Those who maintain that even pure works of literary
art contain either general or singular judgments regard the
rejection of such a view as tantamount to denying that literature can have a fundamental and positive influence on man's
life. They say that this amounts to taking up a formalistic
attitude, according to which the so-called content of the
work is of no consequence, and that they ought to oppose
such so-called "aestheticism."

To draw such conclusions from the position that I have
here tried to justify is completely groundless, as will be
clear from everything that I have said about the "idea" of
a literary work of art. The question as to the character
that predicating sentences have in literary work has nothing
to do with the role played by the content-forming elements
and especially by its ideas, and with what their relation is
to the value of the work. One can ascribe the greatest
possible significance to the work's content element (having,
of course, previously established what in fact constitutes
the work's "content") while at the same time acknowledg-

ing that this work does not contain judgments in the strict sense, and, conversely, one can agree that such judgments do appear in a literary work, while at the same time claiming that form (which in turn must also be clearly defined) constitutes the only value of a literary work. For we must not suppose that the "content" elements of the work, especially the idea in the work, play a role in the value of the work only when such content consists of true judgments or is concerned with certain real objects. It is worth noting that the commonly accepted standard of literary excellence is the degree of similarity between the objects presented in the literary work and a certain extra-artistic reality. But if the point of literary works were to make objects presented in them resemble those appearing in extra-artistic reality, we would, contrary to those who defend the thesis that judgments do appear in literary works, have to agree that such judgments do not in fact appear. This is because true judgments do not refer to objects that resemble real objects, but simply to real objects as such. We must therefore either agree with those who see an artistic value in the resemblance between the presented object and reality, and consequently agree that such works contain quasi-judgments, or we must accept the existence of judgments in literary works but at the same time abandon the view that the resemblance of presented objects to reality contributes to the work's value. The relationship of resemblance assumes that there are some differences between similar objects but that these differences are comparatively so small that they do not cancel out the similarity. One who maintains that objects referred to in literary works, say in drama or in historical novels, resemble real objects, must also maintain that they are at least numerically different from objects that they resemble.

And if such objects are to appear in literature at all and if the reader's attention is to be drawn to them rather than to real objects, the sentences that describe them must not be judgments. Otherwise, the intention would be aimed directly at real objects, while the created purely intentional ones would escape the reader's attention altogether. But neither can these sentences be pure Meinongian "assumptions," that is, sentences completely devoid of assertive power and therefore not conveying any belief regarding the reality of what they designate. For if they were "assumptions," objects presented in literature would have been deprived of all character of real existence and, although they would as regards their properties perhaps resemble real objects, they would not have been able to pretend to be such objects and would not have imposed themselves as real. All artistic illusion would then become impossible. A so-called realistic work (this is admittedly an ambiguous expression) would lack all expressive power and would in no way suggest to the reader that he is being confronted with a certain reality.

So the only explanation of the fact that there are works of literature in which the presented world gives us an impression of being real, although "in fact" it is not, is the suggestion that predicating sentences in literary works are intermediate between "assumptions" and judgments, namely, quasi-judgments. In other words, if someone wants to accept the existence of "realistic" works and attaches a special value to their realism, he must abandon the view that literary works contain logically true sentences and if he nevertheless wishes to ascribe truth to such works, he must do so in a new sense compatible with the quasi-assertive character of predicating sentences in literature. The discussion of what this meaning of "truth" would be lies beyond the scope of this study.

The function of art in general and of literature in particular is not to teach man by means of judgments what the real world is like, and in performing its task it does not have to resort to judgments in the strict sense. Its chief function is to show the possible and necessary connection between the qualitative endowment of objects, and of man in particular, and values and to enable man to enter into a direct commerce with values by acting upon his emotional life. Such values are quite varied and their presence in particular cases depends on the content of the given work of art. Their experience is made possible by, among other things, the aesthetic attitude in which the work of art places its consumer. In this action of the work upon its consumer, quasi-judgments form one of the means contributing to the development of the aesthetic experience. Whether this exhausts the role of art in man's life is a new question, which I do not here propose to resolve.

NOTES

1. In what manner this new world exists, whether and to what extent it frees itself from creative acts and becomes an entity that is accessible to cognition and feeling by other mental subjects, all these are ontological problems which I tried to elucidate in *Das literarische Kunstwerk*. These problems go beyond the scope of this study but it has to be emphasized that the reduction of purely intentional objects, which form one of the strata in a literary work, to "illusory" objects is quite a serious simplification.

2. I distinguish between material and formal content in paragraph 15 of *Das literarische Kunstwerk*.

7

NOMINAL EXPRESSIONS AND LITERARY FICTION*

by

Jerzy Pelc

Translated from Polish by
OLGIERD WOJTASIEWICZ

Jerzy Pelc was born in Warsaw in 1924. He studied logic and Polish philology at the University of Warsaw and Jagiellonian University in Krakow. He was a pupil of Kotarbiński, Ajdukiewicz, and Tatarkiewicz, and received his Ph.D. from the University of Warsaw. From 1945–1950 he held the Chair of History of Polish Literature at that institution, and since 1951 has taught logic there. His books in Polish are: Laws of Science, *1957;* Carnap's Views on the Problems of Meaning and Denotation, *1960;* On the Concept of Theme, *1961;* Logic and Language, *A Collection of Papers of English and American Authors, edited and translated, 1967.*

1. *Fictitious Subsistence*

Literature is sometimes described as the art whose works are those of fiction. They refer to an imaginary world, and

---

* This essay was originally published under the title "Wyrażenia imienne a fikcja literacka" in *Studia Estetyczne* 4 (Warsaw: Polish Scientific Publishers, 1967) :317–36.

not to a real one. That imaginary world is supposed to consist of *fictitious objects*. But in what does their fictitious nature consist? In what does physical existence differ from fictitious subsistence? Are all fictitious objects alike as to their mode of subsistence, or can they be classified in distinct categories?

Answers to these questions can be found in logical analyses concerned with the problems of existential quantification. Here is one of the various possible examples of the description of the various modes of *fictitious subsistence*.[1]

The first category of fictitious objects consists of *subjective things,* which, next to the objective, physical ones, form a subclass of direct things. Subjective things are those "seen" in dreams, and also those objects that we treat as objective and real things, although objects different from them are objectively and really given to our observation. Thus, for instance, while watching light and dark points on a screen or a photograph, we "see" persons, buildings, furniture, and the like.

The second category of fictitious objects might include those to which we ascribe *logical subsistence*. We refer to subsistence of this kind when the assumption of physical existence is not self-contradictory. In this sense a unicorn subsists logically, since the existential statement "a unicorn exists" is not self-contradictory. Sometimes another variation of this concept is introduced, when those things and facts that are logically possible are considered to subsist logically. Still another variation of logical subsistence can be found in what are termed judgments about belief:[2] if a person believes that something is so and so, we interpret this as if he believed in the existence of a fact, which practically means logical subsistence, because that *so and so* does not exist physically.

The mode of fictitious subsistence of intentional objects comes close to the last-named concept. Every transitive verb has its object(s), that is, grammatical complement(s); likewise, mental acts, *e.g.,* acts of desiring, willing, and so on, have their complements, namely those intentional objects. An intentional object is what I desire, what I intend to do, what I try to do, what I expect. That intentional object is similar to a subjective thing in its mode of being, but nevertheless differs from the latter by not being connected with our direct ideas and does not form their subject matter. The goal of our intention is not an idea, but a realization of an idea.

At the moment we are most interested in those fictitious objects to which literary subsistence is ascribed. Literary and art theorists as well as theorists of aesthetics pay much attention to explaining that kind of being. But logical papers also provide some information on the subject, because logicians, though not interested in an analysis of a literary work as the principal subject matter of their research, do find in such an analysis elements that are important to them. This is due to certain essential analogies between this or that mode of fictitious subsistence and the being of mathematical objects or the being of abstract equivalents of expressions, such as denotata and extensions.

Literary subsistence may be interpreted by reducing it to the physical existence of corresponding sentences in a given text, or by reducing it to some kind of existence of ideas and emotions in the reader's psyche. In the latter case we have to do with a mode of being similar to that which is characteristic of subjective objects, "seen" by the reader of a literary work.[3] The first case, on the contrary, might consist in a relativization with respect to the author to whom the sentences occurring in a text owe their physical existence.

There are many and various kinds of fictitious subsistence. The foregoing specification does not exhaust them all, and is not meant to do so. The intention is to make the reader watchful when he happens to hear someone say that literature is an art of fiction. The above remarks show that such a statement can be interpreted in many different ways. One of the many sources of such differences is the variety of modes of fictitious subsistence. And it seems that each of those modes may have something to do with literature.

2. *Nominal Expressions*

It would be interesting and instructive to examine the

various modes of fictitious subsistence in literature, without confining oneself to what is termed literary subsistence. But we cannot engage in all that here, since we wish to concentrate upon the relationship between *nominal expressions,* especially those used as singular, and *fictitious subsistence.*

The traditional explanation of the problem of literary fiction consists in linking it with the problem of the truth-value of the sentences occurring in a literary work. This is a good method of analysis, but I think that it can be usefully expanded by the study of the function performed by non-sentential expressions in creating fiction; we mean here nominal expressions in the grammatical sense of the term, that is, first of all nouns and adjectives. We are concerned with one-word expressions, such as "John," "Hamlet," "table," "Death" (with a capital "D," as a personification), "rich," with compound expressions treated as if they were single words ("John Smith," "New York," "Newcastle-on-Tyne," and perhaps also "Dr. Jekyll"), with expressions consisting of two or more words, such as "My Fair Lady," "he who has climbed Mt. Everest," "the death of a salesman," "captain's daughter," and also such pronouns as "he," "this," and so on.

In logic, these expressions are divided into certain subclasses, but the criterion of division varies from case to case.[4]

For instance, we may speak of *empty, singular,* and *general* expressions, according to the number of the designata they have: an empty expression has none, a singular expression has one, and a general expression, more than one. Moreover, according to definition, by a designatum is meant either the concrete, real, individual object that corresponds to a given expression in its given meaning and in a given language, or an object that need not necessarily be concrete and real, but is interpreted in some other way. The problem of designatum becomes still more complicated when we come to consider what an individual is. At any rate, this classification of expressions depends, as can be seen from the above, on a state of things in extralinguistic reality.

The second classification refers to an immanent, linguistic criterion to introduce the following subclasses: *expressions with a singular intention* and *expressions with a general intention;* here the distinction is based on the way the meaning of a word or phrase determines its extension. For instance, the description "John's only son," as it makes the proviso of uniqueness, has in this sense a singular intention regardless of whether the John in question has only one son, or more than one, or is childless. General intention is ascribed to the expression "red object on my desk,"[5] without an article, and that regardless of whether on my desk there are more red objects than one, or just one, or none. It seems that within this classification we might take into account the third subclass, namely *expressions with an empty intention.* It would consist, according to one of the many possible opinions, of self-contradictory expressions, absurdities like "square circle," because their very meanings account for the fact that they cannot be applied to anything that could be conceived in a noncontradictory manner. They would, of course, be empty expressions—also in the sense of the previous classification.

The third classification adopts a syntactic, or rather logical syntactic, criterion, that is, one belonging to the field of logical syntax. Following Aristotle,[6] expressions are classified into *individual* and *general.* Aristotle classified entities —it is not clear whether he meant extralinguistic entities, or linguistic expressions, or logical analogues of linguistic expressions—into those about which we may predicate (Socrates), but by means of which we many not predicate, and those by means of which we may predicate (man). It is difficult to decide whether for Aristotle Socrates, or "Socrates," or "Socrates" but only in the function of the (grammatical? logical?) subject of a sentence, or all three were an individual entity. Similar doubts pertain to man or "man." In any case, the interpretation of his views tended to make distinctions between expressions, and not between extralinguistic entities, and thus drifted away from ontology. It also resulted in the following distinction: individual expressions are those which may occur only in the function of the subject, and general expressions are those which may occur in the function of the predicate. It probably remains a mystery whether in this formulation reference is made to subject and predicate in the grammatical or the logical sense of the terms, and to which of the many meanings of those terms. Typical examples of individual expressions would be provided by one-word proper names, even were they empty in the sense of the first classification (*e.g.,* "Aphrodite"). As examples of general expressions we might quote "table," "John's father," "Hercules' father," "Hercules' son," that is, general, singular, and empty expressions in the sense of the first classification, and along with them those which are marked by singular intention and by general intention.

In addition to the foregoing classification, the following distinction will prove useful: *a token of an expression, the use of an expression, and expression.*[7] The word *dog,* as written here, is one of the many tokens of that expression; as can be seen, a token of an expression is a concrete thing, located in space and time. The set of all tokens of an expression, conceived as an abstraction, is an expression. And now the use of an expression. I have a dog whose name is "Trot." Now, whenever I use a token of the expression *dog* with reference to my Trot, I have to do with the same use of the word *dog.* When, on the contrary, I use a token of the word *dog* to refer to Kazan, my dog friend from Zakopane, this is a different use of the word *dog.* Still another use is exemplified by the insertion of a token of the word *dog* in the sentence "the dog is a friend of the man," where not any definite dog is meant, but reference is made either to every dog or to the dog "in general." Finally, in all those cases when a token of the word *dog* has occurred in this text, it has not been used with reference to any dog, but has served as an example, which is still another use of that expression.

It must be realized that the semantic properties singled out above: singularity, singular intention, individual character, and the like, are associated, not with an expression, but with the use of an expression. Hence the same expression may be singular in one use (*e.g.,* the word *chair* in the sentence "Offer me the chair, please") and general in the other (*e.g.,* the word *chair* in the sentence "Not every piece of furniture is a chair"). Likewise, it may have a singular intention in one use, and a general intention in any other; it may be individual in one use, and general in another. On the other hand, meaning is associated with the expression, and not with its use or its token. The meaning of an expression may be defined as the general rules of a use of that expression such that it should refer to certain things.

By analogy, the distinction may be made between *a sentence, the use of a sentence,* and *a token of a sentence.* We then shall say about a given use of a sentence, and not about a sentence, that it is true or false, or that the question of its truth-value does not arise at all. To the sentence itself we shall ascribe a meaning, understood as general rules of using that sentence to construct true or false statements.

An isolated expression that occurs as a dictionary item is ascribed *a dictionary meaning,* distinct from the *meaning shaped by the linguistic context,* in which an expression used in thus and such a way occurs, and also by the *extralinguistic situation* that accompanies a given use of that expression. Hence, the expressions that we encounter in definite acts of speaking and writing have their dictionary meanings modified by the context and factual circumstances. The general rules of the use of a given expression, as mentioned above, then become specialized.

The distinctions listed above will be used in an analysis of the functions of nominal expressions in works of fiction.

3. *Nominal Expressions versus Real Use (U_R) and Fictive Use (U_F)*

A comparison of a literary and a nonliterary text helps to grasp the difference between the denoting function of nominal expressions in each of them.

Should we make a list of such expressions, drawn from a literary work, whether poetry or prose, and compare it with a list of items drawn from a scholarly work, it would turn out that it is not the choice of the types of expressions, but the semantic functions of expressions of the same type that decide whether a given work creates fiction or not. The items on the two lists would be much alike. It can be expected that a list of expressions drawn from a Napoleonic epic or a historical novel about the Napoleonic period would much more resemble a list of nominal expressions drawn from a scholarly monograph on Napoleon, than would the latter list resemble a third list, namely, that of nominal expressions occurring in a scholarly monograph on Copernican discoveries in astronomy. And yet both a history of the Napoleonic period and a history of Copernican discoveries refer to real facts, whereas a Napoleonic epic or a historical novel about the Napoleonic period creates fiction. It can also be expected that, should we draw two lists of nominal expressions, one including the items drawn from all past and present written and spoken literary works and the other including the items drawn from nonliterary texts, then the two lists would not differ essentially from one another. The vocabulary of the artistic language, used in creating fiction, does not differ essentially from the vocabulary of the nonliterary language, used in describing reality. This applies, however, at the most to the shape and the dictionary value of expressions.

If the class of the extralinguistic elements corresponding to a language, that is, all that to which all the expressions of that language refer, is termed the *model* of a language, then the previous observation can be formulated as follows. The fact that the model of a language is fictitious, in the sense that it consists of fictitious objects, need not affect the lexicon of that language. A *real model* (M_R) and a *fictitious model* (M_F) may both correspond to the same lexicon. On the other hand, it may happen that two different real models correspond to two different lexicons; the same applies to two different fictitious models.

The question arises whether we have to do with the same language if a fictitious model (M_F) and a real model (M_R) are counterparts of the same lexicon. Hence, is the language L_R , which consists of the expressions E_{R_1} , E_{R_2} , . . . E_{R_n} and has the the real model M_R , identical with the language L_F , if the latter has the same grammar as L_R and consists of all and only those expressions which are equiform with those mentioned above, namely of the expressions EF_1 , EF_2 , . . . EF_n such that EF_1 is equiform with ER_1 , EF_2 with ER_2 , and so on, and if the language L_F has the fictitious model M_F ? It seems that the answer should be in the negative. Even if the models M_R and M_F are isomorphic in the sense that each *real object* O_R , which is an element of the model M_R , has its counterpart in the *fictitious object* O_F , which is an element of the model M_F , and conversely, and if every relation between objects O_R in the model M_R has its counterpart in a corresponding relation between objects O_F in the model M_F , and conversely, the languages L_R and L_F are not identical. The identity of lexicons, the identity of grammatical structures, and the isomorphism of models are necessary, but not sufficient conditions of the identity of the languages L_R and L_F .

Why are L_R and L_F not identical? To answer this question we have to compare a pair of corresponding nominal expressions, ER_1 of the language L_R and EF_1 of the language L_F .

"The horse broke off through the trees dragging him, bumping, face downward, and Robert Jordan stood up holding the pistol now in one hand."[8]

This sentence from *For Whom the Bell Tolls* is an example of the language L_F . The part "the horse broke off through the trees" might equally well belong to the language L_R . The nominal expressions *the horse* is equiform in both cases and has the same dictionary meaning. But when it is spoken in current speech (L_R), then the context and/or extralinguistic circumstances of the statement modify the original dictionary meaning of that nominal expression in another way than happens in the case of a literary statement. Hence in L_R we have to with a singular use. The word *the horse* (ER_1) has its counterpart in one concrete horse, and the word *the pistol* (ER_2), one concrete pistol. In the literary passage, on the contrary, we have to do with an empty use with singular intention. Nothing in the model M_R corresponds to the words *the horse* and *the pistol* (EF_1 , EF_2) ; hence they are empty in terms of that classification.

On the other hand, in the model M_F each of these expressions has its counterpart in a fictitious individual or in an intentional object; this is why we say that they are used with singular intention.

It might be added that in the fictional language (L_F), the role of the context as the modifier of the dictionary values of the expressions used is relatively greater than in the language L_R . This is because in the fictional language concrete extralinguistic situations that accompany the utterance of words and/or sentences cannot affect their use in this way as they can in the case of current speech (L_R). In L_R the presence of a real object O_{R1} often settles the fact that a given expression E_{R1} is used ostensively, *i.e.*, as if the speaker pointed to that object. If a person is in his home and says: "The bulb in the bathroom is gone," then the proximity of the bathroom (O_{R1}) and the bulb (O_{R2}) determines that the general names in the dictionary sense *the bathroom* (E_{R1}) and *the bulb* (E_{R2}) occur here in an ostensive singular use. On the contrary, in the language L_F , the context is often the only, and usually the principal, modifier of the dictionary value of expressions: the competition of factual, extralinguistic, circumstances is incomparably weaker.

Let it be agreed that the term *fictive use* (U_F) is used in such cases as *the horse* (E_{F1}) and *the pistol* (E_{F2}), where those expressions occur as *empty* and with *singular intention,* and are elements of the fictional language (L_F).

The fictive use understood in this way can sometimes be encountered outside literature as well, and in literary works we also sometimes have to do with uses of other kinds. But nonetheless that fictive use must be considered characteristic of poetry and artistic prose. By using nominal expressions in such a way, we call *fictitious objects* to life. On the other hand, when those expressions occur in *real use* (U_R), then they serve to point to, or to identify, a given concrete object O_R . They do not create fictitious subsistence, but refer to objective existence.

By using the terms "fictive use" and "real use," we may say that the languages L_R and L_F are not identical in spite of the identity of the lexicon, the dictionary equisignificance of corresponding expressions, the identity of grammatical structure and the isomorphism of the models M_R and M_P ; they are not precisely because equiform and lexically equisignificant expressions may occur in different uses: in the real use (U_R) in the language L_R , and in the fictive use (U_F) in the language L_F .

4. Nominal Expressions in Fictive Use (U_F) versus the Real Model (M_R) and the Fictional Model (M_F)

When those nominal expressions which occur in the fictive use (U_F) are defined as empty but having a singular intention, then at least the first part of this characteristic, which refers to emptiness, is formulated with reference to the real model (M_R).

It might be disputed whether it is correct to characterize the word E_{F1} in its use U_F and belonging to the language L_F , which has its model M_F , with respect to the model M_R that corresponds to the language L_R . Consequently, would it not be correct, instead of claiming that the word *the horse,* when used as E_{R1} in the language L_R , is singular, and when used as E_{F1} in the language L_F is empty but with a singular intention, to say that it is singular also in the use U_F , within the language L_F , because in the model M_F it has a counterpart, even though that counterpart is fictitious? Now, characterizing the expressions E_F in the language L_F as empty by referring to an alien model M_R , has its traditions and arguments in its favor.

For instance, Russell[9] claims it vigorously, when he says:

The question of "unreality," which confronts us at this point, is a very important one. Misled by grammar, the great majority of those logicians who have dealt with this question have dealt with it on mistaken lines. They have regarded grammatical form as a surer guide in analysis than, in fact, it is. . . . It is argued, e.g. by Meinong,[10] that we can speak about "the golden mountain," "the round square," and so on. . . . In such theories, it seems to me, there is a failure of that feeling for reality which ought to be preserved even in the most abstract studies. Logic, I should maintain, must no more admit a unicorn than zoology can; for logic is concerned with the real world just as truly as zoology, though with its more abstract and general features. To say that unicorns have an existence in heraldry, or in literature, or in imagination, is a most pitiful and paltry evasion. What exists in heraldry is not an animal, made of flesh and blood, moving and breathing of its own initiative. What exists is a picture, or a description in words. Similarly, to maintain that Hamlet, for example, exists in his own world, namely, in the world of Shakespeare's imagination, just as truly as (say) Napoleon existed in the ordinary world, is to say something deliberately confusing, or else confused to a degree which is scarcely credible. There is only one world, the "real" world: Shakespeare's imagination is part of it, and the thoughts that he had in writing Hamlet are real. So are the thoughts that we have in reading the play. But it is of the very essence of fiction that only the thoughts, feelings, etc., in Shakespeare and his readers are real, and that there is not, in addition to them, an objective Hamlet. When you have taken account of all the feelings roused by Napoleon in writers and readers of history, you have not touched the actual man, but in the case of Hamlet you have come to the end of him. If no one thought about Hamlet, there would be nothing left of him; if no one had thought about Napoleon, he would have soon seen to it that some one did.

In addition to more general philosophical considerations, which include the admission of the real world as the only reality, there is also another reason for which we are inclined to compare the language of fiction (L_F) with an alien real model (M_R). Now, the truth-value of propositions is determined in classical two-valued logic by applying the Aristotelian criterion of agreement with reality, precisely that reality to which M_R belongs. A comparison of sentences from the language L_F with the world of fiction that includes the fictional model M_F would introduce different concepts of truth and falsehood, which would also be based on the agreement of a sentence, or, strictly, a given use of a given sentence, with reality, but with a reality of another kind. Likewise, it would become disputable whether such a sentence is a form of a proposition, since the latter is defined in terms of truth and falsehood, but in their previous interpretation.

But the law of excluded middle and the principles of classical two-valued logic could be renounced, and it could be assumed that there are uses of sentences such as are devoid of the properties of truth and falsehood, although the sentences as such are meaningful, because in other circumstances they could be used to state something true or false.[11] According to that theory, we come across such an alleged, apparent use, a use that might be termed a dud, when the subject of a given sentence is a nominal expression that does not refer to anything in the real model M_R , and does not identify any real individual O_{R1} but—being an expression with a singular intention—refers to a definite single fictitious object O_{F1} , to a single element of the fictitious model M_F . From that point of view it would be a misunderstanding to compare statements belonging to the language of fiction L_F and the real model M_R . In particular, it would be a misunderstanding to say, having read in *For Whom the Bell Tolls* about Maria that "her teeth were white in her brown face and her skin and her eyes were the same tawny brown. She had high cheekbones, merry eyes and a straight mouth with full lips,"[12] that it is not true. From that point of view it would also be a misunderstanding to say that it is true.[13] This follows, of course, if the terms *truth* and *falsehood* are used in the traditional interpretation. For if we interpret these terms this way, the issue of truth and falsehood in such cases does not arise at all.

The advantage of this theory is that it complies with the current intuitions associated with the term *false*. We are inclined to treat as false those statements in which something is predicated counterfactually about somebody or something existent, but not those in which anything—no matter what—is predicated about something nonexistent.[14] Another advantage is the fact that it grasps a certain peculiarity of our attitude toward literary fiction, namely that to which Ingarden[15] draws attention: fiction is not taken quite seriously, which results in the quasi-truth of the sentences belonging to a literary work, sentences that accordingly are described as quasi-propositions. The disadvantage of the theory is that it renounces the law of excluded middle. The disadvantage, however, can, it seems, be eliminated while the advantages can partly be saved. For that purpose it suffices to make use of Russell's distinction between the *primary* and the *secondary* use of *descriptions*.[16] The secondary use of a denoting phrase is defined as such in which the phrase occurs in a proposition (p), and p is an element of the entire proposition. For instance, the denoting phrase "the present King of France" occurs as secondary in the sentence, "the present King of France is not bald," if that statement is interpreted according to the formula "it is not true that p"; in other words, "it is not true that there exists a person who is now King of France and is bald." On the other hand, we have to do with a primary use in the case of the following interpretation: "There exists a person who is now King of France and is not bald." The first interpretation, which includes a secondary use, yields a true sentence; the second, which includes a primary use, yields a false sentence. As can be seen, the law of excluded middle has been preserved. But the price to be paid would be the treatment of all empty nominal expressions with a singular intention, and hence nominal expressions in a fictive use (U_F), so common in literature, as descriptive expressions in Russell's sense. Moreover, Russell's theory of descriptions would have to be adopted. Finally, which would perhaps arouse the least protest, all independent declarative sentences that occur in a literary text would have to be treated as elements of a larger whole being taken into account. Only such an operation results in the secondary character of a denoting phrase. Thus, for instance, "Her teeth were white . . ."[17] would require the following interpretation: "Hemingway, as the author of *For Whom the Bell Tolls,* imagined that the heroine of his novel, whom he gave the name 'Maria,' had white teeth. . . ." In this interpretation the word *Maria* occurs as a latent description, and moreover, that description is included in an element of a proposition; we thus are dealing with a secondary use, and with a true statement. Not everyone would decide to accept such interpretational complications, and not everyone would be willing to adopt Russell's theory of descriptions.

A simpler solution—also without a renunciation of the law of excluded middle—would consist in making a distinction between *a weak and a strong interpretation of general categorical sentences, e.g.,* S a P. In the weak interpretation, such a sentence merely states the inclusion of the class S in the class P, without any assumption as to the existence of a real designatum of the name S. Hence, the sentences may be true also if S is empty. This is, however, not a universal solution, since only general and singular statements can be presented after the S a P pattern. The pattern does not apply to particular statements, which are always subject to the strong interpretation. And literary texts do include such statements, too. In view of the emptiness of S, they would be false. Moreover, that emptiness is established by a comparison of the nominal expression in question with the real model (M_R), which has been the subject matter of controversy.

It seems, however, that there is no need to settle that controversy in a decisive way, for neither is the fictional model (M_F), consisting exclusively of fictitious object (O_F), the proper model of literature; nor is the real model (M_R), consisting exclusively of concrete objects (O_R), a model entirely alien to literature; nor are the fictive use (U_F) and the language of fiction(L_F), as consisting solely of expressions of the type E_F in such a use, the specific use and the specific language of the verbal art.

5. *Literary Use* (U_L), *Literary Language* (L_L), *and Literary Model* (M_L)

Literary context modifies the original, dictionary value of the expressions it includes in a number of ways. True, the modification that turns an expression that, from the dictionary point of view, is general or singular into an expression used as fictive (U_F), and hence into an empty one with a singular intention, is very significant, yet it certainly is not the only modification. At most, it strikes the eye because it differs from that in current speech, where the context and the extralinguistic situation modify expressions in a different way, so that, for instance, what by its dictionary value is a general nominal expression becomes a singular expression in a given real use (U_R).

It suffices to examine a number of sentences, drawn from a historical novel, that have as the *subject* the *proper name* of a historical person. It turns out that even in the same syntactical function we have to do with the real use (U_R) on one occasion, and with the fictive use (U_F) on the other; thus, on one occasion the expression is used as singular, and on the other, as empty with a singular intention. Some sentences are about the real Napoleon, whereas others are about (in a different sense of the word) an imaginary Napoleon. The same applies by analogy to the expressions occurring as object (*i.e.,* complement) or apposition, and not only to the proper names of persons, but also to the proper names of places and events, and even to common names. The well-known fragment of Stefan Żeromski's novel *The Ashes,*[18] which describes how Napoleon stooped over the wounded Cedro, one of the heroes, reads: "The Emperor stood still over him for a long while. He looked into his face with stony eyes. Finally he raised his hand to his hat and said, 'Soit.'" This sentence creates an imaginary situation, and the term *the Emperor* occurs in a fictive use (U_F) as an empty name with a singular intention. But when in the same novel Żeromski refers to Napoleon's stay in Bayonne and writes: "The Emperor lived here in Marrac Castle and kept the Spanish kings, Carlos IV and Fernando VII, with him,"[19] the sentence refers to the real Napoleon, and the term *the Emperor* occurs in a real use (U_R) as a singular name. While the adjustment of the former sentence, in the use U_F given in this case to the real model (M_R), would be a misunderstanding, since the result of such an operation is known in advance, the adjustment of the latter sentence to the same model is fully justified.

In addition to this *oscillation of uses* (U_R and U_F) of the same expression as it occurs in the same syntactic function, we can notice in literary texts a difference between the use of a given nominal expression when it functions as the subject and its use when it functions as the predicate. This is connected with the characteristics inherent in the said classification of those expressions into individual (to be used only as subjects) and general (to be used also as predicates). The principal semantic function of an individual expression, such as pure, one-word, nondescriptive proper names, is to indicate a certain individual, to mention him or to identify him. A nominal expression that occurs in literary texts in that syntactic and semantic function very often occurs in a fictive use (U_F) and thus creates a fictitious entity (O_{F_1}). When, however, it occurs as a general name, *e.g.*, in the predicate, it often occurs in a real use (U_R). Hence, in the former case we are concerned with its being used as an empty expression with a singular intention, and in the latter, *e.g.*, as a general name. Thus, even such a short literary context as a single sentence may modify the same expression in semantically different ways in accordance with the syntactic function of the word in question. Within a given sentence the gap is, as it were, bridged between the world of fiction and the real world: the extralinguistic counterpart of an individual expression (in the sense of the classification referred to above) is among imaginary entities, whereas the extralinguistic counterpart of the general expression constitutes part of reality. If we have the sentence in a novel: "John was a secret emissary,"[20] its subject, the proper name *John* occurs in a fictive use (U_F) as an empty expression with a singular intention; its counterpart is the imaginary hero of the story. But the predicate "secret emissary" occurs in a real use (U_R) as a general name, and the whole sentence may be interpreted so that it states the inclusion of the class of the subject in the nonempty and nonsingular class of the predicate. It would be contrary to the intention of the author to interpret the sentence as stating that fictitious John was a fictitious secret emissary; no, fictitious John was a "true" secret emissary. Likewise, if it is said that "Tom was a short, spry man of seventy, a veteran of the Crimean War,"[21] then Tom is an imaginary person, created by the expression *Tom*, empty and with a singular intention. On the contrary, the properties of being a spry man of seventy and a veteran of the Crimean War are real in the sense that they are ascribed to real individuals as well.

The individual or general use of a given nominal expression need not coincide with the occurrence of that expression as subject or predicate, respectively, although those cases are typical. On the other hand, the coincidence of the individual use with the fictive use (U_F), and of the general use with the real use (U_R) is notorious. This applies also to pairs of equiform expressions, or put in another way, to the different uses of the same expression. Suppose there is a story about Ivan, who was a Cossack, and it is said about him that: "He knew how to be a courtier among courtiers, a Cossack among Cossacks, and a brigand among brigands."[22] Here the word *Cossack* occurs as a general, *i.e.*, predicative, expression, and also as a general name in a real use (U_R). If later on we read about Ivan that ". . . the nobleman was enraged by the fact that the Cossack was so impudent,"[23] the same word *Cossack* (if we disregard the use of articles) occurs as an individual expression in a fictive use (U_F); it creates a fictitious entity, namely, Ivan(O_{F_1}) and hence occurs as an empty expression with a singular intention.

Here again we have to do with oscillation, this time between an individual and fictive use, when a given nominal expression occurs as empty with a singular intention, often in the function of subject, and general and real use, when a given nominal expression occurs as general, often in the function of predicate. Thus even within a single sentence such a small literary context as the subject part of that sentence may modify the original, dictionary value of a given nominal expression in a way different from that which the predicate part would do in the case of the same expression. As a result, in the subject position we may obtain an individual, fictive, and empty use with a singular intention, while in the predicate position we obtain a general and real use. Such sentences are, as it were, *bipolar:* they have both a fictitious and a real referent. Hence, in such cases it is difficult to decide that the model proper for them is fictitious

(M_F), while the real model (M_R) is to be rejected, or vice versa. Both models are, each in a different respect, suitable as the criteria of the truth of such a sentence, interpreted in the classical sense on one occasion, and in the coherential on the other. And both are in some respects useless. Hence neither of them may be either accepted or rejected without reservation.

The fictive use (U_F) of a nominal expression is not the only kind of use that may be encountered in a literary work. The real use (U_R) occurs there as well. *They are imposed* alternately upon one and the same expression and modify its original, dictionary value in different ways. How it happens is determined by the literary context, and this is what is characteristic of literature, and not—as it is currently believed—the fictive use only. Let this oscillation between U_F and U_R , this *shifting* of the fictive and the real use, be termed *literary use* (U_L). A nominal expression that occurs in the literary use (U_L) will, according to the context, be either empty with a singular intention, or singular, or general. On one occasion it will create a fictitious entity, and on another it will mention a real entity or will predicate. On one occasion it will occur as an individual expression, and on another as general.

The language of literary works is not a language of fiction (L_F) consisting solely of expressions occurring in a fictive use (U_F), and hence of expressions symbolized as E_{F1} , E_{F2} , E_{F3} , and so on. It also includes expressions occurring in a real use (U_R), and hence expressions symbolized as E_{R1} , E_{R2} , E_{R3} , and so forth. It is thus a mixed language. We shall term it *literary language* (L_L), of course in a sense different from that in which a literary language differs from dialects.

The model of the literary language (L_L), *i.e.,* of the artistic language of works of literature, is not, as is often believed, the fictitious model (M_F), consisting solely of fictitious objects (O_{F1}, O_{F2}, O_{F3}, etc.). It consists of both fictitious and real objects (O_{R1}, O_{R2}, O_{R3}, etc.). In that sense it is *heterogeneous.* We adopt for it the term *literary model* (M_L). In that model we can indicate various relations. Some hold between fictitious objects; others hold between real objects; but there are also those that associate a fictitious object with a real one. The last-named find their formulations in the "bipolar" sentences of the language (L_L), mentioned above. Thus the model M_L accommodates both real existence and fictitious subsistence of various kinds: of subjective things, of intentional objects, of entities endowed with logical subsistence, and so forth.

Literature—poetry, and novelistic prose—is referred to as an art of fiction, and it is believed that the world of literary fiction is an imaginary world that—as opposed to reality—consists of unreal entities only. But in fact that world includes concrete objects in addition to imaginary ones. Literary fiction is not pure imagination: it combines that which subsists only in fantasy with what exists objectively. Such at least is the conclusion reached as a result of the foregoing semiotic analysis of nominal expressions occurring in literary use (U_L) within the literary language (L_L) that has a literary model (M_L).

Summary

1. *Fictitious subsistence.* When it is said that literature is an art of fiction, various things may be meant by that, since there are various modes of fictitious subsistence, *e.g.* the subsistence of subjective things, "seen" in dreams; logical subsistence, when the supposition of physical existence is not self-contradictory; the subsistence of intentional objects; the literary subsistence of persons and objects that appear in poetry and prose works, which is reducible to the physical existence of corresponding sentences in the text or to the mental experiences of the author and/or readers.

2. *Nominal expressions.* The concept of literary fiction is usually explained by an analysis of the truth-value of sentences occurring in a given literary text. But it may be based as well on an analysis of the semantic function of the nominal expressions occurring in that text. Those nominal expressions include nouns, adjectives, pronouns, and noun and

adjectival phrases. They are classified in several ways: into empty, singular, and general—according to the number of the designata of a given nominal expression in a given language and a given use; into those with a singular, a general, and an empty intention—according to the way the meaning of a given expression determines its denotation; into individual and general—according to whether they can function only as subjects of sentences or as predicates as well. It is also useful to make a distinction between a token of an expression, a use of an expression, and an expression. The first is a definite thing, the third, the class of all tokens, and the second, a subclass of the latter, consisting of those tokens which in the same way perform the function of referring to their extralinguistic counterparts. Finally, a distinction will be made between the dictionary value of an expression, as isolated from the context and the situation accompanying its use, and the contextual value, modified by the context and the situation.

3. *Nominal expressions versus real use* (U_R) *and fictive use* (U_F). When a nominal expression is used to refer to a real object, then that expression occurs in a real use (U_R) and is symbolized E_R . When it refers to a fictitious object (O_F), then it occurs in a fictive use (U_F) and is symbolized E_F ; in such a case it is an empty expression with a singular or general intention. Expressions E_R combine to form the real language (L_R), which as its linguistic model has a real model (M_R) consisting of real objects (O_R). The language of fiction (L_F) consists of expressions E_F and has as its counterpart a fictional model (M_F) that is a set of objects O_F . L_R and L_F are different languages, even if their lexicon is the same, *i.e.,* if their expressions are pairwise equiform, if their expressions are pairwise equisignificant, if the grammatical structure of both languages is the same, and if the models of those languages are isomorphic. This difference is caused by the fact that in the language L_R we have to do with a real use of nominal expressions, whereas in L_F we have to do with a fictive use of those expressions.

4. *Nominal expressions in fictive use* (U_F) *versus the*

real model (M_R) *and the fictional model* (M_F). If a nominal expression that occurs in a fictive use (U_F) is classified as empty, this is done so with respect to the real model (M_R), although that is not the proper model of the language of fiction (L_F). We can, however, in this way characterize a sentence drawn from a literary text as to its being true or false in the classical interpretation of those terms. But it is also possible to renounce the law of the excluded middle with reference to the truth-value of such a sentence and to claim that if an expression in the use U_F occurs as a subject of such a sentence, then the sentence is neither true nor false. If the expressions E_F are interpreted in the light of Russell's theory of descriptions, it is possible—unfortunately in a complicated and nonintuitive way—to save the law of the excluded middle. The weak interpretation of universal statements in a literary text yields an analogous result, but is not valid for all occasions.

5. *Literary use* (U_L), *literary language* (L_L), *and literary model* (M_L). Expressions E_F , the use U_F , and the language L_F , although characteristic of literature, are not specific for it, since they also occur outside literature. Moreover, in a literary text itself we can encounter expressions E_R and the use U_R . Frequently the same expression E_1 , in a given place of the text occurs in the use U_R , and hence as E_{R_1} , and in another place of the same text it occurs in the use U_F , and hence as E_{F_1} . It is the literary context that in each case modifies in a different way the original, dictionary value of a given nominal expression. For instance, it is a typical situation that a given expression occurs in the subject position in the use U_F , that is, as E_{F_1} , and in the predicate position in the use U_R , that is, as E_{R_1} . There is a coincidence between the individual nature of an expression and its fictive use, and between its general nature with its real use. This is accompanied by an oscillation, or shifting, of the uses U_R and U_F . This alternate imposition of U_R and U_F upon the same expression E_1 is termed literary use (U_L) and is claimed to be characteristic of literature. The term *literary language* (L_L) will be used with reference to the mixed language consisting

of both expressions E_R and expressions E_F , that is, the language in which nominal expressions occur in the literary use (U_L). This is the language of literary works. Its model is the literary model (M_L), which is heterogeneous, as it consists both of objects O_R and of objects O_F . Various relations hold between objects of a given type, and also between objects of different types. M_L is the model of literature, sometimes also called the world of literary fiction. It combines that which subsists only in imagination with that which exists objectively.

NOTES

1. Cf. Hans Reichenbach, *Elements of Symbolic Logic* (New York: The Macmillan Company, 1948), §49.

2. Cf. Bertrand Russell, *Inquiry into Meaning and Truth* (New York: Norton, 1940), pp. 22 and 336–42.

3. Cf. Reichenbach.

4. Cf. Tadeusz Kotarbiński, "On the Classification of Names," *Gnosiology* (Oxford: Pergamon Press, 1966), pp. 389 ff.

5. Cf. C. I. Lewis, "The Modes of Meaning," in *Philosophy and Phenomenological Research* 4, no. 2 (Buffalo, N.Y. 1943) :236–49.

6. Cf. Aristotle, *Categories* 5.

7. Cf. P. F. Strawson, "On Referring," *Mind* 59 (1950) :320–44.

8. Ernest Hemingway, *For Whom the Bell Tolls* (New York: Scribner, Overseas Editions, Inc., 1940), p. 266.

9. Cf. Bertrand Russell, "Descriptions," chap. 16 of *Introduction to Mathematical Philosophy* (London: Allen and Unwin, 1919).

10. A. Meinong, *Untersuchungen zur Gegenstandstheorie und Psychologie* (Leipzig: J. A. Barth, 1904).

11. Cf. Strawson.

12. Hemingway, p. 22.

13. Cf. Leonard Linsky, "Reference and Referents," *Philosophy and Ordinary Language,* ed. Ch. A. Caton (Urbana, Ill.: University of Illinois Press, 1963).

14. Cf. Alfred J. Ayer, "Proper Names and Descriptions" (in Polish), *Studia Filozoficzne,* no. 5/20, *PWN* (Warsaw, 1960).

15. Roman Ingarden, *The Literary Work* (in Polish), *PWN* (Warsaw, 1960).

16. Cf. Bertrand Russell, "On Denoting," *Mind* 14 (1905).

17. Cf. n. 12 above.

18. Ad hoc translation of chapter, "Widziadła" (Nightmares), from Stefan Żeromski's *Popioly* (*The Ashes*), vol. 3 (Warsaw: Czytelnik, 1964).

19. Ad hoc translation of chapter "Szlak Cesarski" (The Imperial Route), in *ibid.*

20. Example invented ad hoc by the translator on the analogy of the original example drawn from Polish literature.

21. *Ibid.*

22. *Ibid.*

23. *Ibid.*

8

THE WORLD OF ARTS AND
THE WORLD OF SIGNS*

by

Mieczysław Wallis

Translated from Polish by
the author

*Mieczysław Wallis was born in Warsaw in 1895. He studied art
history and philosophy at the University of Heidelberg with Wil-
helm Windelband, and at the University of Warsaw with Jan Łukasiewicz, W. Tatarkiewicz and T. Kotarbiński. He received his Ph.D.
in 1921, and for many years was art critic for various periodicals.
After fighting against the Germans in 1939, he spent five years in a
prisoner-of-war camp. He subsequently received the Chair for Aesthetics and Art History at the University of Lodz and taught there
until his retirement in 1965. His books include:* Expression and
Mental Life, *1939;* Canaletto, the Painter of Warsaw, *1954;* Polish
Art Between the Two Wars, *1959;* Painters and Cities, *1961;* Self-
Portrait, *1964;* The Self-Portraits of Polish Artists, *1966;* Art Nou-
veau, *1967;* Experience and Value, *papers on Aesthetics and the
Science of Art of the years 1931–1949 (in print).*

* This essay is a revised and partly abbreviated, partly enlarged version
of a paper in Polish under the same title (Świat sztuk i świat znaków),
Estetyka 2 (1961) :37–52. A short English summary appeared under the title
"The World of Arts and the World of Signs" in *Proceedings of the Fourth
International Congress on Aesthetics* (Athens, 1960), pp. 397–400.

I. Terminological Explanations

By "the arts" we usually understand today such activities as poetry, music, painting, sculpture, architecture, dance, theater, or the products of these activities.[1] This concept of "the arts" is the result of a long history. For the Greeks poetry, music, and dance were arts, but not architecture, sculpture, or painting.[2] The range of phenomena included in one or another of the particular arts also varied in the course of time. In the seventeenth century folk-poetry hardly ranked as art, nor did Negro carving until the early twentieth century. Today opinions differ as to whether the works of the "naïve" painters and dilettanti, the compositions of the insane, the drawings of children, or the songs of birds shall be regarded as art or not. Like all empirical notions, the notion of "the arts" is a vacillating one, having a distinct nucleus and blurred edges. For our purposes, it is sufficient to state that certain activities and their products are today usually regarded as arts.

These activities and their products are in many ways connected. They act one upon another. They form a large whole, a "world": the world of arts. This world is not a closed one. New arts arise again and again. Industrial design, artistic photography, film drama, radio drama, the television show may be quoted as some examples of new arts that came into being in the last hundred years.

Let us now turn to "signs." By a "sign"—I am giving here a deliberately simplified definition of this term—I understand a sensuously perceptible object produced or used by a "sender," an object that, owing to its peculiar properties, is able, by itself or in connection with other similar objects, sometimes in a particular context or situation, to evoke in a "receiver"—a spectator or a listener—a definite thought— an image, a notion, a judgment, or a complex of them—of an object other than itself. If an object does this on the basis of resemblance, I call it a "likeness" or an "iconic sign." If an object does this on the basis of a custom or convention, I call it a "conventional sign." The drawing of a horse is an iconic sign; the English word *horse* is a conventional sign. There are various intermediate forms between iconic and conventional signs.

By a *symbol* I understand a sensuously perceptible object, man-made or not, that evokes the thought of an object other than itself. This is neither on the basis of a custom or convention, like a conventional sign, nor on the basis of resemblance, like an iconic sign, but on the basis of an analogy, often vague and difficult to grasp. The lion as a symbol of power, courage, or pride, flame as a symbol of revolution are examples.

Symbols may be unfixed, vacillating, shimmering (the "blue Flower" of the Romantics or the crippled wild duck in Ibsen's play are "unfixed symbols"). Symbols may be fixed by a custom or convention (for instance, the symbols of medieval liturgy and art codified in special treatises). Fixed symbols approach in character conventional signs.

Semantic is to me the same as "being a sign" (or "constituted of signs" or "using signs"). On the contrary, *asemantic* is the same as "not being a sign" (or "not constituted of signs" or "not using signs").

Signs form manifold combinations, complexes, and systems. Ethnic languages are, for instance, vast systems of conventional signs. Within the larger human world signs constitute a peculiar sphere or stratum of exceptional importance—"the world of signs."

Neither "the world of arts" or "the world of signs" is an isolated, autonomous sphere, existing independently of other realms of human activity. In calling the complex of arts and the complex of signs "worlds," I want to stress, however, the fact that they constitute large coherent wholes —within the larger whole of the world.

Let us now ask how these two great spheres, the world of arts and the world of signs, are related to each other. It seems that the world of arts is connected with the world of signs at least in a triple way: *1*) Some works of art are signs or complexes of signs, *2*) some works of art may be recorded by means of signs, *3*) some works of art may be reproduced by means of signs.

II. Semantic and Asemantic Works of Art

Is it possible that the works of certain arts are signs or complexes of signs, while the works of other arts are not signs; is it possible to divide the arts into semantic and asemantic arts?

Hippolyte Taine, in his *Philosophie de l'art* (1865/69), had already opposed painting, sculpture, and poetry as "imitative arts," to architecture and music as "nonimitative arts." Similarly, in 1910 Sydney Colvin, in his article "Fine Arts" in the 11th edition of the "Encyclopaedia Britannica," proposed as one of three modes of classification the division of the arts into "imitative" and "nonimitative arts." In 1907 Theodor Lipps divided the arts into "concrete" and "abstract arts"; in 1923 Max Dessoir into "the arts of imitation, of definite associations, of real forms" and "the free arts of indefinite associations and unreal forms." In 1925 Johannes Volkelt divided the arts into those concerned with things (*dingliche Künste*) and those not concerned with things (*undingliche Künste*).[3] In English literature on art, the "representative" or "representational arts" were often opposed to the "nonrepresentative" or "nonrepresentational" ones; in French literature, the "arts représentatifs" or "figuratifs" to the "arts non-représentatifs" or "non-figuratifs." In other words, in nineteenth- and twentieth-century aesthetics, the arts were often divided into two groups: into arts whose works have a semantic character and those whose works do not possess such a character. Painting, sculpture, poetry, theater were usually included in the former group; architecture and music in the latter. The decorative arts and dance were most of the time included in the asemantic arts.

Such classification is, however, for many reasons untenable. There are arts of which some works are asemantic, some others semantic. Dance is usually included in asemantic arts. Certainly there are dances that have a purely asemantic character. Their beauty consists in rhythmic transformations of movements and attitudes, in the mobile arabesques traced by the bodies of the dancers. Each of these dances is, in the

words of Paul Valéry, "l'acte pur des métamorphoses."[4]
Along with such dances there are, however, numerous dances
of an iconic character. All dances representing in the form
of gestures and mimicry, even in an only adumbrated, allusive way, the symptoms of psychic life are iconic. Also
iconic are numerous "animal dances": the dances imitating
the movements of various animals—of bear, fox, peacock,
salmon (in archaic societies often of a magic character);
the dances representing actions connected with the tillage
of soil—sowing, mowing, threshing; the erotic dances representing in a more or less stylized form courting and the act
of love. A historian of dance, Curt Sachs, therefore divides
all dances into "figurative and nonfigurative dances" (*bild-
hafte und bildlose Tänze*),[5] in our terminology, into iconic
and noniconic dances. Many ritual or martial dances contain symbolic elements and conventional signs as well.

It is also impossible to classify the diverse branches of
so-called decorative arts simply as asemantic. A fabric may
have a purely geometric pattern, but it may also have a
pattern of stylized flowers or represent scenes from antique
myths or from the Bible, as, for instance, the tapestries
designed by Raphael. A jug, a vase, may have no ornament
or a geometric, strictly asemantic pattern. But it may also
be decorated with plant or animal ornaments, with scenes
from myths or from everyday life, as, for example, are
many Greek vases. There are also works of pottery shaped
as iconic signs, for instance, the Greek rhytons in the form
of animal heads (the so-called theriomorphic vases) or the
Peruvian vessels in the form of eared human heads.

According to the traditional view, architecture is an
asemantic art. The investigations of the recent three decades
have, however, shown that in many cultural spheres and
epochs a considerable number of buildings, especially the
houses, the tombs, the temples, and the palaces—the Early
Christian, Byzantine, Romanesque, Gothic, Renaissance, and
Baroque churches, the temples and palaces of Imperial
Rome, the Egyptian temples, the Babylonian ziggurats, the
Hindu, Chinese, and Mexican temples—were conceived not
only as places serving definite utilitarian purposes, in the

broadest sense, and artful configurations of volumes and spaces, but, moreover, as iconic signs, or symbols, or images (by *image* I understand here something intermediate between an iconic sign and a symbol) of objects other than themselves—of the Universe, of Heaven conceived as the seat of the gods or the God, or of the community of the faithful. In other words, they had a semantic or symbolic character.

Not only the buildings as a whole, but also the particular parts of buildings, often had an iconic or symbolic character. The columns or consoles were formed as human figures (the "caryatids" and the "atlantes"), the gargoyles of Gothic cathedrals as animal jaws. The pillars of the Hindu temple at Tanjore have the shape of horses risen on their hind legs. The dome was usually conceived both as a likeness of the sky and as a symbol of Heaven. The towers, the gate, the porch usually had a symbolic meaning.

The ground plans of buildings were also often conceived as iconic signs or symbols. The ground plan of the Romanesque and Gothic churches in the shape of a Latin cross, *in modum crucis,* was above all a schematic iconic sign of Christ crucified. The Italian Renaissance dreamt of a round temple, mainly under the influence of Neoplatonic philosophy, in which the circle was the perfect figure and a symbol of "the unity, infinite essence, the uniformity and injustice of God" (palladio).[6] There are Baroque chapels on the ground plan of a triangle—the symbol of the Holy Trinity. Escorial, the palace and St. Laurence monastery, was built on its ground plan in the form of a grill, the tool of the martyrdom and the attribute of this saint. In the Chinese and Indonesian temples, the ground plan in the shape of a square symbolizes Earth, the ground plan in the shape of a circle symbolizes Heaven.[7]

The traditional view that architecture is an asemantic art should therefore be abandoned. Similarly, musical compositions are not always asemantic. In the history of music a great variety of forms and types of musical works have been produced. We may distinguish here at least five groups: *1)* strictly asemantic works of purely instrumental music, as, for instance, some symphonies by Haydn or Mozart that are only artful structures of tones, with an emotional coloring; 2) works with a vague symbolism, like the symphonies of Beethoven; 3) so-called program music, which acquires a definite meaning only in connection with some literary text—the title of the composition or the author's pronouncement—as in the symphonic poems by Berlioz or Richard Strauss; 4) various forms of vocal and vocally instrumental music like song, oratory, cantata, opera—forms in which a musical composition is coupled with a literary text, that is, a semantic structure, a complex of conventional signs, like some compositions of Baroque court and church music, the Gregorian Cantus Firmus of the medieval polyphony, or the works of the Hindu, old Chinese, Japanese, and Indonesian music. All these works are fully understandable only to initiated listeners belonging to definite social or national circles and acquainted with the meaning of these symbols and conventional elements.[8] Finally, in the works of program music, but not only in them, there are sometimes enclaves of an iconic character, passages imitating, usually in a more or less stylized way, real sounds: the voices of birds, the murmur of a brook, the tumult of a market.

The traditional view that architecture and music are non-representational, asemantic arts was challenged by recent investigations on the history of these arts and by a more intimate acquaintance with non-European architecture and music. The traditional view that painting and sculpture are representational, semantic arts was overthrown by new developments in these arts.

Since about 1870 we can watch in one of the main currents of Western art a process that in a most general way may be described as "desemantization." This process had as it were two aspects. On the one hand, the stimulative elements of pictures and sculptures—colors, lines, shapes, texture—began to play an increasingly important role. On the other hand, there took place a progressive degradation of the representative elements of these works. Arrangements of colored areas, the rhythms of lines and shapes became and finally ceased to be the chief subject matter of a picture.

They became small, insignificant, indistinct, often lost in the immensity of a landscape, or they disappeared completely. This process led first, in late Impressionism, Fauvism, and Cubism, to the suppression of the representative elements and subsequently, in the years 1910/20, in the works by Kandinsky, Delaunay, Kupka, Mondrian, Arp, Gabo, Pevsner, and others, to their total elimination. There arose a "nonobjective" (called also "abstract," "pure," or "absolute"), or, in other words, asemantic painting and sculpture. Since that time objective, semantic painting and sculpture one the one hand, and nonobjective, asemantic painting and sculpture on the other hand have been two great realms of painting and sculpture, each split into many currents and trends.

For all these reasons the simple traditional classification of arts into semantic and asemantic ones is no longer tenable. Is it possible, with all the media the artists have at their disposal, to create both semantic and asemantic works of art?

This idea lies at the basis of a system of arts construed in 1947 by Etienne Souriau. Souriau distinguishes seven principal sensory qualities (*sensibles propres, qualia*) that may be used in the arts: line, volume, color, luminosity, movement, articulated sound, musical sound. Each of these sensory qualities gives birth to two arts: to a nonrepresentative art or an "art of the first degree," and to a representative art or an "art of the first degree" and to a representative or an "art of the second degree" (these terms have no evaluative significance here). Line gives rise to the art of arabesque and the art of drawing; volume produces the art of architecture and of sculpture; color gives rise to pure painting and representative painting; luminosity, on the one hand, yields the art of lighting and luminous projections and, on the other hand, wash drawing, photography, and cinema; movement gives rise to dance and pantomime, articulated sound to pure prosody and poetic literature. Finally, musical sound produces music, including dramatic and descriptive music. These seven couples of arts Souriau places within a circle divided into seven sectors. That of the nonrepresentative arts occupies the inside parts of these sectors, and the corresponding representative arts occupy the outside ones.[9]

It is not difficult to criticize this ingenious but rather superficial system of arts. This has been done in detail by Thomas Munro. Munro points out that Souriau, in order to construe his pattern, is obliged to connect together rather different fields, for instance, cinema and wash drawing, and to separate fields usually treated as a whole, for instance, drawing and wash drawing. Further, Munro observes, we meet each of these principal sensuous qualities in many arts: color, for example, occurs not only in painting, but also in sculpture, architecture, dance, photography, cinema, lighting, arabesque. Finally, the predominance of this or another sensuous quality in an art depends to a considerable degree upon the style of a certain school or a certain artist: color predominates in late Venetian and still more in Impressionist painting, while Botticelli or Ingres emphasize line.

Munro admits, however, that "the Souriau system deserves credit for having emphasized an important fact, often ignored—that within each realm of art . . . there is a place for non-representative as well as representative forms." According to Munro, "the term 'non-representative' can be applied only to particular works of art and to certain types and styles of art; not to whole arts. . . . It is misleading to speak of 'the representative arts' with the implication that any arts are wholly non-representative. . . . One can say more correctly that certain arts such as poetry, painting, and sculpture, are more strongly or frequently representative; while other, such as architecture, furniture, and music, are less strongly or frequently representative."[10] I should think that within many realms of art there is a place both for asemantic and semantic forms, but not within all. It is difficult to realize a purely asemantic poem or theatrical spectacle.

Asemantic and the semantic works of art may be connected together in the most various ways. A building may be decorated with statues, reliefs, mosaics, or murals representing men, animals, or plants. A poem and a melody make up a song; a play and a musical composition make up an opera. Works of art using conventional signs and works of art using iconic signs may also be connected in various ways. For instance, a poem and a set of drawings or prints may make up an illustrated book.

III. The Recording of the Works of Art by Means of Conventional Signs

1. Poetry and Writing

Some works of art may be recorded, "noted" by means of conventional signs. Poetic works may be fixed and transmitted by means of writing, a system of signs devised for noting the expressions of a language that is itself another system of signs. The invention of writing was, as is well known, one of the turning points in the history of mankind. It has also had various and important implications both for the reception of poetic works and for poetic creation. Let us sketch at least some of them.

The recording of poetic works and the multiplication of these records, first by hand, later by printing press, made possible an entirely new way of communing with these works. Until then such communing came through the medium of the ear, by hearing. But now it was effected through the medium of the eye, by reading—first by an oral reading, later by a silent one.

The sound aspect of a poetic work is at its hearing immediately perceived and its oral reading reproduced by the reader in a more or less precise way. A rapid reading usually leads to an incomplete reception of the sound aspect of a poetic work and thus to an impoverishment of the aesthetic experience of the receiver. Some late nineteenth- and early twentieth-century writers complained about the decline in sensitivity to the sound aspect of poetry caused by a communing with it exclusively through the medium of eye. In 1886 Nietzsche wrote in "Jenseits von Gut und Böse": "Der Deutsche liest nicht laut, nicht für's Ohr, sondern bloss mit den Augen: er hat seine Ohren dabei in's Schubfach gelegt. Der antike Mensch las, wenn er las—es geschah selten genug—sich selbst Etwas vor, und zwar mit lauter Stimme; man wunderte sich, wenn Jemand leise las und fragte sich insgeheim nach Gründen. Mit lauter Stimme: das will sagen, mit all den Schwellungen, Biegungen, Umschlägen des Tons und Wechseln des Tempos, an denen die antike öffentliche Welt ihre Freude hatte" (p. 250). Some years later, in 1891, Oscar Wilde expressed a similar thought:

Since the introduction of printing (. . .), there has been a tendency in literature to appeal more and more to the eye, and less and less to the ear, which is really the sense which, from the standpoint of pure art, it should seek to please, and by whose canons of pleasure it should abide always. We, in fact, have made writing a definite mode of composition and have treated it as a form of elaborate design. The Greek, upon the other hand, regarded writing simply as a method of chronicling. Their test was always the spoken word in its musical and metrical relations.[11]

In 1926 Lascelles Abercrombie, poet and theorist of poetry, stated:

Poetry consists absolutely of the word spoken and heard: the printed word must always be frankly the symbol of articulated sound. We must hear what the poet has to say; if we are reading ourselves, we must hear it mentally. Otherwise we shall miss half his technique; and that means, we shall miss half of what he is trying to express. . . . Mental hearing is never quite as good as actual hearing; the sound of poetry is always more impressive and expressive when it is actually sounding than when it is imaginary.[12]

If there are possible losses when one is communing with a poetic work through the eye, there are some benefits as well. Let us quote Abercrombie once more:

We read poetry to ourselves more often than hear it aloud; and poets, consciously or not, have taken advantage of this. Poetry will always take advantage of anything that will increase or refine its expressive power. . . . Eye-language is a much subtler and nimbler affair than ear-language. We can get, in printed language, in the appeal through the eye, a more instant and more certain apprehension of fine associations of ideas, of delicate shades of significance, than we can ever get through the ear. One of the chief differences between such an art as Homer's and such an art as Dante's or Milton's is that Homer never thinks of any appeal but through the ear; whereas Dante and Milton both know their verses will meet with eyes as well as ears. Their art is certainly not greater than Homer's, but it has finer modulations of significance. The thing is, that Dante and Milton, like every other printed or written poet, take advantage of the eye-appeal without losing the ear-appeal.[13]

Since the invention of writing and printing the poets began to introduce into their works elements destined, not for the potential listener, but for the potential reader. They explored possibilities offered by writing or printing for the enriching or refining of aesthetic experience. Owing to the graphic arrangements of a paragraph in prose or a stanza in poetry, a glance at a written or printed page teaches us at once, even before we read it, that we have in front of us prose or verses, a sonnet or a poem in octaves. We enjoy the fine regular structure of a sonnet and we grasp this structure more by the eye than by the ear.

Some artistic devices are possible only in written or printed poetic works. The conventions concerning the use of capital and small letters vary in diverse languages and periods. A writer can elicit peculiar effects by using capital and small letters in conformity with current conventions (the English eighteenth- and early nineteenth-century poets used to capitalize the personifications of mental states or abstractions in order to enhance their emotional coloring) or by deliberately breaking these conventions (the German poet, Stefan George, did not capitalize the beginning of nouns, contrary to an ancient tradition of German language). A writer may employ italics, varied spacing, and the like for definite effects. He may use copious and subtly differentiated punctuation marks or he may, as some modern poets do, omit them entirely (the reasons for this omission may be various: awareness of the insufficiency of the traditional punctuation; a wish to leave the articulation of a poem to the reader and, by the same token, to give him greater freedom in its interpretation).

In Egyptian, Chinese, Japanese, and Arabic poetry, the graphic aspect of poems engraved on stone, written or painted on parchment, paper, or silk, their "calligraphy," was an essential component of the poems themselves. In the Western world at the turn of the century the Art Nouveau artists laid great emphasis on the visual aspect of a printed page, and tried to elicit peculiar decorative effects from it. In the early twentieth century, Arno Holz in Germany and Stanisław Wyspiański in Poland disposed the lines of a lyric poem or the dialogues of a drama symmetrically on both sides of a vertical axis.

Let us mention again some frolics or jokes made possible by writing or printing, namely, poems whose lines are arranged in the shape of diverse objects: from the medieval *carmina figurata* in the form of a bottle throughout the verse by Rabelais, or the sonnet by John Donne in the shape of an altar, to the "Calligrammes" by Apollinaire.

The invention of writing has had still other implications for poetic creation. Prose works of greater length have become possible and new literary genres, such as the novel, nonstage drama, and poetic letter, could arise.

Since the invention of writing, even the poet's work on a small lyric poem is unthinkable without the aid of manuscript: The drafts of many eminent poets with their numerous modifications and corrections bear eloquent witness to this. Balzac and Proust were often stimulated by the view of the proofs of their books, and made profuse supplements to the initial version. An outstanding Polish poet, Józef Czechowicz (d. 1939), confessed that the most intensive part of his work on a poem began only when this poem had been typed.

2. Music and Musical Notation

The implications of the invention of musical notation for music were no less important, although they were of another kind. There are some relevant differences between writing and musical notation. Writing is a system of conventional signs originally invented for practical purposes and used for the recording of poetic works. Musical notation was invented specifically for the recording of musical works. Writing is a system of conventional signs to record works that are themselves signs; musical notation is a system of conventional signs devised to record works that, for the most part, are not signs. Writing fixes and makes possible the reproduction of the sounds of language only insofar as it is indispensable for the distinguishing of the smallest sound units having a definite meaning (the phonemes). Musical notation fixes in a much fuller way the sound structure of a musical composition: notes, the pitch of the particular tones, their duration and volume, the tempo of their succession, the instrument by which a certain tone shall be produced, and so on.[14]

In connection with the differences between writing and musical notation, there were different implications of the invention of writing for poetry and the invention of musical notation for music. Just as, owing to the invention of writing and printing, it has become possible to commune with poetic works by reading their written or printed texts, so, owing to the invention of musical notation, it has become possible, in principle, to commune with musical works by "reading" their written or printed scores. Communing with musical compositions by the "reading" of their scores is, however, more difficult than communing with poetic works by the reading of their texts. It requires not only a thorough acquaintance with the musical notation itself, but also a good ear, a reliable musical memory, a capacity to imagine the various harmonies, motifs, themes, rhythms, and timbres of diverse instruments. The invention of musical notation did not, therefore, revolutionize the way of communing with musical compositions to the extent that the invention of writing did in communing with poetic works. Hearing remains the main way of communing with musical works. Communing with them through the medium of sight by "reading," is, at least until now, restricted to a relatively narrow circle of professionals. Nevertheless, some composers, for instance, the sixteenth-century Netherland masters of polyphonic style or Bach in the first half of the eighteenth century, sometimes introduced into their scores things intended more for the eye than for the ear.[15]

The implications for the development of Western music of the invention of musical notation, however, particularly of the perfected mensural notation, were of utmost importance. This impact was brilliantly demonstrated by Max Weber in his paper "Die rationalen und soziologischen Grundlagen der Musik" (1924). According to Weber, the invention of mensural notation mainly contributed to the magnificent development of Western music, both polyphonic and monophonic, gave Occidental musical culture an immense superiority over the no-less-intensive musical cultures of Ancient Greece or Japan. Without mensural notation it is impossible either to create, to transmit, or to reproduce a fairly complicated work of modern music. Without such notation a more complicated work of modern music can nowhere and in no way exist, even as an internal possession of its creator.[16]

IV. The Reproducing of the Works of Art by Means of Iconic Signs

Some works of art may be reproduced by means of iconic signs.

A work of visual art—a painting, a statue, a building—may be reproduced by means of a drawing or a painting. A statue may also be reproduced by means of a cast, a building by means of a model.

Since the invention of various graphic techniques—of woodcut in the fifteenth century, of engraving in the sixteenth century, of lithography and wood-engraving in the nineteenth century—it has become possible to multiply the drawn or painted reproductions of the works of visual arts. Owing to the invention of black-and-white photography about 1830, and later of color photography, and to the invention of the photochemical methods of reproduction, it has become possible not only to obtain far more accurate reproductions of works of the visual arts, but also to produce these reproductions in any number of copies.

Since the invention of the phonograph in 1877 it has further become possible to record and to reproduce the executions of musical compositions and the recitations of poetic works. Since the invention of film in 1895 it has, moreover, become possible to reproduce the performances of theatrical spectacles and dances. The invention of the sound film about 1928, and later of the color film, considerably contributed to the improvement of these reproductions.

For several decades we have, moreover, had at our disposal powerful means to transmit the iconic signs of works of art. The reproductions of the executions of musical compositions or of the recitations of poetic works may be broadcast. Photographs of works of the visual arts, films representing the performances of dances or of theatrical spectacles may be transmitted by television. Owing to these transmissions, the reproductions of works of art can be made accessible to an almost unlimited number of spectators or listeners.

A reproduction of a work of art may serve various purposes. It may be used as a source of information or as an instrument of scholarly investigation. It may give an aesthetic delight and as such it may be a powerful means of aesthetic education and, like all works of art, a generator of various social ties.

Now, it is difficult to deny that even the best reproduction of a picture or the best reproduction of the execution of a musical composition from a "high-fidelity" record reproduces the original work in a somewhat, if even slightly, deformed and therefore degraded way. Something is always lost in a reproduction. There is therefore a danger that the spectator or listener will judge the original work, not on the basis of an acquaintance with this work itself, but on the basis of an acquaintance with a reproduction of this work—that the reproduction will, as it were, place itself between the original work and the receiver.

In spite of these deficiencies, however, the impact of the reproductions of the works of art and of the transmissions of these reproductions has been immense. The new techniques of recording and reproducing works of art and of transmitting these reproductions have surrounded the sphere of works of art with a sphere of the reproductions of the works of art and a sphere of the transmissions of these reproductions. These reproductions and transmissions give spectators and listeners today an incomparable chance to get acquainted with works of visual arts, musical compositions, theatrical spectacles or dances, with which a direct communing is for them, for this or for some other reason, impossible. They make it possible to get acquainted with works of art of various nations, continents, and epochs— one may say, with the artistic heritage of mankind.

André Malraux has called the totality of the reproductions of works of visual arts an "imaginary museum." In a similar way we may call the totality of the records of musical compositions an "imaginary concert hall" and the totality of the films representing theatrical spectacles and dances an "imaginary stage." This imaginary museum, this imaginary concert hall, and this imaginary stage today bring in touch with the works of art of various nations, countries, and periods, not only ordinary spectators and listeners, but the painters, sculptors, musicians, dancers, actors or stage-managers as well. They enlarge their horizons and stimulate their imagination. They foster the exchange and interaction of forms, contents, and techniques on a heretofore-unknown scale. One may quote Japanese or Indonesian painters who never saw an original picture by Matisse, Modigliani, or Klee, but have been stimulated by the reproductions of their works. Sometimes this may lead to a superficial eclecticism; sometimes, however, it may prove a valuable source of inspiration.

This is not the only benefit creators may draw from reproductions of works of art. The new techniques of recording and reproducing the executions of musical compositions, the recitations of poetic works, the performances of theatrical spectacles and dances, often in various interpretation, have made possible a minute examination, analysis, and comparison of these executions, recitations, and performances, and this examination has become a help of great worth to executioners of musical works and composers, to reciters, to actors and stage-managers, to dancers and choreographers.

V. Conclusion

Archaic man believed in the magic power of words, that is, conventional signs, and of likenesses, that is, iconic signs. He was convinced that somebody who knew the name of a person or thing had command over him or it. He was similarly convinced that somebody who mutilated a carved or painted effigy of a person, by the same token mutilated or destroyed the person himself. Today we believe no more in the magic power of likenesses or words. But words and likenesses, the conventional and the iconic signs, signs in general, are still for us something miraculous. They allow us to make present the absent and the past, to transcend what is "here" and "now." By means of signs we communicate our thoughts; we perpetuate and transmit them through space and time. Incessantly we perceive and form signs, we "send" and "receive" them. We live and move in the realm of signs, we are enveloped by a "semiosphere." Without signs there would be no culture, no human world, no Man.

There have been many attempts to define Man. For the medieval schoolmen he was *animal rationale*. Rabelais saw the specific feature of Man in his ability to laugh. For the following centuries Man was successively *homo sapiens* (Linnaeus), *homo faber* (Bergson), *homo ludens* (Huizingo). One modern philosopher characterized Man as the being that transcends the limits (*der Grenzüberschreiter:* Simmel), another as the being that is able to say "no" (*der Neinsager:* Scheler). Ernst Cassirer defined Man as *animal symbolicum*. In a similar spirit I would suggest that Man be conceived as the "sign-maker."[17] Man is not only a sign-maker, but also an art-maker. The arts have made human life richer and deeper. It is an attractive task both for semiotician and for the theorist of art to explore the manifold connections between these two great realms of human creativeness—the world of arts and the world of signs.

NOTES

1. The term "the arts" is often used also in a narrower sense, restricted to painting, sculpture, architecture, and the like (sometimes called also the "visual" or "plastic arts"). Here the term "the arts" will be used always in the broader sense.

2. On the history of the concept of "the arts": W. Tatarkiewicz, "Art and poetry, a contribution to the history of ancient aesthetics," *Studia Philosophica* 2, (Leopoli [Lvov], 1937):367–419. T. Munro, *The Arts and Their Interrelations* (New York, 1951), chap. 2.

3. T. Lipps "Ästhetik," in *Kultur der Gegenwart,* vol. 1 (Leipzig, 1907), p. 6. M. Dessoir, *Ästhetik und allgemeine Kunstwissenschaft* 2¹ Aufl. (Munich, 1925), vol. 3, pp. 390–94.

4. Quoted by M. T(assart) in *Dictionaire du ballet moderne* (Paris, 1957), p. 211.

5. C. Sachs, *Eine Weltgeschichte des Tänzes* (Berlin, 1933).

6. A. Pallasio, *I quattro libri dell'architettura* (Venice, 1570), vol. 4, p. 2.

7. Main investigations on the semantic and symbolic elements of architecture: H. Sedlmayr, *Die Entstehung der Kathedrale* (Zurich, 1950); O. Von Simson, *The Gothic Cathedral* (New York, 1956); R. Wittkower, "Architectural Principles in the Age of Humanism," *Studies of the Warburg Institute* 19 (London, 1949); E. Baldwin Smith, *The Dome. A Study in the History of Ideas* (Princeton, 1950); L. Hautecoeur, *Mystique et architecture —le symbolisme du cercle et de la coupole* (Paris: A. et J. Picard, 1954).

8. On the conventional signs in Baroque music: M. Bukofzer, "Allegory in Baroque Music," *Journal of the Warburg and Courtauld Institutes* 3 (London, 1939-40). On the conventional and symbolic elements of the Gregorian Cantus Firmus and of Asian music: Z. Lissa, "Evolution of Musical Perception," *Journal of Aesthetics and Art Criticism* 24 (1964–65):285.

9. E. Souriau, *La correspondance des arts. Eléments d'esthétique comparée* (Paris, 1947), pp. 73–113.

10. T. Munro, pp. 205, 408.

11. O. Wilde, *Intentions* (1891). Reprinted in O. Wilde, *The Works,* ed. G. F. Maire (London and Glasgow, 1948), pp. 955–56.

12. L. Abercrombie, *The Theory of Poetry* (New York, 1926), pp. 118, 119.

13. *Ibid.,* pp. 118, 119.

14. An essential feature of modern musical notation is its "semantic field" in the form of pentagram. The pitch of a tone is here indicated by the place of a small oval on a certain line or between certain lines. Cf. M. Wallis, "La notion de champ sémantique et son application à la théorie de l'art," *Sciences de l'Art,* Numéro spécial (Paris, 1966), pp. 3–8. Musical notation has yet to be investigated in a comprehensive way from the semiotic point of view. I, for my part, know only one paper dealing with it from this point of view, namely the paper "The Description of a System of Musical Notations," by M. Langleben, published in *Works on Semiotics 2, Transactions of the Tartu State University,* no. 181 (Tartu, 1965), pp. 258–73, in Russian; an English summary, p. 354.

15. Manfred Bukofzer writes about a composition by Bach: "In the cantata 'Hercules am Scheidewege' the words 'for the snakes which tried to seize me with their lullaby' are represented by winding figures in the bass. To be sure, one hears this rise and fall, but the allegory of winding appears in its clearest shape only in the musical notation." Bukofzer, pp. 12, 13. Thomas Mann in his novel *Doktor Faustus* (1948), lets a personage invented by him, Wendell Kretschmer, give a lecture under the title "Music and Eye" and summarizes one of the main theses of this lecture in the following way: "Wie der Title besagt, sprach unser Redner darin von seiner Kunst, insofern sie sich an den Gesichtssin, oder doch auch an diesen wendet, was sie . . . schon damit tue, dass man sie aufschreibe: durch die Notierung also, die Tonschrift. . . ." The lecturer tried to demonstrate "wie manche Redensart des Musikanten-Jargons garnicht aus dem Akustischen, sondern aus dem Visuellen, dem Notenbild abgeleitet set. . . . Zu allen Zeiten hätten die Komponisten in ihre Satzschriften manches hineingeheimnisst, was mehr fur das lesende Auge, als für das Ohr bestimmit gewesen." T. Mann, *Gesammelte Werke* (Berlin, 1955), vol. 6, pp. 84, 85.

16. M. Weber, "Die rationalen und soziologischen Grundlagen der Musik" (1924). Reprinted in M. Weber, *Wirtschaft und Gesellschaft,* 4 Aufl. (Tubingen, 1956), pp. 911, 913.

17. My concept of "sign" is narrower than Cassirer's concept of "symbol."

9

ON MIMETISM AND REALISM IN THE ARTS*

Stefan Morawski

Translated from French by
LEE BAXANDALL

Stefan Morawski was born in Krakow in 1921. He studied in the Departments of Philosophy and English Philology at the underground University of Warsaw from 1942 to 1945. He received his M.A. in Philosophy in 1946. After the war he studied further in English Philology at University of Krakow and at Sheffield from 1946 to 1947, where he received a diploma. He received his Ph.D. at the University of Warsaw in 1948. His dissertation was on English aesthetics of the eighteenth century. He held a research professorship in the section of art theory at the State Institute of Arts, Warsaw, from 1952 to 1958. From 1960 to 1968 he held the Chair of Aesthetics at the University of Warsaw. In 1955 he received the docent's degree for studies on twentieth-century Marxist and non-Marxist aesthetics, and in 1964 he became full professor.

His major publications include: Essays on Marxist Aesthetics, *1951;* The Development of Aesthetic Ideas from Herder to Heine *(German Art Theories), 1957;* Studies in British, French and Polish Aesthetic Thought of the 18th and 19th Centuries, *1961;* Polish Art

---

* This is a part of the author's book on André Malraux's aesthetic doctrine, *The Absolute and Form,* translated from the original French.

Theories of the Romantic Period *(Anthology); preface and commentaries with E. Grabska, 1962;* Between Tradition and the Vision of Future *(on Recent Soviet Aesthetics), 1964;* The Absolute and Form *(on Malraux's Aesthetic Views against the Background of Existentialist Aesthetics), 1966; and* Assoluto e Forma *(an enlarged and revised version of the Polish original), 1971. His articles in scholarly journals have been primarily on theoretical and historical problems of Marxist aesthetics.*

Marxist aestheticians are not unanimous in their understanding of the term realism. Among the opinions now current, all maintain, however, that realism constitutes a *transformation* of reality—a transformation, since it entails the selection of phenomena, the extraction of the characteristic and typical features of reality, and the representation of these in a "condensed" manner that makes their meaning evident. And a transformation, since—within limits determined by, and with the aid of, a distinct subject matter—it organizes the formal structure that absorbs the other values, *i.e.,* the values *de fond* (of content), bestowing on them an autonomy in relation to the world of their real referents. The artistic operation provides then a double domination of the world: psychosocial and technico-material. For this reason, realism is synonymous with the notion I have termed elsewhere (in controversy with A. Malraux): *creationism.*[1] Only when realism is reduced to the particular creative method of the nineteenth century and the formular procedures that accompanied it, does *creationism,* in view of the ensemble of the artistic attitudes and procedures of the twentieth century, appear opposed to realism. In present-day Marxist aesthetics, more and more scholars are abandoning this anachronistic notion of realism.[2] The artist, as it is now understood, does not imitate *natura naturata,* but rather more a *natura naturans, i.e.,* he contributes to creating the social reality while at the same time being created by it.

Regarded as an artistic category, realism provides a

complex problem. This cannot be the occasion for a thorough analysis of the question; but I should like at least to sketch my point of view. I regard what I wrote on this topic in 1963 as inadequate.[3] I now believe that the following assertions are essential. The problem of realism cannot be correctly posed unless one at the same time defines what he means by mimetism, the more so if, at times, one virtually reduces realism to mimetism. The two categories both refer art to exterior reality and invoke a definite relationship of analogy (of correspondence). It does not seem to me, however, that a proposition respecting mimesis in the manner of Democritus can be persuasive, since it is here less a matter of a reproduction than it is of a production, a construction of modeling. True, the Democritan theme concerns an imitation of nature's activity and not of its content. But when Lévi-Strauss (*La Pensée sauvage*) speaks of a portrait by Clouet in terms of a "reduced model," in this instance one can surely deem the structuring activity a mimetic activity, since it treats of a definite external system of relationships, which is simplified and transformed in the process of creation. By mimetism, then, I shall mean a relationship of analogy that in some way reconstructs the existing elements, their totality and their internal connections, within the ordered universe, the space and time requirements of artistic structure. And realism, by contrast—if we follow out our conclusion, takes into account a distinctly modern aesthetic tradition, and stresses the distinction between a philosophical perception of art and its strictly historiographical perception —realism is a special category that invokes a relationship of analogy, decisively determined neither by the form and exterior aspects of objects, nor by the rigor of the course of events—even if this is acutely conveyed—nor by particular linkages of objects, persons, or events, but rather by *typical moments*—i.e., for realism the evocation of certain essential aspects of reality proves decisive. The essential analogical relationship obviously does not exclude other criteria, but the latter are not indispensable to constituting realism in the artistic sense. As for mimetism, it has at least two manifestations: *a*) as the reproduction of external asspects and the form of objects or of persons, and as well of particular relationships existing somehow discernibly among these; *b*) as an apprehension of the polyvalent, open, and contingent structure of the world we inhabit. Due to the continuum running from nonfigurative to figurative art, we are able to speak of the quasi-mimetism or the part-mimetism of many avant-garde art works of the twentieth century. Similarly, between mimetic art and the art I here regard as realist, there exists a realm of intermediary phenomena. Mimesis, as realism too, may be termed an artistic category only in the sense, and only to the extent, that a represented segment of the world is linked, more or less intimately and organically, with a subject matter and an ensemble of expressive means. In a word, we are not speaking of an interpolated element that constitutes within a given work of art a distinct cognitive structure; for this meaning-structure (representation) does not itself become constituted and eventuate if it does not simultaneously embrace the elements stemming from that fundamental source of a given art which we term its specific "language." Reproduction, if we understand the term literally, precludes the bringing into being of a work of art. In film and television too, one never sees the pure and simple reproduction of an existing reality. The degree of modification and transformation (in reference to the exterior world) of the elements and of their ensembles increases proportionately as one turns away from a mimesis based on forms and external configurations and draws near the semi-mimetism of avant-garde art on the one hand and realism on the other. In either case, a specific deformation of the directly sensuous reality occurs, but the deformation is effected according to different principles. Granting that every artist—to use the idiom of Ingarden— transforms the potential raw material of a work into artistic matter, then the semi-mimetist transforms, blurs, and trims both the existing elements and the relations among them, while the realist condenses and selects these. Both processes transform reality, but where the former moves away from it, the other tries to plumb it. Mimetic elements then are distributed unequally through the immense scope of the arts,

and, given that the history of art offers the proof of a reproduction of reality to be found equally in architecture and
the applied arts, one would be hard pressed to defend the
thesis that considers the bonds between art and reality of
small importance. Moreover—and this must be forcefully
stressed—we do not refer here to a mode of presentation;
the success of a copying of reality is not better described
than in the terms of the technical means of its execution,
and it is in this sense that one can speak of, say, the maker
of a museum of wax figures as a virtuoso. Nor do we refer
to what is termed the beauty of natural objects, or of an
ensemble of events or elements to which one should attribute
aesthetic value owed simply to the nature of their being.
Mimesis, in this case, would entail above all the discovery
of such objects and their most efficient transposition to the
field of the work. I reject such a possibility, for I deem this
so-called beauty of nature to be a projection of artistic
values, *i.e.,* I consider the aesthetic values discovered in
nature to be an effect of the optics of culture, while otherwise I look upon mimetic values rather as artifacts, as a
stratum that constitutes a fictive world, thus producing at
most the illusion that one is responding to reality itself. The
degree of fidelity to this reality defines the strength of the
illusion. The transitional scale here reaches from the art
that actualizes the very rhythm of life—thus from television
spectacle and the art of film *à la camera vérité* or Godard—
over to allusive works, whose relation to reality in general
or its essential aspects is not really discernible, *e.g.,* many
works by Klee on the one hand, and by Beckmann on the
other. However, in works of this type, and also in those
with a high degree of fidelity to a specific reality, one cannot
help noting a striking antinomy. Without fail, such works
are constituted by a system of signs that in some fashion
asserts two simultaneous references: one of these interior
and closed, the other, exterior and open. The resulting tension between the semantic-structural plane and the structural-
semiotic plane, *i.e.,* between the form and content of the
work on the one hand, and the content referring to the
sociocultural system on the other—between the *signifiant*

and *signifié*—seems to characterize all works of the mimetic and realistic type. This antinomy in found alongside a tension between the virtual world that is represented and the real world that the former refers to.

What we have just now said, together with the earlier remarks on the apparent opposition of realism and creationism, suggests that in fact we are faced with a philosophical problem. Mimesis and realism are categories arising at once from art and from cognition; what must concern us here is a specific truth bearing upon reality—not reducible to truth in the logical and scientific sense. The first question that presents itself, then, is: may one speak in general of a strictly unequivocal reality? In Poland, the conception of the plurality of realities was defended at the beginning of the twenties by Leon Chwistek. He demonstrated that, inasmuch as our reflections bear reference to things and events, to impressions, or to ideas, and we base on one of these elements our conception of the world, accordingly different philosophical viewpoints appear, with the artistic tendencies that parallel them. Chwistek further added that in various periods of history, owing to the perspectives of cognition then dominant, different philosophical and artistic attitudes held first place. Chwistek was influenced by the *Principia Mathematica* of Russell and Whitehead. We find ourselves here at the source of some present-day theories of semiotic models, which assume a conventionalist mode of thought. Is there in truth no empirical premise that might justify us in having recourse to a single notion (model) of reality? Is reality nothing but the projection of a particular methodological strategy? Observing events and things concretely, do we each time interpret works of art in a different way, as mimetic or nonmimetic, realist or nonrealist, and so on, according to the cultural stereotypes and assumptions raised by them, as, for example, E. Gombrich maintains in *Art and Illusion* (1961)?

I reject the notion of an unalloyed "mirror reflection" of reality, which excludes the intermediary role of a historically specific social *praxis;* I equally agree with those who hold that the analysis of the relation of art to the extra-artistic

world cannot be based on the Gestaltist concept of the "innocent eye." Still, one must not thereby infer that the idea of
the real is reducible to mere conventions. This sort of reduction would seem especially illusory if we consider certain
aspects of the category of *mimesis*. Thus, for example, a
red contrasted with a green, the rounding of a face, something set in the background in relation to objects in the
foreground, something grandiose, and the like—these are
some data of perception that we should respect when the
content of the work of art is treated as the analogon of
reality. It could immediately be replied to me that such an
atomization of the acts of cognition is an anachronistic
interpretation; no perception occurs in isolation; we always
see with the optics of a determinate mode of knowledge;
the exterior world always is a given "world for us" and not
a world in itself; the pure or contrasted colors either are
associated with, or are directly interpreted as, symbols within
the framework of a determinate code; the depth or the
absence of relief in a painting is, in accord with the cognitive
attitudes of a particular epoch, considered the most consistent with natural vision; and so on. The line of argument
is accurate, no doubt at all. It accents the semiotic and historical conditionings that—let us note well!—have to be
considered in all contact with art, as we analyze the process
of creation and its results. This convincing argumentation
does not preclude, however, a notion of reality (in the macro-
scopic sense) that will allow us to discern the iconic sign for
the color blue or for a horse. One may perfectly well emphasize—as has been done probingly by both P. Francastel in
Peinture et société (1951) and the Polish painter and art
theoretician W. Strzemiński in *Teoria widzenia* (Theory of
Vision, 1958)—that the visual consciousness is a historically
variable element and that the *costruzione legitima* of Alberti, say, cannot define for everyone and for all time the
artistic vision (and the reactions, which parallel it, of the
public). Nonetheless, a reference to "near-far" spatial
structure—translated virtually to the work of art, thanks
to methods of rendering perspective—possesses validity as
a reference of mimetic structure. For the fact that in an-

cient Persian culture, for example, or in our contemporary culture, the dominant code sanctions an aperspectival space in painting, and that for this reason even the moderately prepared spectator finds no difficulty in responding to this mode of communication, implies in no way that a table, say, and a person seated before or behind this table, the two elements being superimposed and perceived in the same plane, will be congruous with a perception seeking in the work the confirmation of real relationships. Gombrich, in the work cited, is indeed inclined to recognize—doubtless contrary to his own theory—that Constable's paintings more nearly approximate nature in England than do paintings by children who freely deform the same motif. We may note that Edward Fry—I am familiar with his volume on Cubism in the German translation of 1966—by reproducing photos of the houses at L'Estaque painted by Braque in 1908, and a view of Horta de San Juan known to us from a Picasso painting of 1909, irrefutably proved that mimetic values, even where their fidelity to the original is attenuated appreciably, do have a determinate and verifiable point of reference. Matters stand otherwise for a characteristic that certain film theoreticians *e.g.,* Kracauer and Bazin, stress, and which we may term authenticity, *i.e.,* the fact of conveying entirely the impression that reality itself is being contacted. Where mimesis, whether understood as the reproduction of exterior aspects and the form of given objects and their directly given relationships, or as the reproduction of the content and extension of a given occurrence, can be related to generically given cognitive faculties and to an entrenched mode of comprehending reality, we may observe —equally so, as concerns authenticity—the decisive, historically formed role of a mode of interpreting the structure of the whole of reality. To accept the concept that reality authentically is polyvalent, constituted of contingent events, and chaotic, that we strive to give it a meaning, and that this activity of creating significance is a relentless effort of man to rescue his life from defeat, would seem to be a philosophical (ideological) deed. Contemporary creative work based on these premises (the films of Antonioni, for exam-

ple) may appear mimetic or realist to those who comprehend the actual world in this manner. But if other principles
are admitted at the outset, this work will appear anti-
mimetic and anti-realist. This notion of authenticity is ambiguous. But it is equally possible to relate it—and this
seems to have been the intent of Bazin and Kracauer—to
some precise fragment of reality, wherein appear some
elements that are important and others that are not, some
out of which we shall make a totality endowed with meaning
and others which will disappear forever, borne on the instant. This this apprehension of the world is mimetic will
doubtless be agreed. Where we have this authenticity won
by means of the television or motion-picture camera, we can
speak of a mimetic limit, beyond which point there com-
mences a further continuum moving toward less confused
and more and more ordered wholes. Moreover, given the
viewpoint concerning us here, it is not relevant to discern
whether this effect is gained by improvisation, employing a
camera-vérité while maintaining an indispensable quantum
of the creative element, or whether it is obtained with an
intentional refinement as, say, in the opening sequence of
The Eclipse. Nothing is more instructive than the case of
Dziga Vertov, founder of the "Kino-Eye," who, aspiring
to a purely documentary art, yet put the creative moment,
i.e., a quasi-improvised authenticity, unaware to the fore
(cf., his manifesto We of 1922).

Prior to coming back to the problem of realism, we must
stop again on the question of verbal (literary) signs. The
category of mimesis does seem, in fact, especially applicable
to the arts that rely on iconic signs; these facilitate, if they
do not flatly impose, the construction of analogical models.
Nonetheless, beyond doubt the use of the term "mimetism"
is equally justified in regard to literary works (and particularly epic prose). In place of the traditional and primitive
phrase ut pictura poesis and the attempts following upon it
to justify the "imagistic nature" of an especially chosen
verbal material on the grounds of psychological analyses,
contemporary theories have concentrated rather on the
analysis of specific semantic functions. If the literary sign is

conventional, still it is possible—in context of a given linguistic tradition and a determinate conjuncture in time and
from the viewpoint of the culture—to attribute to it a
signifiant function and, at the interior of that, a determinate
denotative (*i.e.,* designative) function. It seems that the
latter of these functions permits a mimetic orientation in
literary works, with a certain number of indices of denotation (of designation) having the appropriate properties.
In this domain, it does not prove possible to examine the
fundamentals of mimesis or realism by a method of seg-
menting the semantic parts. Failure has met every effort
to date by scholars who have tried to solve the question of
the cognitive content of literary works through analyzing
the logical value of the propositions, whether in isolation
or their ensembles. In this respect, Anglo-American writings
(of the analytical school) are characteristic, *i.e.,* those of
Weitz, Margolis, or Beardsley, notably; they have yet to
succeed in deducing the represented world by means of
dividing propositions of a type they discern as fictional from
the purely predicative propositions. An "implied truth" and
"implicit meaning," such as to indicate a truth distinct from
that of the sciences, cannot be deduced from logical analysis
of propositions that, say, speak of Mr. Pickwick and his
adventures. It seems that we can only determine the global
compass of such intricately interconnected unities, and relate
this to extra-literary reality, if we make place at a higher
level for the "semantic figures" or "semantic systems" (the
characters, leitmotifs, events, action, etc., and the relations
among these elements)—to use the terminology of the
Polish works of a structural-semiological orientation. Struc-
turalism generally contents itself with examining the internal
semantics of the work—a semantics that, to be sure, is
comprehensible in context of a given system of literary
traditions and the conventions current within the domain.
Recently some Soviet scholars (cf. *Troudy po znakovym
sistemam,* vols. 1, 2 and 3, Tartu, 1964-1967) and Polish
scholars (Stefan Zółkiewski, for one) have moved toward
practicing a historical semiotics, as does P. Francastel of
France. The semiotic content of a given work is related to

other sign systems within the limits of a single cultural model, whose basis is a historically defined, globular social structure. Instead of the idea of an expression of the vision of the world belonging to a given social group, or to the whole of the social system, there is introduced the idea of a system of homogeneously encoded interdependencies. This apprehension appears to remove the quandary for mimetism and realism (although the Soviet and Polish scholars in no way wish to eliminate it). We indeed do not know for certain on which reality it would be necessary to define the cognitive content of a literary work. It seems that the world presented in the literary work should be considered in terms not so much of a code as of a concrete system of coordinates, defined by a given social reality. Although there are irrefragible reciprocal dependencies between the metaphorical character both of the parts and the totality of the work and its particular polyvalent relation with reality, I shall omit here the complicated problem of the specificity of the literary language, untranslatable as it is into the "literal" idiom of any given ethnic terrain. Suffice it to state here that in the scope of the literary work, not only the signifying function, but the denotative function as well (interdependent with the *designata*) is distinctly modified. The analogon in the case of a literary work differs, moreover, from that applicable, for instance, to a pictorial work. It is certainly possible to examine the relation to reality of the proposition: "A man descended by a winding street toward the steps leading to the largest square in the city," by reflecting on an imitation *in abstracto* of definite activities in a determinate context. It seems nonetheless that one can speak of mimetism in literature only when this type of proposition is come upon in the bounds of a depicted world, *i.e.,* it is considered within a more extensive semantic totality. In other words, the above relation of reference (which is inseparable, we may note, from the "emotive response" in I. A. Richards's sense) can be treated only within a context. Thus, the equivalent of a situation of reference in a literary work is not—as is possible in the case of a pictorial work— any offhand fragment with distinct contours and a relation of analogy to objects or persons in the real world; rather, it has to be the entire structure of the particular work. Mimetism in literature is manifest, then, at the level of integral semantics. If we may use the comparison of a landscape, what parallels it is not the affirmation: "There stands a tree on the shore of a lake," but rather the definition of the subject of a painting, *e.g.*: "Landscape on the bank of the Vistula, near Warsaw." Mimetic value, let us add, is never the offspring of "proper names," for even in a historical novel or a work of artistic reportage, the real person and the real events are transformed, due to their situation in a fictive world that—as Ingarden says—has its own objective logic. Every literary work—if examined for its mimetism—schematizes the world represented and makes use, therefore, of "common names." The rules governing resemblance to the real world or, more precisely, the rules of verisimilitude, here also permit us to establish a continuum, which will extend from fixed limits (reportage elaborated in an artistic manner) over to a fiction appealing to our sense of immersion in a known world, built up in terms of a determinate communicative system between the artist and the public. Here too, we see—and J. Mukařovsky has particularly well analyzed this on several occasions, starting in the thirties—the intervention of the antinomy noted earlier in respect to the plastic arts. An antinomy between the linguistic level and the level of reference and, further, a tension between the virtuality of the depiction of the world (the Soviet scholar J. Lotman here describes metonymy as an abstraction peculiar to artistic cognition) and the depicted world itself. I have not here taken up the differences in the structure of prose from that of poetry, although this problem is essential, since in light of twentieth-century creative work particularly, one must speak, especially in the case of poetry, of specific modifications in the semantic functions. As for the ontology of the literary work, this cannot be the occasion for developing the question of the particular status of the presented world, and I must simply assert the following. The world presented can be constituted only with the aid of propositions (although, as

I have stressed, the fictive reality cannot be reduced to the sum of the semantic propositions and sequences), and cannot be considered apart from the particular linguistic and cultural tradition; thus fictionality shows clearly its semiotic sources. The ontology of this world derives from the ontology of the entire world of the culture, but at the same time, we add in qualification, fiction is to be distinguished from nonfiction in result of a certain code. The fictive world indeed is constituted only owing to our consciousness, which endows it with meaning and value, while at the same time fiction constitutes a transcendence in terms of that consciousness; hence, to use Husserl's term in a modified interpretation, it might be said that every fictive world partakes of an intentional character. Crucial to our position is this, that the mimetic values become manifest owing to this fictive world, and that, vice versa, it is owing to mimetic tendencies that the artist may realize the fictional structure. Max Bense (*Aesthetica,* 1965), within the limits of art understood in terms of a *Mitwirklichkeit,* disinguishes two fundamental types of signs: *von Etwas* and *für Etwas;* throughout the present discussion I have had the latter in mind. I must further stress, once again, that the denotative function pertaining to mimetic works cannot be reduced to denotation in the logical sense, for the reason that their depictions entail as well an evaluation of reality. Thus, the analogon has in this respect at most a certain isomorphic character that is only approximate. If we abstract the difference that appears when interpreting the mimetic character of works that employ iconic signs and those that employ verbal signs, we should nonetheless stress again in conclusion that mimetism, thus understood, is intelligible to a great number of cultures and within the framework of diverse conventions.[4] This—I repeat—in no way means that social praxis does not define the conditions whereby we apprehend the relationship between art and reality. It only means that the thesis of *adequatio rei et intellectus* established once and for all, is insupportable as a general thesis. On the contrary: within the bounds of a particular social praxis, some relationships of analogy (because they *are* that) can be apprehended outside of the prevailing code that determines the reality to which the artist must relate and the manner in which he may do so. If "convention" has a decisive role here, it must be that of the cumulative human culture, developed upon its natural foundation. Mimetism has its appeal, then, through what is generic in the culture, and, mediated by the culture, in nature.

Realism as an artistic category is distinguishable from mimetism in the first place in that it may, but it need not, be comprised solely of mimetic elements. As I here formulate it, the realist creative work does not exclude elements of fantasy, nor even the conviction that such things as God, angels, devils, and the like, exist. For what in the social, psychological, or psychosocial sense is essential, can as well be expressed by means of the world so presented as to up-end or deform its real objects, and persons, and their relations. The evidence to prove this abounds; one thinks of the works of the Polish romantic school, or *The Divine Comedy* of Dante. Thus, the center of gravity shifts over to the problem of the "essential." It should be clear that I do not propose here any form of essentialism, *i.e.,* the viewpoint of those who think it possible once and for all to ascertain some qualitative moments or their systems—whether these be apprehended eidetically or discursively—that will determine any particular given entity. By essential, I mean simply what may be apprehended on the basis of natural and historical laws—these systems of characteristic traits that enable one to differentiate, forever in a relative fashion, one object from another object, one action from another action, this process from that process, relationship from relationship, and so on. To be sure, we are led once again onto philosophical turf. And it should be obvious that if, on the whole, concord in the matter of mimesis is difficult to come by, agreement in this domain is far less presumable in the present matter. The adopted philosophical perspective results in variant understandings of realism, *e.g.,* by the neo-Thomist, the existentialist, the Marxist. Inevitably the controversy entails recourses to arguments of an ideological character. Precisely for this reason, then, I devote—

deliberately—so much space and attention to the philosophical problems. And thus, if we are unable to arrive at
concurrence on the question of realism, we should make
the acknowledgment that behind differences in aesthetic
views are the differences of philosophical attitudes and of
ideological perspectives. For the Marxist, realism pertains
chiefly to the social world, or, more broadly, to the psychosocial world, although *ex definitione* (*i.e.,* on grounds of
"essential" moments), the category may be applied in regard
to natural phenomena. The concept of the "typical," linked
traditionally in Marxist doctrine with the concept of realism,
always is defined functionally, within the framework of a
historically determined human *praxis.* Indeed, the outlook
on the world underlying this notion of realism implies that
authentically the world is only *diesseitig,* but that englobed
within this world one will find religious faith, inauthentic
images of reality, "mythologizations" of every sort, the
conviction that the individual is an absolute, and so forth.
The question, then, that I raise as a Marxist, when faced
with a realist work, does not fix attention upon the particular artist in considering primarily or exclusively his
philosophical or political vision of the world; it rather
attempts, upon the substratum of their epoch, an explication
of the envisionings of the world, whether the phenomena
be in this sense entirely dominant, dominant among others,
or be marginal phenomena. I am not at all interested in the
scholastic controversy that seeks to fix whether the realist
should depict what already is, or what is but in process of
becoming and hence, in the social sense, rare. To the contrary, it would seem that Marx's remark in volume 3 of
Capital, i.e., that many and diverse variations of the typical
(typification) are possible in a given epoch, is fruitful in
scholarly application. For the study of art the remark is
very important; it aids one to concretize the following question: The typical character of a given work is definable in
relation to what? A character of being typical can as well
be ascribed to the work of Kafka as to Gorky's, as well to
Sholokhov's *Virgin Soil Upturned* as to Hemingway's *For
Whom the Bell Tolls,* as well to Mikhail Romm's *Nine*

Days of the Year as to Fellini's *8½*. The reference point in each case here is a social structure treated as a totality (*i.e.,* globally), and, in limits set by this structure, there are perspectives of differentiated consciousness that probe toward the foundation of what is historically problematical in the given epoch. Kafka is a critic of alienation; notwithstanding, he is also its most tragic witness. On this point Garaudy, in his polemic with the Soviet aestheticians, is quite right; for how is one to credit a refusal of the name of realist to this genial writer, if by a realist we mean one who throws light upon key phenomena within a particular sociohistorical perspective? The sole conditions that have to be satisfied are: the artist cannot be a blind instrument of the processes occurring about him, and if he is to reveal these processes conscientiously he cannot acquiesce to their pressure. Kafka's work measures up on both these counts. In contrast, the second condition would not appear to be met by, say, the creators of the *nouveau roman*. But the example of the Fellini film is particularly telling; in a dramatic manner it raises the question of Oneself as Theme, auto-thematism having been, since *The Counterfeiters* by Gide, a fundamental motif of contemporary creative work. What in the works of Robbe-Grillet and Nathalie Sarraute becomes a task of metalanguage, *i.e.,* a novelistic methodology accomplished in tandem with the narration, here is objectified for critical appraisal. It is not enough to confirm that, just now, the question of the mode of presentation has relegated the presentation of reality itself to the secondary plane. Fellini has seen in this phenomenon a symptom of the crisis of spiritual values in our time; raising as he does the question of the meaning of artistic practice, he poses the question of the meaning of our life as a whole. He is a critical realist, as was Kafka for his day. Here plainly we may see that the realist is a creator who never stops with a simple description of reality but evaluates that reality by bringing distinct viewpoints to bear on it. Quite probably a purely descriptive work of art does not exist, generally speaking; even the works termed naturalistic entail a kind of generalization, that is centered on some particular or secondary phenomena or the grouping of these. At any rate, in the elementary manifestations that we earlier discussed, the mimetic tendency angles for a simple description. And nonetheless, the mimetic elements ordinarily serve as a material enabling the expresion of a selective attitude. What chiefly sets apart the realist is his attitude toward reality, an attitude that merges conjunctively (and also independently of his vision of the world in the strict sense) with the structural process of social life, with the transformational rhythms that the realist, though to be sure not he alone, discerns and proposes to our awareness. It would appear that if immanent in the realist method (typification as the mode of presentation) one finds what German classical idealism called *das Allgemeine im Einzelnen das Besandere*—which we may translate either as individualized generalization or as generalized individualization, for let us note we have here again to do with a continuum[5]—likewise this sort of creational attitude (typification as a relationship of analogy) toward the world known to the artist proves to be characterized by a projection of the latter, together with its critical overviewing. As an example, for socialist realism, if understood in its authentic version, this means the affirmation of a particular reality by means of an attitude critical of everything apathetic and inert in it, everything lagging behind the ideals of that society.

It is important that this aspect be distinguished from the idea of realism such as that put forward by R. Jacobson in an interesting essay of 1921 (cf. *Théorie de la littérature; Texte des formalistes russes* . . . , Paris, 1965). The same idea reappears, we should note, in the work of Malraux and as well in Garaudy. If by realism we mean all creative work that is new within the range of a particular social context and therewith the characterizing artistic conventions, we should have to describe every recent current of art as realist, wholly leaving aside the matter of content of the works representing these currents. The opposite of realism would then be epigonism; moreover, the term automatically would assume a meliorative meaning, for all recent art would be thought the best at that particular given moment. Obviously, the definition of the category as analyzed here can be modified; however—as I remarked earlier—I do not believe its equivocality, howsoever notorious, can justify the many arbitrary treatments of its meaning. Withal, this interpretation of the category (realist equated with novelty in a particular historical context) does not appear to represent a continuation of the Marxist tradition.

To sum up. Realism is a notion that implies not only a philosophical, but also an ideological commitment. Inasmuch as this is so, it does not appeal to the generic characteristics of the culture of man, for the "essential" I mean here is historically concrete, and variable. Nor does it appeal to a human nature; rather, it is based on the social reality in its dialectical movement that casts aside past forms in favor of emergent forms of life. A human universality ("truth to human nature"), of which the Anglo-American aestheticians who take up this problem write voluminously, develops—in my judgment—precisely and above all within this perimeter of realism, *i.e.,* in a historical context that is dissimilar for every instance. The identical problems—love, and death, and human failure and triumph—are modified, since the heroes and the circumstances change. A "human truth" is also at times to be perceived inside the limits of mimetism. In such context it would appear to arise in a pure state; but clearly the force of this truth here is very dubious. It is indeed an artificial, sterile, and illusory thing. We must add, in concluding these remarks, that a sharply defining frontier between mimetic and realist art works cannot be fixed.

NOTES

1. In my book examining Malraux's aesthetic doctrine, *The Absolute and Form* (Bari, 1971, in Italian; a French edition is in preparation), of which the present essay constitutes a section.

2. I discussed this question in my book *Between Tradition and a Vision of the Future* (in Polish, Warsaw, 1964, chaps. 3 and 4), where I offer a critical commentary on the viewpoints of Soviet scholars. See also the works of H. Markiewicz and S. Zółkiewski among Polish studies, and

among other works those particularly by E. Fischer, R. Garaudy, and G. Lukacs's *Die Eigenart des Aesthetischen* (Neuwied, 1963). The position of Lukacs appears to be the most persuasive because he is, in fact, the first to date to have brought an analysis of such thoroughness to the specificity of artistic cognition (*das Typische als das Besonderen*) and to have linked with such scientific mastery the analysis of the mimesis phenomenon with the forming of the unique world of art (which in this book he regards as a *Für-sich-sein*). However, Lukacs—mistakenly, in my opinion—extends the mimesis premise into all the arts in asserting this value as a constitutive element of art; and he opposes, howsoever consistently but without resort to adequate argumentation, avant-garde tendencies wherein he sees a clustering of decadent traits. R. Garaudy in his *D'un réalisme sans rivages* (Paris, 1963) correctly defends the organic ties between realism and the avant-garde, albeit the term realism is handled indecisively and with little clarity. Perhaps following Sartre and M. Dufrenne (in his *Phénoménologie de l'expérience esthétique,* Paris, 1953, part 1, chap. 4, and part 4, chap. 4), Garaudy describes, as determinants of realism, the *conscience de ce qui manque* and again, a participation in *l'acte créateur d'un monde en train de se faire.* Art in general becomes identified with realist art, if arbitrarily, in his argument; art is determinately defined as at once myth and cognition, *i.e.,* a projection transcending and sublating present reality, and, at the same time, as a knowledge of its fundamental properties. In other passages we find, as additional determinants, "labor" and "utopia." It would prove difficult to unite into a coherent entity the visionary, technical, and cognitive aspects of this analysis of realism; as I have indicated in detail in my essay "Garaudy—antynomie prometeizmu" (*Współczesność,* Warsaw, 1967, nos. 10 and 11), realism thus grows impossible to catch hold of and slowly it disappears from view, very like the smile and whiskers of the cat in *Alice in Wonderland.* Other instances—as I see it—of an abusive usage of the concept of realism, are the following: *a*) the interpretation by L. Goldmann of *Les Gommes* by Robbe-Grillet and other works representative of the *nouveau roman,* which he treats as realist because the works express a complete reification; and *b*) the idea not uncommon to American theory of art, that a nonfigurative art is the more profoundly realist. The error of the proponents of a "realist" abstract art resides in the thesis they have spread abroad to the effect that these artists are reflecting the structure of a cosmic matter. As concerns Goldmann, he holds that the homology—itself doubtful, let us note!—between the economic structure and the structure of literary consciousness is a criterion more to be valued than is the relation of the particular content/form structure of the works to the given reality. The creators of the "new novel' consider themselves realists, it is true; at any rate they employ this notion in the sense of an overthrow of stereotypes and conventions, in the sense of a fresh and direct apprehension of the world. Whether we are thus presented with new content or with new forms, or both at once, is not clear. Probably the latter solution is favored by Robbe-Grillet and by N. Sarraute, whose views differ in other respects. In any case, the uncertain aspects of this proposition are not what concern us now. Despite the polyvalence of the term as examined here, it would be difficult to accept a definition that would categorize as realist a literature that creates its own independent reality, or assumes basically that while the world *exists,* to be sure, it is the "point of view" defined by the hero that gives it *meaning* in every case, or that, finally, treats human beings impersonally, as but objects emergent from chaotic flux.

3. See my essay "la réalisme comme catégorie artistique" (in *Recherches internationales à la lumière du maxisme,* 1963, no. 38. A fragment of it appeared earlier in the Proceedings of the Fourth International Congress on Aesthetics, which took place in Athens in 1960). In this essay I dealt with the problem of the realist work of art as a specific sign. I still hold to the opinion that every work of art is a sign, and among the artistic signs, the works one calls realist possess properties that are notably, manifestly semantic. However, I would say today that all works of art may be interpreted semantically, that all have a determinate signification. All the same, only works imbued with mimetic and realist values, due to their contents, refer to the extra-artistic *designata* in some degree. What I have essentially had to modify was, in the first place, my approach to idealism vs. mimetism and realism. One has a far easier time of it opposing the aesthetic conceptions of idealism, realism, and naturalism (as discovered in the history of ideas), than in discovering subtle distinctions, labeled idealistic, naturalistic, realistic, etc., among the works themselves. I do not dwell on this problem here. Let me only point out that Lukacs's conception according to which naturalism is founded on facticity and sheer immediacy while idealism (allegorism) on abstract symbolic rendering of reality succumbed to some metaphysical principles, seems to be convincing and worth further elaboration.

4. And, by extension, it will appear that to explicate the mimetic properties of art one need not rely upon an older psychology that, bifurcating the cognition process in terms of two separate units (the subject and object), mechanically totals up in turn the sensations, representations, associations. Rather, one may proceed, in my estimate, by developing the assumption that human perception—due to anthropologically unvarying factors—is remarkably stable. The old psychology has to linger on the stream of data, durations, etc.—everything that lessens, for theory, the identity of subject and object. The conclusions of existential phenomenology lend support to my understanding of mimesis, which is predicated on the Marxist notion of certain invariants that confront human praxis. Precisely if man perceives the world situationally, in active encounter with it (being able to perceive

the field of objects in a synthetic manner, and reaffirming his human *projets,* in large measure thanks to the reiterative nature of the train of situational patterns), mimesis would then appear most credible as an artistic category similarly appealing to individuals from diverse cultures and from different epochs. This is a problem I deal with at full length in my book *The Absolute and Form.*

5. In this case, a continuum, because whereas the general traits prevail in some realistic works (hence the term, individualized generalization), in others an opposite result obtains and the particular traits predominate, making the variant term, generalized individualization, applicable. Of course, the optimal and ideal sphere of typification is that where the *Besondere* (*i.e.,* the special, which is located in the center of the sociohistorical processes and rendered in a unique way) will comprise an entirely organic and compact whole. This happens with the great masterpieces of realistic art. But works of individualized generalization (*e.g.,* the plays of Fr. Schiller) tend toward the kind of art that we may roughly term (after Lukacs) "symbolic" and "abstract," whereas realistic works of generalized individualization tend the other way, toward naturalism (*e.g.,* Zola). Naturally our notion of a continuum here should not be reduced to our two extreme instances selected more or less at random; it is meant to apply to the diversity of realism.

10

ARS AURO PRIOR*

by

Jan Białostocki

Jan Białostocki has been curator of the European Paintings Gallery at the National Museum in Warsaw since 1955 and professor of the history of art at the University of Warsaw since 1962. He is a specialist in European painting of the fifteenth and eighteenth centuries, art theory, and iconography. He has published several books and articles in Polish and also the following in German and French: Europäische Malerei in Polnischen Sammlunge, *Warsaw, 1957;* Stil und Ikonographie, *Dresden, 1966; and* Corpus des Primitifs Flamands: Les Musées de Pologne, *Brussells, 1966.*

Professor Białostocki was a Ford Foundation scholar at Princeton University in 1958, a visiting professor at Yale University in 1965–66, and participated in the twentieth International Congress for the History of Art in New York.

Ernst H. Gombrich in his admirable lecture on *Light, Form and Texture in XVth Century Painting*[1] has recently drawn attention to the fact that Leon Battista Alberti, in

---

* This essay is a part of *Mélanges de Littérature Comparée et de Philologie,* dedicated by several scholars to Mieczysław Brahmer, Professor of Italian and French literature at the University of Warsaw. Published by Państwowe Wydawnictwo Naukowe in 1967. The translations of extracts in Italian, Latin, and French are provided by the editors.

the second book of his *Treatise on Painting*, opposed the use of gold in painting. Alberti wrote indeed:[2]

> Truovasi chi adopera molto in sue storie oro, che stima porga maëstà; non lo lodo. Et benché dipigniesse quella Didone di Vergilio ad cui era la pharetra d'oro, i capelli aurei nodati in oro et la veste purpurea cinta pur d'oro, freni al cavallo et ogni cosa d'oro, non però ivi vorrei punto adoperassi oro però che, ne i colori imitando i razzi del oro, sta più admiratione et lode al artefice.

> There are those who make large use of gold in their paintings, since they believe that it confers stateliness [on them]; I do not commend [it]. Although he painted Dido by Virgil [the Virgilian Dido] as having a gold quiver, her blond [golden] hair held by gold bands, her crimson dress equally ornate with a gold belt, her horse's reins and everything in gold, nevertheless I wish he had not used gold at all because, by imitating the gleam of gold through colors, the artist deserves more admiration and praise.

In his text Alberti takes up an old idea, to be met with in texts concerning art in clasical antiquity as well as in the Middle Ages: namely, the idea that art, artistic skill, is something that can be opposed to gold, to the quality of materials used, and that human ability is more important and valuable than gold. But this *topos*, which I propose to call *ars auro prior*, according to one of its medieval formulations, has of course various meanings, which depend on the changing meaning of the terms *art* and *gold*.[3]

The problem "gold in art" is a many-faceted and very important one. I do not intend to take up all its manifold aspects.[4] My purpose in the present note is to put together some texts and to try to interpret their meaning according to changing aesthetic ideas and doctrines of the times.

I begin with antiquity. In his account of Lysippus's activity Pliny tells the following story. Lysippus executed several statues representing Alexander the Great; one of them showed him in his youth:

> quam statuam inaurari iussit Nero princeps delectatus admodum illa; dein, cum pretio perisset gratia artis, detractum est aurum, pretiosiorque talis existimabatur etiam cicatricibus operis atque concisuris, in quibus aurum haeserat, remanentibus.[5]

Thus, upon seeing this statue and being moved in some way by it, Nero ordered that it be gilded [covered] with gold. Later, since its market value deprived it of its artistic value, the gold was taken off. It was thus felt that it was much more precious, in spite of the breaks and cracks in which gold remained.

In this report, for the first time perhaps, art is opposed to gold, the purely artistic value of a work of sculpture being considered as not only much more important than, but downright contradictory to, the impression of wealth and to the hypnotizing glittering of gold. *Materiam superabat opus,* said Ovid[6] a little earlier, as he expressed the sophisticated idea of art that was characteristic of the refined Roman intellectual milieu. When describing ancient heroes, the Roman poets spread out a quantity of gold, as did Virgil in the passage that Alberti referred to in the sentences quoted above. Virgil speaks, we recall, of Dido's golden quiver, of her golden girdle and the golden trappings of her horse.[7] But this ostentation of precious materials, which was increasing also in the imperial court art of Rome, must have been regarded as an expression of primitive taste. Big idols like those made by Phidias, shining not only with excellent craftsmanship but also with the metallic glitter of gold and the white splendor of ivory, must have seemed barbarian to the aesthetically minded philosophers, writers, and poets of the first century A.D.

Soon, however, gold was to reassume a function similar to that which it had fulfilled when it surrounded the statue of Athene Parthenos with a holy shine. *Splendor* became the main aesthetic principle in the art conception based on Plotinian philosophy.[8] In early Christian and Byzantine art the golden background has replaced, with its reflected light—a symbol of the supernatural—the naturalistic landscape, still to be seen in the late Roman, and in some Catacomb, paintings.

In medieval art gold, used as an abstract background, was well suited for the representation of holy persons or allegories; and as material suited to the making of receptacles for the preservation of holy relics and Sacraments, it had the utmost importance. Its special significance for Imperial art was stressed by Gottfried of Viterbo in his *Pantheon*. He wrote in the chapter *Quid significat aurum in coronis?*:[9]

Aurea materies regalibus apta coronis,
Indicat imperium mundi superesse patronis,
Circulus est orbis forma rotunda soli.

Aurum cuncta suo superat fulgore metalla,
Imperium superat, quos orbis continet aula,
Et bene Romuleo iure gubernet eos.

Suscipit innumeras aurum tractabile formas,
Suscipit et variat Romana monarchia normas,
Flexibilis, facilis, aurea forma suis.

Gold fits royal crowns.
It shows that the domination of the world surpasses its subjects,
and that of the universe the circle [of the crown] alone is the perfect image.

Gold surpasses all other metals with its gleam.
Its authority dominates everything enclosed in the universe.
Therefore let it govern according to the laws of Romulus.

Soft as it is, gold receives innumerable shapes.
It receives and modifies, like Roman monarchy, its laws.
It bends and adapts itself to the need of its subjects.

Claritas was one of the chief aesthetic qualities esteemed in medieval thought. The stars, gold, and precious stones were called beautiful because of this quality.[10] The impact of gòld and precious stones on the medieval imagination is well known. May it suffice to give a few less well known examples of literary records concerning Sicilian monuments, recalled recently by Rosario Assunto.[11] The twelfth-century Arab writer Ibn Giübàyr describes in the following words the church of Santa Maria dell'Ammiraglio in Palermo:[12]

Le pareti interne son dorate o piuttosto son tutte un pezzo

d'oro, con tavole di marmo a colori, che eguali non ne furon mai viste; tutte intarsiate con pezzi da mosaico d'oro: Inghirlandate di fogliame con mosaici verdi; in alto poi s'apre un ordine di finestre di vetro color d'oro che accecavano la vista col baglior de' raggi loro e destavano negli animi una tentazione cosi fatta che noi ne domandammo aiuto a Dio.

The inside walls are gilt, or rather, they are a solid piece of gold, with colored marble tables, the equal of which were never seen. They are entirely inlaid with parts of gold mosaic and they are decorated with garlanded [rows] of leaves of green mosaic. Above, moreover, there opened a row of windows with gold colored glass, which blinded the eyes with their dazzling light. They awakened in the [our] souls such a temptation that we asked God for his help.

That gold could enrapture the mind of medieval man and make him feel as if transported to heaven is suggested by the *Homily* of a Basilian monk (wrongly attributed to Theophanes Cerameus). It was pronounced on June 29, 1140, in the Capella Palatina at Palermo, and concerns the same chapel:[13]

con intagli finissimi disposti a forma di piccoli panieri adornato, e tutto lampeggiante d'oro rassomiglia al cielo.

decorated with very fine intaglio distributed in the shape of little baskets, all glittering with gold to resemble the sky.

In his excellent summary of the essence and of the development of what is unjustly called "minor arts" of the Romanesque period, Hanns Swarzenski formulates in the following words the attitude of medieval man toward precious materials:[14]

In all young cultures gold and jewels embody and convey a magical or symbolical force, a supernatural and impersonal power. And it is due to this quality that they were used in Christian art to enshrine and emphasize the transcendental revelations of the mystery of the liturgy and of the relics. This is the reason why the mediaeval craftsman and his patron found and experienced in those precious materials the appropriate medium for the artistic realization of their purpose. Both were aware that it was an offering pleasing to God, and consequently the artist gave his best to the delicate work—the *opus subtile,* as it was called. For the purer and more precious the material in which he worked, the closer he came to the fulfillment of his consecrated purpose. The very preciousness of the material acquired the value of symbolic significance: crystal and ivory became attributes of the Virgin.

We do not wish, of course, to summarize the problem of the golden background, already thoroughly studied by Bodonyi, Gombrich, Braunfels, and Schöne.[15] We should like only to consider the opinions expressed concerning the relative value of precious material and of artistic skill. When the *Vita Henrici* mentions a (lost) Byzantine golden antependium in the Speyer Cathedral, it gives equal emphasis to the value of the material and to that of "art":[16]

aurea tabula . . . tam artis novitate quam metalli pondere miranda.

table of gold, admirable as much for the novelty of the art as for the weight of the metal.

But the Ovidian formula *materiam superabat opus* was also taken up again. We find it in Abbot Suger's *De administratione ecclesiae Sancti Dionysii,* when—in his polemics against those who are opposed to the richness of the works of art in churches—he stresses the fact that in spite of the lavishness of the barbarian (Lotharingian?) goldsmiths who have done the retabulum in Suger's Abbey Church, the work became not less but more remarkable because of its artistic value, and only to a minor degree because of its material value.[17]

In the well-known poem that he put on the gilt doors of the West porch in his church, Suger admonished:[18]

Portarum quisquis attollere quaeris honorem,
Aurum nec sumptus, operis mirare laborem,
Nobile claret opus, sed opus quod nobile claret
Clarificet mentes ut eant per lumina vera
Ad verum lumen ubi Christus janua vera.

Whoever will sing the beauty of these portals, let him not
marvel at this gold or this richness but rather at the workmanship
in the art.
The work of art shines nobly, but this work, shining with ardor,
illuminates minds, so that, through its true light, they
reach the Real light where Christ is the true door.

The onlooker should wonder not at the expense and not
at the gold, but at the workmanship, the "art." On the other
hand, the awareness of the symbolic significance of gold is
still very strong, and it is expressed in the lines where the
anagogical meaning of *claritas,* leading the minds of ob-
servers up to Christ, is also stressed.

Had gold been conceived always as a symbol of divine
splendor, art would not have been considered as the more
important. But this was not always the case. We find a
negative judgment about gold contemporary with Suger's
texts. This appears in an inscription placed on the fragment
of an enameled shrine ordered by Henry of Blois, Bishop
of Winchester (*ca.* 1150). There we read:

ars auro gemmisque prior.[19]

Art surpasses gold and precious stones.

It is to be deduced from this formula that the ability to
create a beautiful work was considered more valuable than
the material value of gold and gems, while their possible
symbolical meaning is not mentioned. The Ovidian *topos*
recurs in the history of the bishops of Le Mans. The bishop
William built himself, toward 1158, a private chamber,
finely illuminated by windows "the workmanship (of which)
surpassed the quality of the materials." And again we come
across the same *topos* in William of Malmesbury's *Gesta
pontificum Anglorum,* in a passage which is quoted, like the
preceding one, by Meyer Schapiro in his admirable study of
the aesthetic attitude in Romanesque art.[20] When speaking
of the ornaments of the cathedral of Canterbury, of its
cloths and sacred vestments, he says that the skill with which

they have been executed "surpassed the preciousness of the materials."

There must, however, have existed cases where the material value of gold triumphed over "art." We know that many a work of the goldsmith's art perished, having been melted during the wars, when gold was needed for purposes other than art. According to the ingenious hypothesis of Richard Krautheimer, such is the reason for the nonexistence of the works of the famous goldsmith Gusmin, to whom Ghiberti devoted words of the highest praise in his Memorabilia.[21] Gusmin's works are supposed to have fallen victim to the war needs of the Duke of Anjou when struggling for the possession of Naples. In such cases, gold could also have assumed a meaning as symbol of the transience of all material values.

In looking through medieval proverbs, we can find that in the folk wisdom of the time, expressed through proverbs, gold is, in a moralistic way, put rather low in the hierarchy of values. We can quote the following set of questions and answers:[22]

> Auro quid melius?—Iaspis.
> Quid iaspide?—Sensus.
> Sensu quid?—Ratio.
> Quid ratione?—Nihil.

> What is better than gold—Precious stone.
> What is better than Precious Stone—Intelligence.
> What is better than Intelligence—Reason.
> What is better than Reason—Nothing.

The concept of an art based on restraint and simplicity, which satisfies the eyes of the learned, as opposed to the lavishness of color and glittering of gold, which appeals to the ignorant, appears in the famous words of Boccaccio, celebrating Giotto's achievement. It was recently discussed by Gombrich and connected with the development of the idea of "noble simplicity."[23] The tendency to oppose art to the material value of gold and precious stones increased, of course, with the development of artistic naturalism in the

Gothic period and in the Early Renaissance. We can only expect to find some trace of the problem in the first Renaissance treatise, written by Alberti at the time when in many an Italian studio—not to speak of those in Spain, Germany, or the Netherlands—the habit of using golden backgrounds and gilt ornaments in pictures was still current. I have already quoted from this classic text at the beginning of the note, but we can find in it further statements pertinent to this topic.

At the beginning of his second book Alberti gives a perfect—as it seems—formulation of the *topos* *"ars auro prior,"* for he writes:[24]

Et quanto alle delitie dell'animo honestissimo et alla bellezza delle cose s'agiunga dalla pittura puossi d'altronde et inprima di qui vedere, che a me darai cosa niuna tanto pretiosa quale non sia per la pittura molto più cara et molto più gratiosa fatta. L'avorio, le gemme et simili care cose, per mano del pittore diventano più pretiose et anche l'oro lavorato con arte di pictura si contrapesa con molto più oro. Anzi ancora il piombo medesimo, metallo in fra li altri vilissimo, fattone figure per mano di Fidia o Praxiteles, si stimerà più pretioso che l'argento. Zeusis pittore cominciava a donare le sue cose quali, come diceva, non si poteano comprare. Né extimava costui potersi venire atto pregio quale satisfacesse ad chi fingendo, dipingniendo animali, se porgiesse quasi uno id dio.[25]

Besides, what great pleasure in a noble soul and in beautiful things is contributed by painting, one can first see from this: that one cannot give anything so precious to me that it cannot be rendered more valuable and more graceful by painting. Ivory, jewels, and similar valuable things become more precious through the hands of the painter. Also, the gold that is treated through the art of painting is equivalent to much more than gold. Even lead, one of the basest metals, when made into figures (statues) by Phidias or Praxiteles will be considered more valuable than silver. Zeusis the painter began to donate his works, which, as he said, could not be bought. Nor did he believe that anyone could accomplish a worthy work that might satisfy him, who, in painting animals, acted almost as a god.

Leonardo da Vinci also despised those who base their reputation on the splendor of gold and of "azzuro," and this attitude was continued in several utterances of art theorists who represented the classical doctrine, such as Bellori, Dufresnoy, De Piles.[26]

When we look at the process of eliminating the golden background from pictures in the fifteenth and sixteenth centuries, as described by Braunfels and Schone, we can almost paraphrase the medieval *topos* into *ars naturam pingendi auro prior*—for, in art, whose scope it was to create an image of reality similar to the Albertian "view through the window," gold could have conserved its symbolical value only when fulfilling the function of a frame, which gave a tradition-imbued dignity to the new naturalistic projection of three-dimensional reality onto the flat surface of the picture. In the juxtaposition of the golden frame and of the framed, realistically conceived picture, there is almost an explicit challenge to compare *ars* and *aurum*.[27] Some residuum of the sacred meaning involved in the golden shine of the frame may have persisted even in the seventeenth century, since at that time Protestant countries emphatically rejected gold and chose dark black or brown frames for their realistic-baroque pictures.

The art of painting could not, however, have been considered literally as superior to gold earlier than the time when it learned, not only how correctly to represent three-dimensional reality on a flat surface, and even not only how to model the shapes of things with the help of light and shade, but also, finally, how to paint and represent the shine and glitter of light on glossy surfaces and to contrast them with the absorbent surfaces of matt objects—in a word, when it learned to give not only effects of light, but also of lustre: of *lume,* and of *lustro*.[28]

That the art of the painter is infinitely superior to all material richness of his work was, of course, obvious to Italian artists at the beginning of the sixteenth century. Even in the north of Europe, the gilding of wooden sculpture must have been considered a little backward after Tilmann

Riemenschneider ceased to cover his statues with a traditional gilt coat. But this was still not obvious to Julius II,
who, having seen the Sistine Ceiling after its completion,
wanted Michelangelo to put gold ornaments into the fresco,
as was projected.

Il papa, vedendo spesso Michelagnolo, Vasari writes, gli diceva:
"Che la Cappella si arricchisca di colori e d'oro, che l'è povera."
Michelagnolo con domestichezza rispondeva: "Padre Santo, in
quel tempo gli uomini non portavano addosso oro, e quegli che
son dipinti non furon mai troppo ricchi, ma santi uomini, perché
gli sprezzaron le ricchezze."[29] In Condivi Michelangelo says: "Io
non veggio che gli uomini portino oro."[30]

The Pope, writes Vasari, seeing Michelangelo very often, would
tell him: "Let the Chapel be enriched with colors and gold, because it is [looks] poor [inadequate without colors and gold].
Michelangelo would answer courteously: "Holy Father, in those
times men did not wear gold, and those who are painted were
never very rich, but saintly men, because they scorned wealth." In
Condivi Michelangelo says: "I do not see men wearing gold."

The great master of the Renaissance could dismiss with
a verbal joke the demand that might have been authoritative
but was based on an antiquated idea of art.

Gold might have been considered as a symbol of higher
values, but it might also be seen as a material of the artist.[31]
In this second case, gold as "matter" was subordinated to
"form"—to recall Aristotelian concepts. In the classical
theory of the seventeenth century, such an idea was often
expressed. Teyssèdre quotes the words of Nicolas La-
moignon de Basville (1667):[32]

la beauté de la forme surpasse toujours la richesse de la matière."
"L'industrie d'un excellent ouvrier ne perd rien de son prix quand
elle s'exerce sur le bois, ou sur l'argile; de même l'or ni l'argent
ne peuvent rendre plus estimable le travail d'un mauvais artisan.

The beauty of the form always surpasses the richness of the material. The work of an excellent worker loses nothing of its value
when it is applied on wood or on clay. In the same way neither

gold nor silver can make more valuable the work of a bad artisan.

It is amusing to see that in Romantic criticism both these medieval attitudes were revived: the opinion about the priority of art over material preciousness, as well as the conviction that gold acts on people with a magic power creating an aura of holy things. The first opinion was expressed by Duppa in 1806, when he stated, commenting upon the frescoes of the Sistine Ceiling, that "[Michelangelo] felt the importance of a truth best known in an age of simplicity, that the mind, and not the material is the true basis of future fame."[33] The second was represented by Stendhal, who stressed—also in connection with Michelangelo's frescoes—that "La richesse des autels et la splendeur des habits augmentent la ferveur des fidèles qui assistent à une grand'-messe" (The richness of the altars and splendor of the garments increase the fervor of the faithful who attend the High Mass).[34]

But modern art has gone further and further away from emphasis on the value of precious materials, although gold was reintroduced incidentally by the retrospective masters of the Nazarene or Pre-Raphaelite groups, precious stones by such an artist as Klinger, and gold again reappeared even in the work of creative members of the *Art Nouveau* movement, for instance Gustav Klimt.[35] In the works of contemporary artists who know how to bring about the glow of beauty from some old torn pieces of burlap, from broken utensils, destroyed machines, useless tools, and shattered car bumpers, the idea of the superiority of "art" to valuable materials seems to have reached its climax.

NOTES

1. *Journ. of the Royal Soc. of Arts* (October 1964), pp. 826–49, especially p. 831. The problem was also discussed by the same author in his paper "Visual Metaphors of Value in Art," in *Symbols and Values,* ed. L. Bryson et al. (New York, 1954), reprinted in Gombrich's *Meditations on a Hobby Horse* (London, 1963), pp. 12–19, esp. pp. 15–18.

2. L. B. Alberti, *Della Pittura,* edizione critica a cura di L. Mallè (Florence, 1950), p. 102.

3. On the economic and symbolic value of gold recently, see Z. Jeffries, "Gold," *Proceedings of the American Philosophical Society* 108 (1964): 437–42 and F. Machlup, "The Fascination of Gold," *ibid.* 109 (1965): 105–7.

4. They will perhaps form the subject of another, more developed study.

5. Pliny, *Nat. Hist.* XXXIV. 63–64, ed. H. Rackham, in Loeb Classical Library (Cambridge, Mass., London, 1952), p. 174.

6. Ovid, *Metamorphoses* II. 5.

7. Vergil, *Aeneis* IV. 136.

8. See recently R. Assunto, *La critica d'arte nel pensiero medioevale* (Milan, 1961), p. 42.

9. Gottfried of Viterbo, *Pantheon,* Particula 26 (*Mon. Germ. Hist. Script.* 22, 272–76), quoted from P. E. Schramm and F. Mütherich, *Denkmale der deutschen Könige und Kaiser* (Munich, 1962), p. 103.

10. O. G. Von Simson, *The Gothic Cathedral. Origins of Gothic Architecture and the Medieval Concept of Order* (New York, 1956), p. 50. See also W. S. Heckscher, "Relics of Pagan Antiquity in Medieval Settings," *Journ. of the Warburg Inst.* I (1937–1938):212.

11. Assunto.

12. *Ibid.,* p. 115, quoting M. Amari, *Biblioteca arabo-sicula,* vol. 1 (Turin-Leipzig, 1880), p. 162. I give Assunto's Italian version.

13. *Ibid.,* p. 117, translated from Migne's *Patrologia Graeca,* vol. 132, coll. 951F. "In the later Trecento works the transcendent world of the Deity and the Saints glows with gold and is filled with objects of luxurious and sparkling texture. This material richness is concentrated on or around the superior beings, and the hierarchical distinctions that it implies are often augmented by clothing lesser religious figures as well as laymen in contemporary dress" (M. Meiss, *Painting in Florence and Siena after the Black Death* 2d ed. [New York, 1964], p. 46).

14. *Monuments of Romanesque Art* (London, 1954), p. 13.

15. J. Bodonyi, "Entstehung und Bedeutung des Goldgrundes in der Spätantiken Bildkomposition," *Archaeologiai Ertesitö* 46 (1932–1933); E. Gombrich, Review of the preceding in *Kritische Berichte zur Kunstgeschichtlichen Literatur* (1932–1933), pp. 65–76; W. Braunfels, "Nimbus und Goldgrund," *Dos Münster,* III (1950):321–34; W. Schöne, *Über das Licht in der Malerei* (Berlin, 1954).

16. *Vita Henrici,* cap. I (*Mon. Germ. Hist. Script.* vol. 14, p. 271, ed. W. Wattenbach. 3rd ed. 1899, p. 12) quoted from Schramm and Mütherich, p. 62.

17. E. Panofsky, *Abbot Suger on the Abbey Church of Saint Denis and Its Art Treasures* (Princeton, 1946), p. 60f. (*De administratione,* XXXIII).

It is not without significance to note the context of the Ovidian formula. It is to be found in the description of Apollo's palace, to which Phaeton comes in order to beg Apollo to allow him to lead his chariot through the heaven. We find there the following description:

Regia Solis erat sublimibus alta columnis,
Clara micante auro flammasque imitante pyropo;
Cuius ebur nitidum fastigia summa tegebat,
Argenti bifores radiabant lumine valvae.
Materiam superabat opus. Nam Mulciber illic
Aequora caelarat medias cingentia terras
Terrarumque orbem coelumque, quod imminet orbi . . .
(*Metamorph.* II. 1-7)

When he also referred a similar metaphor to the door of his church he might have done it because he conceived of his church as a new *Regia Solis*, a Kingdom of the Light Divine.

The Ovidian formula *materiam superabat opus* is also adduced by Poussin in one of his so-called *Notes on Painting*, but for him *materia* means subject and his opinion is probably connected with the *querelle* that took place about 1635 in the Academy of St. Luke in Rome (see A. Blunt ed., Nicolas Poussin, *Lettres et propos sur l'art* [Paris, 1964], p. 173, note: "Comment on doit suppléer au manquement du sujet").

18. Panofsky, p. 46 (*De administratione,* XXVII). Cf. Gombrich, *Meditations,* pp. 15 f.

19. Swarzenski, p. 13, pl. 195, fig. 446.

20. M. Schapiro, "On the Aesthetic Attitude in Romanesque Art," in *Art and Thought (Essays in Honor of A. Coomaraswamy)* (London, 1947), pp. 140-41.

21. R. Krautheimer, "Ghiberti and Master Gusmin," *Art Bulletin* 29 (1947):25 f.; idem, *Lorenzo Ghiberti* (Princeton, 1956), pp. 62-67; Ghiberti's text: *Lorenzo Ghibertis Denkwürdigkeiten,* ed. J. Von Schlosser (Berlin, 1912), vol. I, pp. 43 f; vol. II, pp. 164 f.

22. *Carmina Medii Aevi Posterioris Latina* II. 1. *Proverbia sententiaeque latinitatis medii aevi. Lateinische Sprichwörter und Sentenzen des Mittelalters in alph. Anordnung,* ed. H. Walther (Göttingen, 1963), vol. I, ad vocem (I owe this quotation to the kindness of Dr. Tadeusz Dobrzeniecki).

23. Gombrich, *Meditations,* pp. 17 f. For a developed discussion of the concept of "noble simplicity," see W. Stammler, *"Edle Einfalt"; zur Geschichte eines kunsttheoretischen Topos,* in: *Werte und Werke. Bruno Markwardt zum 60. Geburtstag* (Berlin, 1961), pp. 359-82, reprinted in Stammler's *Wort und Bild* (Berlin, 1962), pp. 161-92.

24. Alberti, ed. Mallè, pp. 76-77.

25. This story is told by Pliny XXXV. 62, but is referred not to Zeuxis but to Phidias; see Mallè, p. 77, n. 1.

26. Giovanni Pietro Bellori, *Vite dei pittori, scultori ed architetti moderni* (1672) (ed. Pisa, 1821), vol. I, p. 48; Charles Alphonse Dufresnoy, *De Arte Graphica*, vol. 24, pp. 217–18 ("Nec sit opus nimium Gemmis Auroque refertum; /Rara etenim magno in pretio, sed plurima vili.") (1st ed. 1668); Roger De Piles, *Abrégé de la vie des peintres* (1699), ed. 1767, p. 46 (". . . pour éblouir la multitude qui n'avait plus de goût que pour le brillant de l'or et l'éclat des couleurs, on tâchoit de mêler l'or et l'argent aux materiaux qu'on y employait").

27. Alberti agrees that all ornaments that are customarily added to the picture may be made of gold. See p. 102: "Dico bene che li altri fabrili hornamenti giunti alla pictura qual sono colupne scolpite, base, capitelli et frontispicii, non li biasimerò se ben fussero d'oro purissimo et massiccio. Anzi più una ben perfetta storia merita hornamenti di gemme pretiosissime."

28. Gombrich, *Light, Form and Texture*. The terms appear in Leonardo da Vinci. Gombrich indicates: J. P. Richter, *The Literary Works of Leonardo da Vinci* (London 1939), vol. I, plates III–VI, Nr. 133; Leonardo da Vinci, *Treatise on Painting*, ed. Ph. McMahon (Princeton, 1956), pp. 260–63.

29. G. Vasari, *Le Vite* . . . I quote from G. Vasari, *La vita di Michelangelo*, ed. P. Barocch (Milan-Naples, 1962), vol. I, p. 40.

30. Ascanio Condivi, *Vita di Michelagnolo Buonarroti* (Rome, 1553), pp. 112 f., quoted from Barocchi, vol. II, p. 444. See also Vasari's story on Sixtus IV's high appreciation of Cosimo Rosselli's use of gold in his frescoes in the Sistine Chapel. Rosselli's colleagues opposed his practice, but the pope was satisfied by this traditional approach (Gombrich, *Meditations*, p. 17). It should be pointed out, on the other hand, that Botticelli's *Birth of Venus*, one of the most typical pictures of the late Quattrocento, shows an intensive use of gold (leaves, tree, grass, shell, hair of Venus, flowers and so on).

31. On golden color and its use in painting, one finds considerable remarks in such treatises on painting as Carel Van Mander's *Het Schilderboek* (1604; see R. Hoecker, *Das Lehrgedicht des Karel van Mander* [The Hague, 1916], pp. 297 ff.) and Raffaello Borghini, *Il Riposo* (1584) (Florence, 1730), pp. 182–83.

32. B. Teyssèdre, *Roger de Piles et les débats sur le coloris au siècle de Louis XIV* (Paris, 1965), p. 67.

33. R. Duppa, *The Life of Michelangelo Buonarroti with his Poetry and Letters* (London, 1806), from ed. 1870 (R. Duppa and Quatremère de Quincy, *The Lives of Michelangelo and Raphael*, p. 45), quoted after Barocchi, vol. II, p. 444.

34. H. Beyle, *Histoire de la peinture en Italie* (Paris, 1817) (ed. Paris, 1929, vol. II, pp. 279, 299) quoted from Barocchi.

35. See data given in the recent monograph on Klimt: E. Pirchan, *Gustav Klimt* (Vienna, 1956), p. 44, Fig. 34: a drawing representing Tragedy,

executed with chalk and gold, 1897, today in the Historisches Museum der Stadt Wien, Vienna; p. 42, pl. after Fig. 18: Pallas Athene, oil and gold, 1898, coll. Ed. Ast, Vienna; p. 45, Fig. 61: Judith, oil and gold, 1901, Gallerie des XIX Jahrhunderts, Vienna. In 1902 Klimt executed a Beethoven frieze in the Building of the Vienna Secession. This composition was to have served as a background for Klinger's Beethoven monument. Klimt has used genuine gold for that painting.